THE NEW ECONOMIC HISTORY

THE WILEY SERIES IN

AMERICAN ECONOMIC HISTORY

RALPH L. ANDREANO
Editor

Ralph L. Andreano
THE NEW ECONOMIC HISTORY:
RECENT PAPERS ON METHODOLOGY

Louis M. Hacker
THE COURSE OF AMERICAN ECONOMIC
GROWTH AND DEVELOPMENT

70/- A

THE NEW ECONOMIC HISTORY

RECENT PAPERS ON METHODOLOGY

EDITED BY

RALPH L. ANDREANO

Professor of Economics
University of Wisconsin

JOHN WILEY & SONS, INC.

NEW YORK · LONDON · SYDNEY · TORONTO

To Arthur H. Cole

Library of Congress Catalogue Card Number: 72-109393

SBN   471   02902   5   (Cloth)
      471   02903   3   (Paper)

Printed in the United States of America

10   9   8   7   6   5   4   3   2   1

CONTRIBUTORS

ROBERT L. BASMANN, *Professor of Economics, Texas A. & M. University*

STUART BRUCHEY, *Allan Nevins Professor of American History, Columbia University*

ALFRED D. CHANDLER, JR., *Professor of History, The Johns Hopkins University*

ALFRED H. CONRAD, *Professor of Economics, City College, The City University of New York*

LANCE E. DAVIS, *Professor of Economics, California Institute of Technology*

ROBERT W. FOGEL, *Professor of Economics, University of Chicago*

GEORGE GREEN, *Assistant Professor of History, University of Minnesota*

J. R. T. HUGHES, *Professor of Economics, Northwestern University*

GEORGE G. S. MURPHY, *Professor of Economics, U. C. L. A.*

FRITZ REDLICH, *Emeritus, Harvard University*

G. N. VON TUNZELMANN, *A Fellow of Nuffield College, Oxford University*

INTRODUCTION TO THE SERIES

Research in economic history has literally exploded in the past decade. The purpose of this series is to make this research available to students in a set of interchangeable books on American economic history from earliest times to the present. Not only would it take considerable time to bring this research into the classroom in conventional textbook form, but the text itself would be massive in order to fully capture what economists and historians have been writing about America's economic past. The Wiley series aims to give a breadth and depth to American economic development not now possible in a single, unsupplemented, conventional text. The series includes books by both historians and economists that represent new and fresh thinking, that challenge old concepts and ideas, and that contribute to a new understanding of the main contours of American growth and the human welfare consequences of that growth. The past ten years have witnessed not just a "new economic history" but a "new history." The books in the Wiley series will bring to the student and the classroom a needed dialogue between historians and economists that will reshape our thinking about America's economic growth and development.

Ralph L. Andreano

University of Wisconsin
October, 1969

PREFACE

The articles collected in this volume all first appeared in *Explorations in Entrepreneurial History, Second Series*. They reflect the dialogue that has been taking place in the past decade between historians and economists on the methodology of what has come to be called the "new economic history." Many traditional historians have been less than enthusiastic about the methodological impact of the new economic historians. This skepticism has stemmed partly from conceptual misunderstanding on both sides, a missionary flavor in the early work of the new economic historians that was bound to antagonize those who have worked long and hard in traditional historiography where spectacular research findings are harder to come by, and finally from a series of genuine methodological shortcomings in the approach and research findings of both the new economic history and traditional historians. The result has been a quite heated and rich debate on the scope and method of economic history and the spirit of this debate is well illustrated by the articles collected here. Whatever the merits of the critics and proponents in this debate, the field of economic history in this country has never been as fertile as it is at present.

Making this material accessible in convenient form should enrich the classroom experience and hopefully stimulate the research capabilities of both students and professors. The papers are arranged in logical sequence starting first with pure methodological issues, criticisms of method in substantive research, and ending on a critique of quantitative tools used in the new economic history. Obviously, any of the papers can be read independently of each other.

Ralph L. Andreano

ACKNOWLEDGMENTS

I am indebted to all the authors of the papers reprinted here in two specific ways: (1) for graciously waiving royalties (as has the editor) on this volume as a contribution toward the future financial success of *Explorations in Economic History*, successor journal to *Explorations in Entrepreneurial History, Second Series;* and (2) for having permitted publication of their papers in the first instance, in a shaky and fledgling new scholarly journal.

I am also happy to acknowledge the excellent secretarial services in compiling this collection performed by Miss Rosalyn Wick, secretary to the Graduate Program in Economic History at the University of Wisconsin.

Dedication of the collection to Arthur H. Cole needs little explanation. He was the principal architect of the original *Explorations in Entrepreneurial History* and was largely responsible for stimulating a rebirth of the journal into an effective and influential force in economic history.

CONTENTS

SOURCES OF THE ARTICLES

We list below the specific volume and page numbers of *Explorations in Entrepreneurial History, Second Series,* in which the papers collected in this volume first appeared.

THE "NEW" HISTORY

George G. S. Murphy

I

The term "New Economic History" has gained a certain currency.[1] This paper examines the case for saying that current history is new in some senses. It argues that there are good grounds for such an assertion largely because current history is coming close to what a modern empiricist might demand of it, and for the first time has a really defensible set of techniques. It also argues that this is not so much due to a growing philosophic self-awareness on the part of historians, but to other reasons which seem to indicate that the movement towards a "new" history will continue.

II

If we were to outline a form of history acceptable to an empiricist who was demanding on epistemological grounds, the outline would turn on the kinds of sentences admitted to such a history, and the denotations assigned to the terms and symbols of the sentences.[2] Admissible sentences which were descriptive of the world would need to have the property of being adjudged true or false by appeal to some common experience; they could never be derived from *a priori* knowledge. We might derive new conclusions from such admissible sentences by the use of logic or mathematics, but the procedures by which we did this would have to be tautological (in the strict logical sense of the word). Logic and mathematics, themselves, would be held to be languages which were devoid of any truth about the world, and for that matter could bring no new empirical truths. Sentences describing future outcomes could never have a truth value assigned to them, although we might attach to them some indicator

Source. EEH/Second Series, Vol. 2, No. 2. © Graduate Program in Economic History, University of Wisconsin, 1965.

of the degree of confirmation of the whole sentence. Sentences involving an open set of future outcomes could be refuted, as some of the future outcomes were realized, but could not be assigned a truth value. For this reason most "theories" about the world would be held conjectural. Denotative terms of the sentences would have to be well-interpreted either by a prior set of semantic rules, or by explicit, contextual or recursive definitions within a language. Operation symbols of the language would be standardized, and the syntax of the language would be specified. Finally, if ethical judgments were introduced into the language, assigning truth-values to them would be viewed as arbitrary and, in an empirical sense, basically undecidable. A language involving value judgments would have interest only on a logical plane. We would merely want to know whether or not empirical sentences conjoined with ethical sentences led to conclusions which were logically valid. The set of semantic rules restricting language to expressions that denote objects of experience would be viewed as strongest when those expressions had an ostensive quality, or involved intersubjective systems of measurement well-agreed upon, or had the characteristic that the sense of the denotation would immediately force itself upon people dealing with the language. Finally, in order to avoid ambiguity and logical paradoxes, a clear separation would be made between the use of language and the mention of terms and expressions of language. Given an initial set of admissible descriptive sentences about the past world, the techniques used to manipulate and order the set of sentences would in this language have an unambiguous quality to them. For example, we should be able to write them as instructions to the executive unit of a computer.

The modern historian with a firm grasp of the rules of an empirical language would write a particular type of history. If he infringed none of the rules, we would have to regard the results of his work as acceptable as the whole empirical philosophic position itself. Furthermore, he would use a non-controversial language as far as empiricists were concerned.

III

The writer of the "old" history had no such language model in mind. Essentially, he learned to write history by studying earlier historians or by discovering his own rules. From the standpoint of modern empiricism he made persistent and typical errors. The "new" history increasingly becomes free of such errors.

A. EXPLANATION BY DESCRIPTION

The first and most important error of the "old" history was that it explained by describing. Consider the procedure. First the historian usually selected a single time-period and examined it through library materials. In doing this, he might have in mind (1) an explicit hypothesis or a group of hypotheses, (2) a general interest in the causes of an historical event or events, or (3) merely a concern with the time-period.

After searching the materials (rarely a statistical population or sample, but rather histories written by others) he wrote either descriptive history for a given time period (his sentences being purely descriptive, were devoid of explicit or implicit inferences or implications) or he wrote to "prove" a hypothesis or a group of hypotheses which he had started with or which he had formulated during his period of research.

Parenthetically, we might note that the effect of historical research on the historian's "frame of reference" tended to give him great confidence in his method. We may designate the historian's frame of reference as the group of initial hypotheses and value judgments with which he started. We might also include the information he already had about the area of investigation. This frame of reference, naturally, might change over time; as an individual continued his research and reported it, his intuitive assessment of his observations might lead him to revise "explanations" about behavioral change and relationships between historical actors or processes that he formerly held. He might, naturally, also revise his values. Few historians who have done continued research on a given period will be unaware of this process of change in the frame of reference. Further, it is not unusual for the whole group of "explanations" in the frame of reference to undergo transformation at one time. New linkages between them are seen, some may be discarded, new ones may be introduced, all in a sudden once-over change. Kenneth Boulding has called such a change a "revolution in the image." [3] Certainly, historians undergo revolutions in their images of the past, and the fact that they do undergo such striking psychological events tends to assure them of their methodological approach. In a way, they can truthfully assert that they have "felt" their "understanding" of the past to have improved.

Once the historian felt he had mined his materials sufficiently, the time came to communicate results, to convey his "understanding" of his period. If he wrote a purely descriptive history, then he arrayed sentences about a time period by means of a system which pleased him. [4] The sentences could be non-general or of higher levels of generality though generalizations were usually not given precise quantification and often were implicit. Biographical history, for example Eileen Power's *Medieval People,* consists almost entirely of descriptions of individuals. Yet there is implicit generalization in biographical history of this kind. The individuals described are average, interesting not so much for their special characteristics as their representativeness of the whole relevant population. Power's approach, in essence, is a literary way of computing a number of means.

If the historian studied and described social systems or their subparts he merely selected by intuition observations which seemed important to him to record. A typical sentence would be: "labor unions were of size x at time t." Such simple sentences arrayed in a text indicated trends. Were quantitative data available we could replace sentences like these by time-series, and this is what modern history does.[5] Naturally, a statistical table is only a stylistic variant for a set of descriptive sentences. The older descriptive and literary social history might have no major hypothesis or value judgment to urge on the reader. A text like Clapham's *The Economic Development of France and Germany* would come close to such a model. Considerations of charming the reader aside, we could replace such a model by a statistical abstract. It *would* be a clumsy statistical abstract in that there would be a great number of time-series with single or few observations. Generally, modern descriptive histories seeking greater precision compile statistics at the cost of style and concentrate on time-series with many observations. But nothing very significant has happened; fundamentally, nothing has changed.

Were we to continue our examination of the "old" history, we would note sentences not purely descriptive. For example, universal laws such as "every society prescribes its own standard of conduct" [6] might be stated. And usually such general laws have been empty of predictive content. In the example cited all that we learn is that if we examine a society that was previously unexamined, we will find its standard of conduct different from other known standards.

Of course, the "old" historian did not make many general statements of this kind. However, it has been suggested that he did frequently make more restricted generalizations, or "quasi-laws." Joynt and Rescher comment:

> The discovery of such restricted generalizations . . . is perhaps the most central and characteristic task of the historian. . . .
>
> Historians do make generalizations—the military historian, for example, tells us that certain tactics in the use of cavalry in the massive land-engage-

ments of the American Civil War proved particularly effective. Such a statement is no mere description, but has law-like force, in asserting that *if* military conditions and technology were again to be realised, the same tactics would again prove effective.[7]

The law is naturally only implied. It is an unwritten sentence, and although it can be reconstructed, various persons might all formulate it differently. Such laws are not universal laws. They are concerned only with a given time and place, and they are loose since the conditions relevant to their operation are not all listed. Finally, they have little value since their only test is the single instance given.

But even were we to read every general law and reconstructed quasi-law of the "old" history, we would not have captured all the non-descriptive sentences. The "old" historian sometimes used value judgments (although he usually tried to avoid these) and he did attempt "explanation." For example, we might read: "The Industrial Revolution was caused by the expansion of the British colonial market." We will point out later that the use of such sentences was really an appeal to an implicit general law, but of most interest at this point is the method by which the historian attempted to support his sentence.

Such "explanations" did not follow from a train of deductive logic, nor were they explanations resting on statistical inference. The "explanations" were urged upon the reader by a whole mass of descriptive sentences which attempted to warrant the acceptance of the "explanation." The historian appealed to the commonsense knowledge of the reader (which we might view as a huge implicit and unsystematized body of laws) and having made his descriptions demanded that the reader make the necessary conclusions by processes best known to himself. Of course, even if every description were true a conclusion might still not be warranted at all.

In this discussion we should separate very clearly two entirely distinct historical problems. In the one, the historian by reconstructing an event can lead us to accept a new position on the role of an actor in this event. He does this by presenting evidence as a prosecutor does in a case based on circumstantial evidence.[8] Essentially he imputes a general law. To take the analogy of the prosecutor in a murder case hinging on circumstantial evidence, the imputed general law is: "Men not directly observed on scenes of crimes, known to be violent, strongly motivated by personal motives, with fingerprints on death weapons, and with the possibility of being on the scene of the crime, and no other known possibility for their whereabouts, are guilty." The prosecutor establishes all conditions by true descriptions; for example, he shows that Mr. Exman did have a motive. He then asks the jury, on the basis of the knowledge of conditions, and on the basis of the law which springs out of our common-sense knowledge, to make the correct inference that Mr. Exman is guilty. The historian establishes or recovers descriptive knowledge about the past by similar procedures, and does this legitimately. Such a procedure is invaluable to the political and biographical historian.

In a second historical problem, the historian uses the same technique to throw light upon quite a different problem. The techniques of biographical or political history are used to throw light on an explanation like: "Mr. Exman caused World War II," or "Slavery caused the Civil War," or "Rome declined because . . .," or "Western Civilization is doomed because. . . ." Consider the explanation of the Civil War. Behind it, is a general law of the kind: "If social tensions exist, then these create war." The historian of the American Civil War, for example, describes the social tensions of the ante-bellum period, and then asks us to believe that these, all due to slavery, caused the war. Even though logically the form of explanation is the same as in the preceding case, a great gulf separates the acceptability of the two arguments. There are critical differences between the two: the lack of precision of the language in the second instance, the lack of any real body of evidence based on our own experience to confirm the law, and finally the large and open number of conditions which constitute the initial social state which is held to lead to the second one. We can sharpen the difference by considering the counterfactual argument: "If Mr. Exman had not been at the scene of the crime, then we could be sure his victim would still be alive." But can we be sure, out of our commonsense knowledge, that: "If there had been no slavery, then there would have been no Civil War"?

B. COEXISTENCE OF "EXPLANATIONS"

Use of such explanatory procedures have led to very many "explanations" for certain events. Consider the fact that there are over one hundred histories of the American Civil War.[9] Undoubtedly, a survey of them would produce very many "explanations" of the causes of the war. Yet, paradoxically, all these histories on a sentence-to-sentence basis will surely be true, for, generally, historians do not record false sentences. Furthermore, expert opinion cannot tell us which explanation to accept. Expert opinion can tell us who is the more "imaginative" or more "insightful" or more "assiduous" historian, but it cannot judge between the case of the prosecution and the defense. For that matter, it is entirely possible that there may be no "correct" explanation at all because the language of the hypothesis may defy decision about it.

C. MEANINGLESS SENTENTIAL CONNECTIVES

It follows from the preceding that, as Berlin has noted, the sentential connectives of the "old" history sometimes have no meaning within the domain of logic.[10] We cannot reconstruct the logic which permits the use of connectives, except by the unfruitful approach of always arguing they involve implicit general laws. "Therefore," "then," "hence" are really nothing more than an appeal to the commonsense knowledge of the reader. They have, to use Carnap's phrase, psychologistic rather than logical force. This is not to say that all uses of sentential connectives are incorrect; the matter hinges on the nature of the implicit general law appealed to.

D. STRATEGIES OF EXPLANATION OF AN INFORMAL NATURE

Since the inference techniques of the "old" history were never formalized there were important consequences. Consider an economist or mathematician who makes intuitive leaps in his argument. In a proof he may write: "Proof: obvious," or "Clearly . . ." Potentially his argument can be formally reconstructed and tested if it has any logical or mathematical content. Any grounds for doubting the validity of an argument can be removed by appeal of a formalization of the argument. The existence of formal procedures, even though they be so well-known that we can omit them, has an important by-product. Over the course of time it is recognized that a class of problems can be solved by using similar formal procedures. The knowledge of which techniques to use in analyzing a given problem we might call a knowledge of strategy. Such strategies can become quite explicit. A simple example from logic would be the rule by which one assumes a conditional when testing the validity of an argument with a conditional as a premise. But simple examples should not cloak the fact that recognition of classes of problems has emerged in social science and that strategies to deal with them have been evolved. In economics we speak of "optimizing problems," "queuing problems," "inventory problems" and so on. Over the course of time specific strategies for solving well-defined and tractable problems have emerged.

In the "old" history, only "distillations of generalised sagacity" are at the command of the historian as strategies to solve historical problems.[11] An example of one such strategy, or "distillation" if you will, is: "To solve the problem of explaining the causes of a war, ignore great men and focus on social factors." It hardly needs pointing out that this instruction is vague and does not lead to the application of well-known procedures which we can find in any manual of logic, mathematics or statistics. Just how *does* the historian focus on social factors? Furthermore, if he does, is he any nearer correct explanation?

In modern history there is some growing recognition of strategies due to the introduction of more formal techniques. A familiar class of historical problems deal, for example, with living standards. Most historians today automatically turn to price indices to attack this problem.

E. THE STUDY OF THE DEVELOPMENT OF TECHNIQUE AS "HISTORIOGRAPHY"

Another consequence of the use of commonsense methods rather than formal methods is that historical technique has never been standardized. (Consider staging analysis: is there any history of the development of a formal technique of staging? If we read discussions of staging even today, they turn upon a consideration of the differences in approach of historians of prominence rather than on the technique itself.) This implies that history has been deprived of a growing body of technique, and that the history of historical theory is of a biographical rather than a technical nature. In fact the term "historiography" cloaks the fact that this is really a concern with the development of historical analysis.

F. MEANING VARIATION IN TERMS

The next problem in the language of the "old" history, which the "new" increasingly avoids, is that of great variation in the meaning of terms. Partly this is due to the fact that history has been viewed as an art. In science terms are reduced and standardized. In literary arts they are multiplied to serve the needs of euphony, the general architecture of prose, and verbal rhythm. Of course, even in mathematics there is some attempt to avoid repetition and to use stylistic variants, but these are never a source of ambiguity. Without a formal language in which there are exact equivalents, if variants are used it becomes a matter of debate which terms are actually stylistic variants one for the other. In addition, given no standard language, individual terms acquire different meanings. Machlup has investigated this problem in economic language when he calls terms "weasel-words" and "jargon-words." [12] Different writers, as he demonstrates, have used quite differently the term "structure." We might observe, however, that there is no ambiguity in the use of this word by writers used to formal languages.[13]

Historians have compounded the problem by introducing terms which permit a multitude of interpretations. "Industrial Revolution" and "Dark Ages," for example, describe broad time-periods and hence may be taken to describe any one of a vast number of true conjunctions about such periods.

G. MEANING VARIATION IN HYPOTHESES

A related problem which springs from the nature of the terms used in an "explanation" is the variety of interpretations possible in a hypothesis. Actually, most historical "theses" have been hypothesis schema. A simple example will show this. Consider the Turner "hypothesis" which Turner laid out as follows: "The existence of an area of free land, its continuous recession, and the advance of American settlement westward, explain American development." [14]

The Turner thesis has been a subject of continuous debate and clearly, the debate arises partly from the ambiguity of the hypothesis quoted. It is possible to interpret the terms "American development," "free land," and "American settlement westward" in a variety of ways. (As a matter of fact, Turner himself was not always careful to use the same interpretation.) Take the term "American development"; it has been interpreted in at least the following ways:

1.1 The development of typical American personality traits.

1.2 The development of democracy. This term, itself, has had a family of interpretations. One, for example, has been broad participation in community decisions as opposed to leaving community decisions to specialists and choosing specialists at polls.[15]

1.3 Deviations of political institutions at the local, state, and federal level from the "European" model.

1.4 Deviations in the set of laws from those in Europe.

1.5 The time-path of Net National Product and its components.

1.6 Characteristics of economic organizations over time, viz.: firms, banks, industries, labor organizations, agricultural organizations.

1.7 Opportunities for individuals to improve their income and status at one point in time and over time.

1.8 Economic and social relationships of the American polity with other countries.

This is not an exhaustive list but is reasonably representative in character. To take another example, "free land" has been interpreted as:

2.1 Land with no ownership rights existing to it; land for the taking.

2.2 Land easily acquired by displacing its occupants.

2.3 Natural resources easily available.

2.4 Agricultural land disposed without price under the Homestead Act.

Even if these were the only interpretations, they are enough to generate thirty-two interpretations of the hypothesis.

H. SPECIAL OR LITTLE USE OF "THEORY"

The individualism of the "old" historian extended not only to terms but to the use of theory to generate sentences that can be tested. Consider Perlman's *Theory of the Labor Movement*. Perlman's "theory" is not really a theory at all but a set of possible explanations.[16] The method of this little classic is based on the idea that any event of labor history can be explained by one of the explanations in the set below:

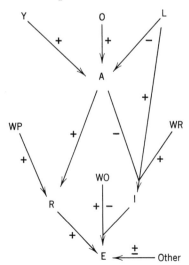

Perlman's Possible Explanation Set [17]

Terms

Y—"maintaining or increasing the relative share of labor"
O—"opportunity"
L—the extent of legislative repression
WP—"the will to power"
A—"acceptance of the capitalist system"
I—"the influence of intellectuals"
R—"the resistance power of capitalism"
WO—"the will to organize"
Other—any event
E—an event of labor history, usually decreased radicalization of unions

Perlman does not use this set as an informal simultaneously-determined model. He selects certain relationships to explain a unique event. Thus we might "explain" the radicalization of the Russian labor movement during World War I by the war itself. We might also explain it by the growing influence of intellectuals in the labor movement when those intellectuals had a strengthened will to resist capitalism. We might also explain it by a declining will to resist on the part of capitalists. We might also explain it by combining all these explanations. All we know in a quantitative sense is the sign of relationships. Thus we might read off for $Y \xrightarrow{+} A$: "maintaining or increasing the relative share of labor has a positive effect on the acceptance of the capitalist system."

Essentially, Perlman asks us to look at each event and see which is the relevant explanation. Hence, we do not have a theory of events for we provide the explanation after the event. Such an approach does permit us to arrive at true descriptions about the past state of the world, which is perhaps the reason why such an approach survived. Sometimes it is asserted that such a way of explaining is "tautological" but this is not correct in the strict logical sense. We could falsify the sentence: "If Y or L or O . . . or Other, then E." But, procedurally, we never do falsify the sentence or some variant of it.

In addition to the special use of "theory," it is also true that the "old" history made very little use of theory at all. For evidence on this we would have to engage in an examination of the written sentences of history. We should either be able to formalize steps in a theoretical argument appearing in those written sentences, or we should be able to formalize implicit sentences. A simple example will demonstrate the latter. Suppose we have an argument of the form: The current worth of gold (y) is 500 billion dollars. The current worth of silver (x) is 200 billion dollars. Exman's law is that the price of silver is always $\frac{y}{x} \cdot 1000$. The conclusion follows naturally that the price of silver is $2500 per unit weight. If Exman's law (which I do not suggest is in any way correct) were widely known then we might write "Gold and silver stocks were 500 and 200 billion dollars respectively and thus the price of silver was $2500 per ton." The truth of this sentence would be widely accepted but if challenged we could reconstruct the argument in full. However, if we examine written history we would rarely find the need to reconstruct such implicit arguments.

Generally, the use of theory has been to give focus to the work of the historian. The various social theories, viz., the theory of the firm, the theory of the consumer, the theory of prices in economics, suggest topics for the historian. They guide his descriptive interest along certain lines. This is to say that the historian talks the same language and discusses the same problems as the economist or other social theorist, but it is not to say that he uses social theory. In the past the usual article stressing the need for application of theory in historical studies was more a pious recognition of the merits of theory than a demonstration of how it was used. This situation is certainly changing in the "new" history but even now it is necessary to view with caution a person's claim that "he is using theory." [18]

I. INFERENCE FROM SPECIALLY SELECTED POPULATIONS

The commonsense approach of the "old" history, and its emphasis on archival sources, made it liable to three further errors. An archives collection will give us the answer to who wrote a secret protocol or a treaty. It will not answer other problems which require some care in the construction of a sample or the investigation of a certain population. Meyer and Conrad have already given interesting and instructive examples of this error.[19]

J. THE ERROR OF REGRESS

We also owe to Meyer and Conrad recognition of the problems which arise when explanations "regress." This is the mistake of "origins of." Consider a country whose investment coefficient is .000001 and whose Incremental Capital Output Ratio is 10/1. If these conditions do not change we know that Gross National Product will grow. Suppose there have been shifts only in the investment rate and suppose we wish to consider the dimensions of today's Gross National Product. The "old" history in examining "Origins of Today's Gross National Product" essentially focused on all shifts of the investment rate rather than significant shifts. Consider per capita income or shifts in the occupational structure. Did the industrial revolution of the English sixteenth century involve large or small shifts in these expressions? Consider modern democracy, did the shifts in freedom granted by Magna Carta have similar dimensions to the great transformations in British society of the latter half of the nineteenth century? To have a minute amount of expanded freedom for six centuries and a great expansion in a matter of decades are phenomena of quite different kinds. Regress in explanation, or the desire to push initial conditions back as far as possible, lacks a sense of quantitative significance. Furthermore, it gives the impression that the dead weight of centuries presses down on us and that social change is slow. The interesting and more optimistic question is what produces significant changes in social variables. In other words we need to focus not on shifts of the investment rate from .000001 to .00001 but from .00001 to .1.

There is another kind of regressive explanation and this is continually to link one set of initial conditions with a preceding one. The following quotation illustrates this:

> We owe the vast industrial system of which we are lucky beneficaries not to the acquisitive instinct and not to the calculating spirit of the "counting house" but to accidents of acculturation through which in early modern times Western Europe became the seedbed of scientific and technological revolution, and also to the unique fluidity of the institutional patterns of Western society—itself a consequence of the turmoil of preceding centuries—by grace of which the technological break-through occurred.[20]

Depending on how we interpret "industrial system" this explanation clearly links some state of today's world with the *Volkwanderung*.

K. THE ERROR OF TIME STANDPOINT

A final error made by the "old" history was always to make value judgments about desirable social policies from the viewpoint of the final income distribution. Welfare economics agrees that we should examine the distribution of income before and after a change before we say it is good or bad according to some criterion for a desirable change. Yet this does not seem to have affected a great number of historical judgments. While, for example, Peter the Great may have committed many enormities, on the other hand it is easy to find opinions that these changes were to the good on the ground that "Russia was stronger thereafter." The genera- tion of the decision-makers of the American Civil War period are deemed wise because they "preserved the Union" without any consideration of the immense social costs of the policies, and of the costs of alternative poli- cies. It seems safe to predict that even Stalin eventually will be judged a good policy-maker because his policies helped to create the potential for modern Russians to enjoy a high standard of life in a powerful nation- state. Such judgments are quite out of tenor with the thinking of modern liberal welfare economics, yet they persist. Undoubtedly the reason for this is that the costs of mistaken policies were shouldered by past genera- tions and the benefits are enjoyed by present generations. But whatever the psychological reasons for certain judgments, they were made because historians have felt that commonsense knowledge in these matters would not lead them astray, whereas perhaps one lesson we learn from welfare economics is that commonsense judgments are usually political rather than ethical, tenable in some reasoned position.

L. PEDAGOGY

As historians demanded that history be description-rich, and believed that they could derive explanations from their detailed descriptions, there were important consequences for pedagogy. Inevitably, the peda- gogy of the "old" history at the undergraduate level was a matter of pumping a great number of trivial truths into generations of passive buckets. Inevitably, the pedagogy of history had to be authoritative, *ex cathedra* so to speak, when it could not be brilliantly aesthetic. One con- vinced an audience by the sheer cumulative weight of facts, not by rea- soned argument. Graduate instruction could only be in the nature of an apprenticeship since there was no body of techniques and knowledge of strategies to communicate to graduate students.

IV

In coming closer to the model of what an empiricist demands, mod- ern history throws off the errors and habits of the "old" history. The growth of formal and axiomatic social theory has influenced the modern historian's language and selection of terminology. The emphasis on quantitative work has reduced the ambiguity and the difficulties over terminology. In economic history, the modern concern with economic growth has certainly speeded up this tendency for in this area it is hard to distinguish who is theorist and who historian. But undoubtedly the major influence on the emergence of new language, procedural, and analytical habits has been and will be the emphasis on bringing all disciplines of knowledge into line with methods practiced by empiricists generally. In the academic world debate on accepted means of establishing knowledge is diminishing; the historian functioning in an intellectual environment which is increasingly agreed on a philosophy of scientific method cannot but be affected, even if unconsciously so. That historical language, historical method, and knowledge will no longer be *sui generis*—this rather than any novelty of style, subject-matter, or emphasis on particular periods or problems, is clearly the most fundamental novelty.

University of California, Los Angeles

NOTES

1. First mention of the term in economic history seems to be in Lance E. Davis and others, *American Economic History* (Homewood, Ill., 1961), p. vii.

2. "Sentence" is used rather than "proposition" because the former is more general and the latter has been objected to by Tarski, for example.

3. Kenneth Boulding, *The Image; Knowledge in Life and Society* (Ann Arbor, Mich., 1956).

4. These systems are extra-logical but can be analyzed and formulated.

5. Even an event which looks as unique as a law can be reduced to serial information, if we focus on the changes introduced by the law. Thus labor legislation, for example, might be resolved into specific changes in a time series describing the permitted set of labor union activities over time.

6. Ephraim Lipson, *Economic History of England* (London, 1956), II, p. lxxiv.

7. C. B. Joynt and Nicholas Rescher, "On Explanations in History," *Mind*, n.s. 68:384-5 (July, 1959). See also Olaf Helmer and Nicholas Rescher, *On the Epistemology of the Inexact Sciences* (Rand Report R-353), (Santa Monica, Calif., 1960).

8. This is not to say that the rules for admitting evidence in history and in law are the same. See Nicholas Rescher and C. B. Joynt, "Evidence in History and in the Law," *Journal of Philosophy*, 56:561-78 (June 18, 1959).

9. *Theory and Practice in Historical Study, A Report of the Committee on Historiography* (Social Science Research Council Bulletin 54), (New York, 1946).

10. Isaiah Berlin, "History and Theory: the Concept of Scientific History," *History and Theory*, 1:12 (1960).

11. *Ibid.*, p. 18. The example given is Berlin's.

12. Fritz Machlup, "Structure and Structural Change: Weaselwords and Jargon," *Zeitschrift für Nationalökonomie*, 18:280-98 (August, 1958).

13. Compare the usages of Siegfried F. Nadel, *The Theory of Social Structure* (London, 1957), p. 3 either with Jacob Marschak, "Economic Measurement for Policy

and Prediction," in *Studies in Econometric Method* (New York, 1953), or with Wassily Leontief, "Structural Change," in *Studies in the Structure of the American Economy* (New York, 1953).

14. Frederick Jackson Turner, *The Frontier in American History* (New York, 1920).

15. This example is taken from Stanley Elkins and E. McKitrick, "A Meaning of Turner's Frontier. Part I: Democracy in the Old Northwest," *Political Science Quarterly*, 69:321–53 (Sept., 1954).

16. In conversation with Professor Arnold Zellner and myself, Perlman remarked that he did not wish to use the title his book was published under but did so at the request of his publisher. He did not feel his book constituted a "theory."

17. The terms given in quotation marks are Perlman's own. I am indebted both to Donald F. Gordon and to Arnold Zellner for this way of diagramming the problem.

18. We can see how little theory was used in one celebrated historical controversy from the discussion in Reuben A. Kessel and Armen A. Alchian, "Meaning and Validity of the Inflation-Induced Lag of Wages Behind Prices," *American Economic Review*, 50:43–66 (March, 1960).

19. John R. Meyer and Alfred H. Conrad, "Economic Theory, Statistical Inference, and Economic History," *Journal of Economic History*, 17:537 (Dec., 1957).

20. Clarence E. Ayres, "A New Look at Institutionalism: Discussion," *American Economic Association, Papers and Proceedings*, 47:27 (May, 1957).

THE ROLE OF THE ECONOMIC HISTORIAN IN PREDICTIVE TESTING OF PROFFERED "ECONOMIC LAWS"*

R. L. Basmann †

"To express my faith I have to say many things which are common-place. I do not try in the least to be original, but to state as simply as possible things which I deem important. I wish they were even more commonplace than they are." —GEORGE SARTON, 1962, p. xi.‡

1. THE DOCTRINE OF CO-RESPONSIBILITY

In a recent monograph I suggested that econometricians—*if* they wish to *test* economic theories—must cope with the economic historian as peer in

Source. *EEH/Second Series*, Vol. 2, No. 3. © Graduate Program in Economic History, University of Wisconsin, 1965.

* Paper presented at Cliometrics meeting, February 4, 1965, at Purdue University.

† I am indebted to J. R. T. Hughes for the many pleasant hours we have spent together discussing history, economic history and economic science. This paper has been composed at his suggestion. E. Ames, C. Lloyd, E. J. Mosbaek and D. H. Richardson and S. Williamson have offered helpful comments. I am indebted also to James A. Papke and E. T. Weiler for helpful comments relating to the role of econometrics in policy-making.

The views expressed in this paper are my own, however, and I take sole responsibility for their inadequacies.

‡ Footnotes in this paper are of two types. Explanatory footnotes are indicated by the usual raised numerals and are arranged numerically at the end of the paper. Bibliographical footnotes include the author's name, the date of publication, and the page reference; the titles can be found in the alphabetically arranged listing of references following the explanatory footnotes.

respect of criticism and assistance (Basmann, 1964, pp. 19–20). If an econometrician announces a statistical test as conclusive, i.e., if he pronounces a given "economic law" to have been disconfirmed by relevant "facts," his pronouncement might be discredited, not only on the ground that his methods of statistical inference are (say) inappropriate or misinterpreted, but also on the ground that the essential *historical investigation* of initial and background conditions is inadequate. I stressed the indispensability of making clear statements of initial and background conditions for the predictive testing of explanatory economic models, and the necessity for suspending judgment, in the event derived prediction statements are falsified, until a really competent job of warranting the statement of initial conditions has been completed. Implicitly, at least, my remarks suggested that the job of establishing the background and initial conditions for predictive testing of proffered "economic laws" requires professional handling—that is, by historians.

The foregoing remark has excited some comment by economic historians, perhaps because it is regarded as a novel admission on the part of one who is reputed to be an econometrician. Therefore I take for granted that there is some interest in this point of view and I propose to amplify in this paper some of my previous remarks.

Although frequent reference is made to topics belonging to philosophy of science and philosophy of history, this paper is not supposed to be a contribution to those disciplines. Nor, of course, can it be considered as a contribution to "hard economic history." It is concerned, rather, with some practical difficulties that stem from the legitimate demand for specialization in research. In particular, this paper is concerned with the fact that there is a more or less hypostatized boundary separating two important fields of specialization, i.e., econometrics and economic history, which *cuts straight through the heart of a natural unit of scientific activity, namely, predictive testing of proffered "economic laws."* Of course, no one ever intended this unnatural cleft to occur, not to mention intending its becoming fixed to the degree it has. The founders of the Econometric Society announced it as their purpose to promote the empirical testing of economic theorems (cf., Tintner, 1952, p. 3); certainly they would assent to the use of any kind of rational procedure that contributes to the goal of testing proffered "economic laws." Yet even Tintner, whose depth and breadth of view on matters of method in economic inquiry are unexcelled, in warning that econometrics cannot claim to be the only method of economic research (Tintner, 1952, pp. 13–14), fails to stress the essential unity of the testing procedure and to emphasize that econometrics alone cannot suffice even where data are abundant. In Tintner's account econometrics and historical research seem to be competing rather than complementary in predictive testing: historical research is said to be more suitable than econometrics in certain subject matter branches of economics; econometrics can, for instance, throw very little light on the problems of economic development; here historical method is much more fruitful (Tintner, 1952, p. 13).

A historical explanation for the unnatural split of the predictive testing activity in economics is beyond the scope of this paper. Root causes must be sought in a period antedating the founding of the Econometric Society. A more immediate cause may be briefly indicated. To begin with, many pioneering econometricians have been eager to get results that would gain the attention of policy-makers (by being of practical use to them, of course). Corollaries of that severe practical orientation are the emphasis on statistical *estimation* of economic relationships, as distinct from *hypothesis testing,* and the controversies that stemmed from the introduction of statistical methods of data reduction more suitably adapted to the form of models which economists already had been formulating for some time. The tendency of policy-oriented econometricians has been to formulate models, to argue in a more or less Aristotelian fashion for the plausibility of the underlying assumptions,[1] and to trust to the efficacy of asymptotically efficient (viz., large-sample) methods of statistical estimation to bring them somewhere near knowing the true values of economic parameters. Gerhard Seiler dates from about 1939 the emergence of the tendency to regard statistically estimated econometric models as sufficiently reliable and effective tools for the making of definite economic policies (Seiler, 1959, p. 8); that is to say, this confidence in reliability of model formulation antedates the development of asymptotically efficient methods of econometric estimation (1940's).

The strong policy-making orientation of prominent econometricians and the emphasis on efficient *estimation* which derives from it; the relatively great prestige that most mathematically untrained economists have been willing to accord to the "invention" of "new and even better" methods of estimation,[2] together with the abundant inventory of methods and results that can readily be borrowed from the previous work of statisticians and applied with little modification to econometric problems, have undoubtedly lured many young econometricians away from investigation of the deeper problems of econometric model-building and predictive testing, even though the latter afford much greater opportunities to find one's own limits in (say) applied mathematics and mathematical statistics, and, I should add, in the weighing of empirical evidence by historical methods.

Economic policy-making is an extremely important matter, of course, and it is requisite that there be available a number of economists who, by reason of their practical knowledge of our country's economy, their perspective as reflected in awareness and acceptance of the limitations and obligations of the expert's natural role, can serve as advisers to the high dignitaries of State (cf., Sorenson, 1963, Ch. 5). To what extent the specific products of policy-oriented econometric model-building are of direct service to public policy-makers I am not qualified to say. Anyway, it is not the purpose of this paper to judge the technological value of econometric model-building, nor to criticize any econometrician's personal decision to specialize in forecasting (see Section 2). Immediate concern is with the fact that a natural unit of scientific economic inquiry is cleft by specialization, and that this cleavage is sustained by the natural consequences of a widespread preoccupation with econometrics as the handmaid of economic policy. Alfred Marshall, you will recall, pointed out the impracticability of seeking in the immediate needs of policy-making the chief stimulus for the pursuit of scientific knowledge (Marshall, 1948, Bk. I, Ch. 1–4). Here it seems appropriate to add this passage from Morris Cohen's *Reason and Nature:*

> To subordinate the pursuit of truth to practical considerations is to leave us helpless against bigoted partisans and fanatical propagandists who are more eager to make their policies prevail than to inquire whether or not they are right. The pursuit of pure science may not completely prevent our initial assumptions from being biased by practical vital preferences. But this is not to deny the aloofness involved in the pursuit of pure science is the condition of that liberality which makes men civilized. (Cohen, 1959, p. 350.)

For the time being let us take it for granted that a considerable part of the work involved in subjecting proffered "economic laws" to predictive test belongs to the *métier* of the historian. What would motivate the historian and economist to cooperate in predictive testing? What are the obstacles to such cooperation? The rest of this section attempts to answer in part these questions.

To begin with, it must be admitted that the views to be expressed here are colored by a specific interest, namely, to subject economic theory, as embodied in a variety of specific explanatory models, to the hazards of predictive test. The motives that lead economists to make predictive tests of explanatory economic models differ in kind and intensity; and the point of view economists adopt towards economic history and its role in predictive testing varies with those motives. For present purposes I should like to stress one kind of motive, namely, the *aesthetic,* which is almost never mentioned except in connection with pure mathematical economics. Historians in particular should be able to appreciate that the aesthetic value of economic theory is not confined to the elegance of style with which it may be expressed in literary or mathematical symbols. Trevelyan is supposed to have said that the poetry of history consists in its truth. Teggart emphasizes the same point: the aesthetic interest of historical narrative depends on its supposed accuracy and the factual character of the events it portrays; the aesthetic value of accuracy is sufficient to justify critical historical inference (Teggart, 1960, pp. 35–39). "The documentary scholar is thus justified in his endeavors. Through his efforts assurance is given to the public that the statements embodied in the most recent history are really true." (*Ibid.,* p. 36.) All great historians from Niebuhr and Ranke to Pieter Geyl have stressed the force of this motive.

Likewise the aesthetic value of an explanatory economic model consists in its truth or, rather, in the warranted supposition of its truth; and (what is intimately bound up with the significance of its supposed truth) in its logical inability to be in agreement with any but a very narrow range of potential facts. In this connection refer to the remarks about equation (3) which appears in Section 2. I mention the aesthetic motive, not merely to argue that the aesthetic value of explanatory economic models justifies the painstaking efforts at thorough deductive exploration and statistical testing of the derived prediction-statements, but rather to suggest that, in common with the aesthetic interest of historical narrative, it justifies undertaking the processes of critical historical inference when they are to be applied to the establishment of the factual character of the background and initial conditions, the fulfillment of which is necessary to render any given predictive test valid.

While I think that the aesthetic parallel between historical narrative and predictive testing of explanatory economic models warrants mention in its own right, there are other practical reasons for laying stress on it. If, as has been claimed, the task of establishing warranted background conditions for predictive testing of explanatory economic models is complicated enough to call for treatment by professional historians, then the habit of continuous close and effective cooperation between historians and test-oriented economists has to be developed. Great obstacles to such cooperation are rooted in divergencies of background and training. However, the common aesthetic interest, e.g., that which motivates efforts to secure logical completeness in explanatory economic models, relevance of statistical tests, and factual accuracy in historical narrative and explanation has a strong tendency to draw those who share it into effective cooperation.

The view that holds historical criticism as important as statistical inference in predictive testing of economic models is colored also by a definite philosophical "bias," which may be broadly stated as follows: every explanatory model that rests on a set of logically consistent economic premises and allows the derivation of prediction-statements whose state of agreement with relevant economic observations is not perceptually obvious, deserves to be subjected to predictive test repeatedly. That is to say, imagination should be free to construct explanatory hypotheses in any form whatsoever, subject only to those restraints that are necessary to secure intersubjective testability and economic relevance. A more or less transparent corollary is that hypothesis formulation must be free of those artificial taboos that appear in the form of methodological prescripts or legislation and choke off rational discussion (it does not matter whether that is the intended effect or not). For the most part, methodological prescriptions in the social sciences are designed to perform in lieu of efforts to disprove hypotheses by predictive tests.

I cheerfully admit that the *anti-limitation* bias of the foregoing policy is strong, and that it might appear extreme to some readers. For all that, I think a strong case can be made for accepting the risks inherent in following a vigorous anti-limitationist policy as preferable to the dangers inherent in a "neutral" policy of allowing limitationist prescriptions to go unchallenged. Actually, the one big risk involved in holding to an anti-limitation policy is largely personal, viz., a risk to the individual only. For it is widely considered by economists to be in bad taste to deliver a riposte to a limitationist sally—or at least quixotic; [3] and neutrals seem rarely to distinguish between the pronouncement of a methodological edict, on the one hand, and a simple denial of the existence of any intellectually compelling reason to heed it.[4] Another risk—though perhaps not really a risk at all—is that an anti-limitation policy tends to provide no easily traced guidelines for decision-making, e.g., in respect of financial support for economic research, whereas methodological prescriptions might seem to do that very well. But if I have not gathered a totally erroneous impression from the *history of science* then it is not too inaccurate to say that the effect of *a priori* methodological limitations on the formulation of scientific hypotheses has been ineffective at best, or at worst, ultimately crippling. (Recall the passage quoted from Cohen above.)

Clear recognition of methodological prescriptions, of their defensive purpose in many instances, is an important initial step in establishing effective cooperation between the historian and the economist. To the extent each one can subject to scrutiny the methodological biases he has absorbed in his own training, and can recognize the absence of any compelling reason to cling to such biases in each and every case, the easier it is for both to concentrate attention on the problems of "hard" economic science. If both the historian and economist have adopted what might be termed an anti-limitation "bias" to begin with, so much the better; effective cooperation is then much easier to achieve.

Less readily overcome are obstacles to cooperation inherent in attempts to satisfy the real need for broad *directive principles* for the guidance of inquiry. These are, in part, broad definitions of the subject matter of given branches of science or, rather, expressions of a consensus in respect of what the subject matter of a given branch of science ought to be. In part, they are heuristic *maxims* for the practical conduct of inquiry, e.g., the Principle of Causality in modern philosophy of science. Directive principles wisely used are not allowed to impose restrictions on the detailed form of scientific hypotheses, nor to entail the employment of specific techniques of investigation. Such principles are not themselves scientific hypotheses; they cannot be logically proved (or disproved), nor can they be disconfirmed by observation.

Historical methods of research are employed in the study of a wide range of very different kinds of phenomena, of course, and it seems only natural that directive principles are used to mark the boundaries between different applications of historical research. Some branches of inquiry are more "historical" than others, e.g., geology and paleontology are certainly more historical than (say) physics in the sense that recourse to historical method to establish facts and to explain infrequently recurring phenomena, is more prominent in the literature of those sciences. In the same sense, most social sciences, including economics, are more "historical" than many branches of natural science. But the directive principles just referred to only mark off branches of scientific inquiry; they do not separate from them a realm of inquiry that is uniquely and specifically *history*.

The reader who is a historian should know better than I the annals of that quest for a science that is uniquely *history:* the scientism of Comte; the search for "historical laws" undertaken by Hegel and Marx (and thought by them to have been successful); history as the science of human development, not as just the handmaid of social science, viz., history as a science, no less and no more (Bury); [5] history as the kingdom of individualities, of details which are not to be repeated and which have value in themselves (Windelband); [6] history, the "ideographic" science that is to be sharply delineated from the "nomothetic" or law-giving natural sciences (Windelband and Rickert); [7] history as recapture of the meaning of the human past as understood (felt) by those who experienced it (Dilthey); [8] history as "explanation" adducing the general "laws" established by the special sciences (Hempel and others).[9] Although this paper is not concerned with the quest for a unique *history*, it is appropriate to mention that, with exception of the positivism of Comte and the prophetic philosophies of Hegel and Marx, each of the foregoing conceptions of *history* has influenced, in one way or another, the view put forward at the beginning of this section, namely, that the economic historian *qua* historian is involved in the predictive testing of proffered "economic laws" in a rather fundamental way. Finally, the very great influence of historical researches and humanistic ideals of George Sarton ought to be mentioned.[10]

To view the economic historian as solely, or even just chiefly, a "user of economic theory," as a scout in the search for examples to illustrate the "economic laws" formulated, and sometimes thought warranted by the intuitions of theoretical economists, is precedented, no doubt, but mistaken, for reasons I shall mention in Section 3. Equally mistaken is the view of the economic historian as primarily a miner of "facts" to set before the econometrician. The whole *métier* of the economic historian, his intellectual participation in every stage of the testing of proffered "economic laws," is required: in the formulation of such "laws," in their empirical interpretation, and in the evaluation of their agreement with what actually happened in the past.

2. HISTORICAL INFERENCE AND PREDICTIVE TESTING

The readers of this essay, being for the most part economic historians, will undoubtedly prefer that any remarks made about the logical structure of "historical explanation" be kept brief. I do propose, however, to discuss the logical structure of explanatory economic models in a little more detail, just to elucidate the respective tasks of the economic historian and general economist when they cooperate in the essential work of subjecting economic theory to sharp predictive test. In examining the logical structure of explanatory models we find justification for a partial division of labor between economist and historian, but, it must be stressed, for *only* a partial, not a complete division.

In order to achieve a degree of concreteness in the discussion of predictive testing I take the liberty of referring to one of the simultaneous equations models on which I have done some work.[11] That model is based on four structural relations, viz., consumption function, investment function, liquidity preference function, and supply of money function. As it is a very small model, it is not fashionably "realistic"; whether it is an accurate representation of the class of economic events it actually purports to explain is, of course, an entirely different matter, and above all, one which has to be determined by the performance of suitable predictive tests. A complete description of the class of economic events to which this model refers is beyond the scope of the present paper. A rather vague and incomplete description of the purpose for which this model has been formulated would be afforded by saying that it is to explain year-to-year changes in the endogenous variables, consumption, gross national product, long-term rate of interest, quantity of money, and gross private investment in terms of bank reserves and autonomous shifts in the *investment schedule*.[12] Of course, in putting forward such a model, we aim to discover and explain much more than just those rather crude events that can be described by year-to-year changes in the endogenous variables. The specific observations that are employed to test the model in question were generated by the American economy during the period 1930–1959. For simplicity of expression, let us say that the historical time-series of observed endogenous variables describe an "event" that happened to the American economy, and let us say that the time-series of exogenous variables describe (in part) the given circumstances under which that event occurred.[13]

It is convenient, however, to describe the foregoing event by a set of *sample statistics*. Sample statistics are mathematical functions of the observed endogenous variables. In certain cases we can construct a set of sample statistics fewer in number than the successive observations in the historical time-series, yet containing all empirical information in the latter that happens to be relevant to the explanatory hypothesis whose truth is in question. Such a set of sample statistics is said to be *minimally sufficient* for the explanatory hypothesis and it can *replace* the immediate time-series observations in the test of the model. A minimally sufficient set of sample statistics can be constructed for the model I am referring to here.

One of the foregoing statistics is the coefficient of bank reserves in the statistical regression of gross national product on the exogenous variables, viz., bank reserves and the autonomous shift variable; let us denote this coefficient-statistic by a_4. In repeated sampling under approximately constant background conditions and under initial conditions essentially the same as those described in part by the historical time-series of bank reserves and autonomous shifts in the investment schedule, the statistic a_4 has a unique *probability distribution;* there is, for instance, a definite probability with which the event

$$(1) \qquad\qquad a_4 < 0$$

occurs. As it happens in the model referred to here, the probability of the foregoing event is very small:

$$(2) \qquad\qquad \Pr\{a_4 < 0\} \leq 0.000001,$$

less than or equal to one chance in a million.[14] Since the statistic a_4 is computed from 30 successive annual observations on the gross national product, we should expect to wait a very long time, indeed, for the American economy to produce the event (1), at least *if* the probability statement (2) is true.

If, upon computing a_4 from one of our very first samples of 30 annual observations, we find that the event (1) has occurred, we should be strongly inclined towards doubting that the probability statement (2) is true.

Undoubtedly the reader is wondering where I got the probability statement (2) in the first place and what, if any, is the economic significance of the event described by (1). The answer is, of course, that the probability statement (2) has been derived, by mathematical reasoning from a set of *initial condition* statements with the help of a set of *economic premises,* the latter being universal statements about economic parameters, e.g., the marginal propensities to consume and spend, the *ceteris paribus* rate of decrease of desired investment with respect to interest rate, and so on.

The statistical regression equation in which a_4 appears is the unconstrained maximum-likelihood estimate of the reduced-form equation for gross national product

$$(3) \quad y_{t,2} = \frac{\beta_2 \gamma_3}{\Delta} z_{t,1} + \frac{\beta_4 \gamma_2}{\Delta} z_{t,2} + \frac{\beta_4 \gamma_1 + \beta_2 (\gamma_4 - \gamma_5)}{\Delta}$$
$$+ \frac{\beta_4 (u_t + v_t) + \beta_2 (x_t - w_t)}{\Delta}$$

where

$$\Delta = \beta_4 (1 - \beta_1 - \beta_6) + \beta_2 \beta_3;$$

$y_{t,2}$ denotes gross national product, $z_{t,1}$ denotes bank reserves, $z_{t,2}$ denotes the autonomous shift variable in the investment schedule, and u_t, v_t, w_t, x_t denote random disturbances in the underlying structural relations. $\beta_1, \ldots, \beta_6, \gamma_1, \ldots, \gamma_5$ denote coefficients in the structural relations. The statistic a_4 is an unbiased normally distributed estimator of the coefficient of $z_{t,1}$ in equation (3). Given the specified initial conditions, the coefficient of $z_{t,1}$ in (3) is at least 6. 23 times as large as the standard deviation of its estimator a_4. From our sharpest formulation of economic premises we can deduce that

$$6 \leq \frac{\beta_2 \gamma_3}{\Delta} \leq 12.5.$$

Thus the economic premises of our model are incapable of being in good agreement with any but a very narrow range of values of the sample statistic a_4.

Statement (2) is called a *prediction-statement*. To show that statement (2) is a prediction-statement one must display the premises of the model in question. Those premises include statements about the coefficients in the consumption function, investment function, liquidity preference function, and supply of money function, and statements about the statistical distribution of the random disturbances in those structural equations.[15] In addition, the linkages among those functions would have to be displayed; moreover, the definite time-sequence of exogenous variables would have to be displayed as part of the statement of *initial conditions*. Finally, the form of a_4 as a mathematical function of potential sample observations would have to be described. All of the foregoing is only preliminary to mathematical derivation, of course. That derivation would have to show that the negation of statement (2), viz., the statement

(4) $\Pr \{a_4 < 0\} > .000001,$

contradicts at least one of the economic premises, *given the statement of initial conditions.*

Since the probability statement (2) is a logical consequence of initial conditions conjoined with economic premises, i.e., since the conjunction of the statement of initial conditions and the economic premises implies that the probability of the event described by (1) is extremely small, the actual occurrence of that event is charged with economic significance. For, *if the statement of background and initial conditions is warranted,* then the actual occurrence of the event described by (1) disaffirms one or more (but perhaps only one!) [16] of the economic premises from which the prediction-statement (2) is derived. It should be noticed, however, that the argument for disconfirmation is enthymematic; appeal is tacitly made to a statistical convention termed by Emile Borel *la loi unque du hasard:* extremely improbable events do not occur (Borel, 1950, pp. 100–101). If the event (1) actually occurs, then we agree to act as if the probability of its occurrence is greater than one chance in a million (decision rule); that is to say, we act to modify one or more of the premises from which the prediction statement has been derived.

Here a parenthesis is in order. I am often asked by students and econometricians why I regard certain kinds of event, e.g., the occurrence of (1), as "economically significant." Frequently inquirers refer to certain passages in the econometric literature in which authors seem to claim that events like that described by (1) have no significance, e.g., that even if the estimate a_4 of a given reduced-form coefficient in a simultaneous equations model turns out to have the wrong sign, it is of no consequence.[17] Such passages must be read in context, however, and in many cases close scrutiny reveals that the authors have formulated a *fore-*

casting problem rather than a predictive test. Clearly, any definite event, the occurrence of which can be regarded as disconfirming a probability statement that is actually derived with help of a set of economic premises, is an "economically significant" event. Of course, if one explicitly disclaims the intention of making a predictive test of the economic premises in question, then one is justified in referring to disconfirming events as "uninteresting," perhaps, but never in referring to such an event as "economically non-significant."

However, it is appropriate to mention that leading predictivists in the economics profession do not agree with me in considering events like (1) as economically significant, nor would they regard the foregoing procedure of examining the state of agreement between observations and statements as (2), which are derived with help of the economic premises, as constituting a predictive test of the latter (cf., Christ, 1952, p. 67; Friedman, 1952, p. 108). For present purposes it will be enough, perhaps, to say explicitly that the conception of predictive testing that is under discussion here has nothing essential in common with that crude form of predictivism vigorously touted by Professor Friedman and the Chicago School.[18]

It is worthwhile, however, to contrast the *forecasting use* of statistical estimates with their use in a predictive test of an explanatory economic model. The contrast should not appear invidious, as the forecaster and testing economist are trying to accomplish two rather different things. Consider once more the statistical regression of gross national product on bank reserves and the shift variable, cf., equation (3). Suppose that the sample from which the foregoing statistical regression is computed happens to yield a large value for the multiple correlation coefficient R^2 and a small value for the estimate of the variance σ_{22} of the disturbance in equation (3); e.g., suppose that $\hat{\sigma}_{22} < 140$. The forecaster might argue rationally that (for some given purpose he has in mind) it would be sound practice to forecast the next several annual values of gross national product y_{t2}, with help of the statistical regression equation, from auxiliary forecasts of bank reserves z_{t1} and of the autonomous investment function shift z_{t2} and the assumption that the random disturbances are equal to zero.

Agreeing that the forecaster's use of the statistical regression equation is sound for the purpose announced, the economist who employs the same regression estimate in making a predictive test of the economic premise from which the reduced-form equation (3) has been derived, would mention that one or more of those premises seems to be in very poor agreement with the observations; for if the appropriate background conditions are fulfilled, then it follows from the economic premises that the probability of the event

(5) $$'\hat{\sigma}_{22} < 140'$$

is very small, since one of the derived prediction-statements is

(6) $$\Pr\{\hat{\sigma}_{22} < 140\} < 0.025.$$

The appropriateness of the foregoing statistical regression as an instrument of forecasting does not rest on its being in good agreement with the premises of some explanatory economic model or other. Moreover, the accuracy with which the mathematical equations appearing in an explanatory economic model represent economic structures is not dependent on the practical suitability of those equations as instruments of forecasting. It might well be that under appropriate background conditions for the explanatory model referred to here, the reduced-form equation for gross national product (3) would not be suitable as a forecasting equation. For the variance σ_{22} of the random disturbance in that equation cannot be smaller than 296 if the model is an accurate representation of the economic mechanism it purports to describe, and might therefore not allow a sufficient degree of precision in forecasts of gross national product computed with help of ad hoc assumption that random disturbances tend to be negligible. (Such an assumption, however, is transparently *not* one of the premises of the model in question.) One means of overcoming this difficulty in forecasting might be to forecast the next few disturbances with help of some additional variables not appearing in the explanatory model but which have been found to be highly correlated with a few immediately previous estimates of the random disturbance in the reduced-form equation. (The rationality of the foregoing ad hoc procedure cannot be overthrown merely by averring that the correlation is without theoretical significance, only temporary, and spurious in the long run).

I repeat: the contrast drawn between the forecasting use of statistical estimates and their use in predictive testing of explanatory economic models has been stressed here solely for purposes of clarification. A few readers of my earlier monograph have interpreted the criticism of predictivism put forward there as an attack on economic forecasting (cf., Bassmann, 1964, pp. 4–5, pp. 55–62). Such an interpretation rests on alien assumptions that have been read into the context of that monograph, and is completely mistaken.

Let us return to our illustration. The conjunction of the statements [19]

(a) *background and initial conditions were fulfilled during the given historical period in question;*

(b) *the event (1), viz.,*

$$a_4 < 0,$$

occurred in the period mentioned in (a);

is called the *falsifier* of the *conjunction* of those economic premises actually employed in the derivation of the probability statement (2) (cf., Popper, 1959, Ch. III). Notice that both (a) and (b) are *singular statements;* [20] both are potential facts.

Any claim that a statistical disconfirmation of one or more of the prediction-statements derived with help of an explanatory economic model is decisive against one or more of the premises must, if it is to be valid, adduce warrant for the appropriate initial and background conditions. The specific historical problem in predictive testing occurs in connection with the conceptualizing of relevant *background conditions* and in determining whether the statement alleging their fulfillment is warranted.

As in the case of natural "laws," we do not expect that proffered "economic laws," even if they are true, will manifest themselves to observation under all conceivable background conditions. Pure water does not always freeze whenever its temperature falls below 0° C., even under carefully controlled laboratory conditions; no geophysicist, intending to collect observations for the testing of some proffered "lays" of earthquakes, would locate his seismograph in the switching yard of a rail terminal. By the same token, if there is warrant for the statement that government controls distorted the functioning of the American economy during the Second World War, then there is excellent reason for regarding a forecasting test (for the years 1946–1947) of L. R. Klein's early dynamical model as logically invalid (cf., Basmann, 1964, p. 59).

To every explanatory economic model there corresponds a set of more or less definite background or external conditions that must be fulfilled in a given period of economic history if observations recorded for that period are to be deemed appropriate for predictive testing of that model. Those conditions, which must remain approximately constant over the period in question, are suggested in part by the structure of the model (cf., Basmann, 1964, Sec. 2.4). But the conceptualization of relevant background conditions is a task for which the economic historian *qua* historian is equipped by training, experience, and general point of view, at least potentially. The ability to conceive of events not represented by operationally interpreted symbols in a given mathematical economic model, yet which, if they occur, invalidate a proposed empirical test thereof, is not adequately cultivated by the training, formal and informal, that mathematical economists and econometricians normally undergo. The ability to conceptualize relevant background conditions for the predictive test of a given explanatory economic model is not to be confused with mere ingenuity in imagining and naming "factors" that *might* interfere with the normal functioning of the economic mechanisms the model is supposed to represent. The conceptual ability of which I speak is professional; in that respect it is like that of the mathematician in formulating problems for which there is a good chance of solution and yet which are non-trivial and worthy of attention. The conceptualization of background conditions requires the simultaneous operation of the imagination and critical foresight of the practical steps that must be taken in order to give them substance and verify their presence or absence, as the case may be. This conceptualization also requires the touch of the true artist; as the creator of Sherlock Holmes has put it, the knowledge of when to stop. For it is possible, of course, to go on indefinitely specifying background conditions that are to be fulfilled if a given test of a given explanatory model is to be considered valid. Hence the conceptualization process is open to abuse; economic theories can be "saved" by inventing background conditions, on an ad hoc basis, which, not being fulfilled, can be supposed to invalidate any predictive test that has ever been performed.

Discouraging as it might seem to be, the economist can no more expect his statistical tests of hypotheses to be valid predictive tests unless he provides adequate warrant for initial background conditions that can (say) the physicist. In this connection it is appropriate to mention that theoretical physicists are quite dependent on the specialized knowledge of laboratory physicists and the experience of the latter with scientific equipment; even if the experimental physicist is not consulted in the formulation of the proffered "law" that is to be tested, he is almost always called in to interpret the documentary record of experiments performed some time back; frequently he is expected to correct that documentary record, to infer from it what actually happened in a past sequence of experiments that might be too expensive to repeat without especially good reason. No doubt the technology that the laboratory physicist commands usually permits him to control the background conditions to a sufficient degree of approximation; but

> To tell the truth, there are times when this or any kind of work seems dull, exhausting, even fruitless. When, after days of trying, you still can't find the leak in the vacuum system, or when, after you patiently have fitted an elaborate piece of apparatus together, an oscilloscope suddenly picks up a lot of meaningless "noise" from some unknown source, . . . then of course the work is unattractive. This is no different from the difficulties and frustrations to be expected in any serious undertaking. (Bitter, 1963, pp. 26–27.)

For all that there is a grain of truth in the excuse frequently advanced by social scientists, namely, that natural scientists have it easy with their technological control of background conditions and the rapidity with which their experiments can be repeated; but it should not be forgotten that this is first and foremost an excuse. The extended time-scale in accordance with which the unplanned "experiments" on a real economic mechanism can take place, and the various ethical restraints which prohibit economists from experimenting where they can, are serious obstacles to be sure. But it is only the exceptional difficulty of surmounting the problem of background conditions, not the problem itself, that seems to be peculiar to the social sciences and economics.

The practical skills by means of which the presence (or absence) of changes in conceptualized background conditions are detected (or verified) belong to the *métier* of the historian. (If the requisite ability to conceptualize background conditions is not adequately cultivated by the training the mathematical economist or econometric statistician normally undergoes, it is true a fortiori that neither his training nor experience provide him with adequate command over the tools of historical inference.) In the first place the time of occurrence of such perturbations of background conditions has to be conjectured, viz., a hypothesis about timing has to be formulated, and tested by reference to a documentary record and the weighing of evidence that can be gleaned therefrom. While the presence of background perturbations will often be suggested by the failure of prediction-statements, which are derived with help of the explanatory model, to be in good agreement with observations (Basmann, 1964, p. 19), this failure cannot be viewed as cogent evidence for the occurrence of such a perturbation. Other data, logically independent of the endogenous observations from which test statistics are computed, have to be found, interpreted, and shown to warrant the statement that the given perturbation actually has (or has not) occurred.

It is worthwhile to illustrate briefly the sort of conceptualization and subsequent historical inference I have in mind, and for that purpose it is appropriate to mention the paper "English Pre-Industrial Population Trends" by G. L. S. Tucker (1963). Suppose that a break in the long-run trend of English population growth is conceived of as a relevant change in the background conditions for some economic hypothesis, in the formulation of which population does not itself enter explicitly as a variable. Suppose, too, that the hypothesis is to be subjected to predictive test, the sample statistics having to be computed from 18th century observations (say) because we have already used up all subsequent observations without succeeding in disproving the hypothesis in question. Tucker's investigation, his test of the generally accepted hypothesis that such a sustained break occurred about 1750 against the alternative hypothesis that no break occurred about 1750 but one did much later in the century; his *explanation* of the appearance of the Griffith and Brownlee population time-series (Tucker, p. 207) with help of a model local epidemic that moves from place to place over a period of decades; then illustrates the sort of investigation of background conditions I have in mind. Of course, Tucker was not seeking to validate background conditions for some definite explanatory model, and reference to his paper is made here for illustrative purposes only.

Historical studies of a more general nature are contributions to the work of conceptualizing, and finding warrant for, background conditions for predictive tests of specific explanatory models. For instance, Schlote (1952) and Imlah (1958) not only provide valuable new quantitative data, but also valuable reference material for conceptualization of background conditions, the latter in the form of narratives of significant and more or less unique events such as changes in government economic policy. This kind of contribution is, however, traditional and well-understood; it will be sufficient just to mention it.

Let us consider sample statistics again. Recall that a_4, defined at the beginning of this section, is a function of observations. I said that the event described by (1) had "economic significance" because its actual occurrence, in conjunction with warranted historical statements of background conditions and initial conditions, constitutes a "falsifier" of one or more of the underlying economic premises of a given explanatory model. There is another sense in which the event (1) can be said to possess or lack economic significance, which, for lack of a more definite terminology, I shall refer to as its *economic interpretation*. From a purely logical point of view the symbols for observations in an economic model are completely arbitrary, of course, and some decision in respect of what they are to stand for has to be made. The significance of the event (1) is only that it disconfirms, under appropriate conditions, one or more of the underlying premises as statements about whatever it is that happens to be measured by the observations from which the sample statistic a_4 is to be computed.

Thus (to take a different example), on the basis of one given operational definition of exchange-rate, a given theory or model purporting to predict the gold points [21] might appear to be disconfirmed by observations. On the basis of a different operational definition of exchange rate, however, the same theory might be in good agreement with observation. The critical evaluation of Morgenstern's calculations of the gold points (1875–1914), and some of his conclusions about the empirical truth of exchange-rate theory, which has been offered by Davis and Hughes (1960, cf., pp. 62–64), illustrates the participation of economic historians in the formulation of operational definitions of the symbols that appear in pure economic theory and explanatory economic models. But such participation is more or less informal and, from the point of view of its close connection with the formulation of definite theories and models, very infrequent. (In this regard I do not mean to undervalue the achievements of economists working on the national accounts.) The formulation of operational definitions of economic variables is, however, part and parcel of theory and model formulation. It is an essential part of theory formulation for which economic historians are by training and knowledge particularly well suited. While it cannot be separated from the formulation of economic premises and their deductive elucidation into theorems that can serve as prediction-statements, it is equally true that the formulation of operational definitions of economic observables cannot be separated from the conceptualization of background conditions.

I do not mean to suggest by the foregoing remarks that economic historians will be able to cooperate effectively in predictive testing of proffered "economic laws" without reflecting deeply on the nature of scientific prediction and explanation in general. The economic historian has to bring to this enterprise more than a mere kit of tools.

3. SOME CONCLUDING REMARKS

In contending that the determination of what of significance actually happened in economic history is a task equally as fundamental in predictive testing of proffered "economic laws" as the derivation of prediction-statements (mathematical economics) and the manipulation of statistical computations (econometric statistics), I have not overlooked the fact that traditional historiography offers other uses for the facts that become warranted by *historical inference*. For one thing, historians offer *explanations*—by doing so they present modern philosophy with one of its most perplexing problems (Gardiner, 1955)—that are in many respects found to be original when viewed against the background of accepted opinion in their own time.

Much of the value of historical explanations resides in the fact that they are not always derived entirely from "that vague amalgam of currently recognized generalities, derived from common experience and more or less confirmed by our own (Walsh, 1960, p. 66), or deduced solely from the sociology, psychology and the economics that theorists in those fields claim to "know." I have the impression that the competent historian is not so content with the existing degree of empirical confirmation of proffered "economic laws" that he will hesitate to offer generalizations and hypotheses of his own making if the latter seem better to account for the facts at his disposal. In this attitude towards economic theory the historian is right. To be sure, he risks that supposedly devastating charge of not "knowing much economics," which the general historian, at least, knows that he can safely ignore. At any rate, historians immersed in facts produced by historical inference often frame explanations that might contradict some proffered "economic laws" or other. I plan to say more about that possibility later. For the time being I should like just to say that, from the point of view of one involved in the predictive testing of such proffered "economic laws," new alternative hypotheses, hypotheses that really contradict old ones, are always welcome from every quarter.

It should be recognized, however, that most explanations offered by historians are not explanatory hypotheses, at least not in the sense that a well-articulated and deductively rich explanatory economic model is. I do not intend this comparison to be invidious. Hempel has coined the term "explanation sketch" to describe the explanations commonly put forward by historians (Hempel, 1942, p. 351); he reminds us of the fact that most explanations offered in history involve only tacit reference to the general "laws" or regularities those explanations presuppose. (See also Gardiner, 1955, pp. 96–108.) Very often the generalizations tacitly referred to in historical explanation are those of common sense, as we have already noted. But very often those underlying generalizations are potential universal hypotheses which, in their newness, are not sufficiently precise to support strict derivation of feasibly testable prediction-statements. By way of illustration, I should like to mention a recent article by Nathan Rosenberg, "Technological Change in the Machine Tool Industry" (Rosenberg, 1963). The explanatory intent and pattern is clear and prominent in Rosenberg's paper. The *explicandum,* the object of explanation, is a historical sequence of economically significant innovations. Most of the general premises are explicitly indicated; they are mechanical, thermodynamical, and chemical "laws" as well as general economic principles. Moreover, Rosenberg contributes an original concept of "technological convergence" and the elements of a theory to account for it. Finally, the pattern of reasoning is tightly woven. Rosenberg's "explanation sketch," while certainly not a deductive explanation of the kind described in Section 2 is richer in argued conclusions and, in that sense, "better testable" than a great many policy-oriented econometric models, and, therefore, of greater value, at least to economic science. In this connection it is worthy of mention that Rosenberg does not make much use of explicit "economic laws."

In suggesting that historians can do much for economic science by continuing to offer their own "explanation sketches," I am not departing from an attitude of strong skepticism regarding the existence of *purely historical* "laws."

Economic historians are often exhorted to make greater use of economic theory and econometric technique, and they are almost as frequently condemned for failing to do so. Whether it is appropriate to raise against a piece of research in economic history the criticism that it does not "make use of economic theory" depends in part on the purpose of that research, but, more importantly, just what piece of economic theory the critic has in mind that the historian has failed to use. If the historical research is an "explanation sketch," it will hardly be clear that it contradicts any given piece of economic theory except, perhaps, when it specifically does so at the level of announced premises. But even if a contradiction of that sort can be found, it will always be appropriate to point out to the critic that premises are logically remote from the empirical evidence that might tend to disaffirm them, and to ask the critic at least to supply reports on the predictive tests the allegedly superior premises have survived. Of course, it would hardly do for the critic to reply that most economists, or at least, some prominent economists believe that the theory in question is approximately true, or that an acquaintance at the "Fed" or National Bureau of Economic Research has some classified data that confirm it. The only really sound argument against a piece of research in economic history is of the same nature as a cogent argument against an explanatory economic model, namely, that at some point or other its assumptions or conclusions are at variance with publicly available independently warranted statements of fact (or, of course, that it is internally self-contradictory).

It is a fact, however, that economic historians—at least those carrying on in the "new economic history"—*do* make considerable use of economic theory and models, and thereby involve themselves in the matter of predictive testing of the strictly universal economic premises they employ. Whenever economic premises are invoked to explain an event or sequence of events that occurred in the past, or are adduced as an argument for the claim that such-and-such an event "must have occurred," two questions have to be answered in the affirmative before the proposed explanation or claim can be considered as cogent:

(1) Has at least one stringent predictive test of the adduced economic premises already been carried out, and have those premises survived all of the predictive tests that have been made up to now?

(2) Were the background and initial conditions allegedly appropriate for application of the foregoing economic premises actually fulfilled

for the time-period during which the fact to be explained or inferred is supposed to have occurred?

The scientific value of research in economic history depends on the extent to which the economic premises borrowed or invented by the economic historian for explanatory purposes have withstood fairly rigorous predictive tests; it also depends on the quality of the historical investigation of the background conditions under which the economic historian proposes to employ those economic premises.

The critical appraisal of econometric practices, which appears in Section 2, is meant primarily for the economic historian who regards himself as chiefly a user of, and not responsible for, economic theory invented and established by others; as a producer of research in economic history, he cannot afford to be indifferent to the suitability and quality of the inputs he employs. For if his proffered explanations of the economic past come to naught, and his work collapses, because he has borrowed uncritically from the great catalog of inadequately tested economic models, he, and no one else, will be blamed. It has been suggested in this paper, however, that economic historians can do a great service to economic history and to economic science generally by taking a closer and better informed interest in the formulation and predictive testing of explanatory economic models, contributing his own special skills at all levels of that enterprise.

Purdue University

NOTES

1. According to this ancient conception of scientific explanation one is supposed to argue from well-known and established premises to hitherto unknown facts, the latter being supposed established by deduction. In econometric studies it is common to find statistical estimates labeled "reasonable" on the basis of their agreement with *a priori* theory, a procedure reminiscent of that of the surveyor who, having laid out a small right-triangle on Earth's surface, checks the accuracy of the figure by adding his measurements to the acute angles and comparing their sum with 90°00′. The surveyor's confidence in Euclid has long ago been justified by experience, of course.

2. Rondo Cameron has commented favorably on the graduate program in economics here at Purdue, so perhaps it is not out of place for me to mention that all students are required to take a considerable number of courses in which continuous use is made of mathematical deduction, previous courses in differential and integral calculus usually being a requirement for admittance. Of course, the purpose is not to make (say) a future economic historian into an econometrician but to give him background for judging intelligently the true worth of the statistical and mathematical contributions of others.

3. Syncretists often suppose that the response of the outspoken skeptic is intended to convert the partisan of methodological legislation. Such an aim is almost never the skeptic's intention, it being so very unlikely to succeed. What the skeptic is usually trying to do is persuade the bystanders, particularly the inexperienced, not to give up their methodological freedom. Partisanship on behalf of methodological legislation is not a *crimen laesae majestatis divinae,* and the skeptic has, therefore, little motivation to save the partisan from himself, charitable as that might seem to be; rather it is the prospect that a new "school" will be formed, with its clients generating a lot of dull studies in accordance with a rigid formula and phrased in colorless in-group slang, that motivates open criticism and a pointing-out of specific dangers (cf., Boring, 1963, p. 252).

4. It is unfortunate that many economists fail to distinguish between philosophy of science and methodology—between philosophical clarification, on the one hand, and methodological legislation, on the other. The ability to make such distinctions is a real asset in econometricians and historians who seek to cooperate effectively. For there are encountered in economics and history many real questions which, not being susceptible of answer by logical demonstration or by reference to empirical facts, yet call for systematic *clarification.* To be sure, many such perplexities are muddles that have been produced by earlier attempts to legislate method for the conduct of scientific inquiry, and generally by economists seeking short-cuts to the achievement of success in research, cf., Nagel, 1954, p. 47. Attempts to clear up such muddles are not themselves efforts to introduce competing methodological prescriptions, although they are frequently taken for such. In a recent paper (Basmann, 1963) I pointed out that the Principle of Causality cannot be adduced in support of the claim made by H. Wold and R. H. Strotz (Strotz-Wold, 1960) that "causal chain" models are in some relevant sense better paradigms for causal explanation in economics than "interdependent" models. Some readers have taken my arguments as a prescription *against* the formulation of "causal chain" models in economics. Of course, I did not say that "causal chain" models are in any way inferior to "interdependent" models as potentially accurate representations of economic mechanisms. What I did claim (primarily for the benefit of graduate students in search of a methodology) was that the Principle of Causality in no way singles out the "causal chain" model as an *ideal form* of causal explanation to which we economists ought to strive to make our explanatory models approximate as closely as possible, cf., Nagel, 1961, pp. 316–324. By the way, I said nothing original in that paper.

5. Bury's inaugural address is reprinted in Stern, 1956, pp. 209–223.

6. Possibly the most readily accessible short statement of Windelband's views of historical research, its nature and method, is given in *History of Philosophy* (1893), Chapter 1, Art. 2, pp. 8–18 (Windelband, 1958).

7. For a brief account of the epistemological theory that underlies the analysis of history by Windelband, Rickert and their followers, and its connection with the neo-Kantian movement in philosophy, see Bochenski, 1947, pp. 101–111.

8. See H. P. Rickman's introduction to selected passages from Dilthey's works (Rickman, 1962).

9. Papers by Hempel, White, Nagel, Gallie, Dray, Frankel, Donegan and Scriven on historical explanation are reprinted in Gardiner, 1959.

10. The case for humanization of science is stated most eloquently by George Sarton in his essay, "The History of Science and the New Humanism," reprinted in Sarton, 1962, Chapter III, and, of course, the idea is pervasive in all of his writings. Two additional essays of Sarton's that are especially pertinent here are "History of Science" (1956) and "Four Guiding Ideas" (1947); they are reprinted in Stimson, 1962. In the same connection, see the essays by Bronowski, 1956.

It is worthwhile noting that T. H. Huxley, in his *Progress of Science* (1887), *Science and Culture* (1880), and *On the Advisableness of Improving Natural Knowledge* (1866), in addition to explaining with great clarity the humanistic value of the pursuit of science, explains with equal clarity the relation between the technological and humanistic functions of science.

11. Basmann, R. L., Lectures on Quantitative Economics, I. Purdue University, Econ. 670–671, 1964–1965.

12. The shift in the investment schedule is a hypothetical construct. The investment schedule for the American economy is assumed to have shifted downward in 1939, 1942, and 1945, and upwards in 1953, remaining constant between shifts. At the present juncture, the hypothesis about shifts has not been established; that is to say, the statement of timing, direction and magnitude of the investment schedule shifts has not yet been confirmed by independent methods of historical inference.

13. In this paper we shall distinguish between *initial conditions* and *background conditions*. The former are represented by exogenous variables which appear explicitly in the mathematical functions of an explanatory model; the latter do not appear explicitly and might not even be measurable.

14. That is to say, the relative frequency with which the economy is supposed to generate a sample of endogenous observations yielding $a_i < 0$ is less than 0.000001.

15. For instance β_1, β_6, and β_3 are coefficients of gross national product in the consumption function, investment function, and liquidity preference function respectively. Among the economic premises that underlie the explanatory model in question are the following inequalities

$$
\text{(a)} \quad
\begin{cases}
0.75 \leqq \beta_1 \leqq 0.85, \\[4pt]
1.0 \; < \beta_1 + \beta_6 \leqq 1.03, \\[4pt]
0 \quad < 2\beta_6 \leqq \beta_3 \leqq 0.5.
\end{cases}
$$

These inequalities, together with other premises, are actually employed in the derivation of the probability statement (2).

The economic premises state also that the structural disturbances u_t v_t, w_t, x_t are independently normally distributed with zero means and very small variances; viz.,

$$
\text{(b)} \quad
\begin{cases}
1 \leqq \dfrac{\omega}{u^2} \leqq 2, \\[8pt]
1 \leqq \dfrac{\omega}{v^2} \leqq 2, \\[8pt]
1 \leqq \dfrac{\omega}{w^2} \leqq 2, \\[8pt]
1 \leqq \dfrac{\omega}{x^2} \leqq 2,
\end{cases}
$$

Nonetheless the variance σ_{22} of random disturbance in the gross national product reduced-form equation (3) shown above is not small; for, with the help of all economic premises we derive the statement

$$
\text{(c)} \qquad 296 \leqq \sigma_{22} \leqq 40{,}494,
$$

From the foregoing restriction (c) we learn that our original economic premises fail to make a very definite claim in respect of the average magnitude of the random variation in gross national product. Consequently I have undertaken to sharpen the economic premises to the extent that one can derive the more precise statement

$$(d) \qquad 296 \leqq \sigma_{22} \leqq 925.$$

16. An important goal sought in deductive exploration of explanatory economic models is—as far as possible—to prepare to single out just those economic premises that are to be regarded as having been disconfirmed by a given predictive test. Poor agreement between a prediction-statement and observations disaffirms a conjunction of several premises. In logic a conjunction is false if one or more of its constituent statements is false. In many cases it will be possible to account for the poor agreement between a prediction-statement and relevant observations by attributing the poor agreement to the falsity of just one or two specified economic premises. It would be very inefficient procedure to scrap the entire model in the face of a predictive test that disconfirms the *conjunction* of economic premises. It is equally inefficient to try to find the disconfirmed premises by trial and error experimentation with alternative premises.

For econometric models that contain many equations and many parameters, however, thorough deductive exploration appears to be infeasible; at least, no one seems to attempt it.

17. For an illuminating case see the paper by Stojkovic, 1964, p. 404.

18. For a general critique of predictivism see Toulmin, 1963.

According to predictivists, the procedures followed by the (say) testing economist, the close examination of economic observations and test statistics to determine whether there has occurred one or more theoretically very improbable events like (1) and (5) are "essentially tests of internal consistency" and "perhaps should not be called tests at all" (cf., Christ, 1952, p. 67). Predictivists do not ordinarily *derive* probability statements like (2) and (6); instead the calculated disturbances from equations like (3) or the statistical estimate $\hat{\sigma}_{22}$ are to be "examined to see whether they are very large according to some intuitive standard of how large they are expected to be" (cf., Christ, 1952, p. 67). (Just whose intuition is to be received as more cogent than mathematical derivation is not specified.) Thus predictivists seem to be content to remain ignorant of all but the most transparent testable consequences of the economic premises in their models and sometimes rationalize this content by methodological prescriptions that depreciate the employment of mathematics as an instrument of exploration of theoretical economic premises. Unfortunately the offhandedness and obscurity with which the predictivist doctrine has been retailed makes it exceptionally difficult to clarify the nature of arguments that might have been brought forward on its behalf.

19. For more detailed accounts of the logic of scientific explanation see the paper by Hempel and Oppenheim, 1948, and the book by Nagel, 1961, Chapters 2 and 3.

20. A *singular* statement asserts that a specified event has occurred at a given time and place.

A universal statement is of the form: *For every x, x has the property P.* Some universal statements can be verified by exhaustive enumeration of a finite class of individuals, viz., as a conjunction of a finite number of singular statements. For example: *For every x, if x is the infinitive of a currently used regular French verb, then x forms the future tense by adding -ai, -as, -a, -ons, -ez, -ont.*

Ideally, however, scientific "laws" are supposed to be strictly universal statements; such statements are not expressible as conjunctions of a finite number of singular statements and cannot be verified by exhaustive enumeration. For example: *For every x, if x is a demand function with positive own-price elasticity, then x has negative income elasticity.* We do not know *a priori* that the class of all demand functions with negative own-price elasticities is finite (cf., Hempel-Oppenheim, 1948, pp. 338–341).

Prediction-statements, which are singular statements, cannot be derived from universal statements (economic premises) alone, but with the help of other singular statements (initial and background conditions).

21. The gold points are theoretical constructs, of course, and not directly observable. Hence any decision in respect of their operational definition is central to the formulation of a model of exchange rates.

REFERENCES

1. Basmann, R. L., 1963, "The Causal Interpretation of Non-Triangular Systems of Economic Relations," *Econometrica,* 31:439–48, 451–53 (July, 1963).
2. Basmann, R. L., 1964, *On Predictive Testing of a Simultaneous Equations Model: The Retail Market for Food in the U.S.,* Institute for Quantitative Research in Economics and Management, No. 78, Purdue University.
3. Basmann, R. L., 1964–65, *Lectures on Quantitative Economics,* I, Purdue University, Department of Economics.
4. Bitter, Francis, 1963, *Mathematical Aspects of Physics,* Garden City, N.Y.
5. Bochenski, I. M., 1947, *Europäische Philosophie der Gegenwart,* 2te Aufl., Bern.
6. Borel, Emile, 1950, *Elements de la Theorie des Probabilités,* Paris.
7. Boring, Edwin G., 1963, *History, Psychology, and Science: Selected Papers,* ed. by Watson, Robert I. and Campbell, Donald T., New York.
8. Bronowski, J., 1959, *Science and Human Values,* New York.
9. Christ, Carl, 1952, *A Test of an Econometric Model for the United States 1921–1947,* Chicago, Cowles Commission Papers, New Series, No. 49.
10. Cohen, Morris R., 1959, *Reason and Nature,* 2nd ed., Glencoe, Illinois.
11. Davis, Lance E. and Hughes, J. R. T., 1960, "A Dollar-Sterling Exchange. 1803–1895," *Economic History Review,* 2nd Ser., 13:52–78 (August, 1960).
12. Feigl, Herbert and Brodbeck, May, eds., 1953, *Readings in the Philosophy of Science,* New York.
13. Friedman, Milton, 1952, "Comment" (See 9, pp. 107–114).
14. Gardiner, Patrick, 1955, *The Nature of Historical Explanation,* London.
15. Gardiner, Patrick, 1959, *Theories of History,* Glencoe, Illinois.
16. Hempel, Carl G., 1942, "The Function of General Laws in History," (Reprinted in 15; pp. 344–356).
17. Hempel, Carl G., and Oppenheim, Paul, 1948, "The Logic of Explanation," (Reprinted in 12; pp. 319–352).
18. Huxley, Thomas H., 1893, *Method and Results: Essays,* New York.
19. Imlah, Albert H., 1958, *Economic Elements in the Pax Britannica,* Cambridge, Mass.
20. Marshall, Alfred, 1948, *Principles of Economics,* 8th edition, New York.
21. Muller, Herbert J., 1953, *The Uses of the Past,* New York.
22. Nagel, Ernest, 1954, *Sovereign Reason,* Glencoe, Illinois.
23. Nagel, Ernest, 1961, *The Structure of Science,* New York.
24. Popper, K. R., 1959, *Logic of Scientific Discovery,* New York.
25. Rickman, H. P., 1962, *Wilhelm Dilthey: Pattern and Meaning in History,* New York.

26. Rosenberg, Nathan, 1963, "Technological Change in the Machine Tool Industry," *Journal of Economic History*, 23:414–43.
27. Sarton, George, 1962, *The History of Science and the New Humanism*, Bloomington, Indiana.
28. Seiler, Gerhard, 1959, *Ökonometrische Konjunkturmodelle*, Stuttgart.
29. Schlote, Werner, 1952, *British Overseas Trade from 1700 to the 1930's*, Oxford.
30. Sorensen, Theodore C., 1963, *Decision-Making in the White House* (Foreword by John F. Kennedy), New York.
31. Stern, Fritz, ed., 1956, *The Varieties of History*, New York.
32. Stimson, Dorothy, ed., 1962, *Sarton on the History of Science*, Cambridge, Mass.
33. Stojkovic, George, "Market Models for Agricultural Products," (in 41; pp. 386–418).
34. Strotz, R. H. and Wold, H. O. A., 1960, "Recursive *vs.* Non-Recursive Systems: An Attempt at Synthesis," *Econometrica*, 28:417–27 (April, 1960).
35. Teggart, Frederick J., 1960, *Theory of History*, Berkeley, Calif.
36. Tintner, G., 1952, *Econometrics*, New York.
37. Toulmin, Stephen, 1963, *Foresight and Understanding*, New York.
38. Tucker, G. S. L., 1963, "English Pre-Industrial Population Trends," *Economic History Review*, 2nd Ser., 16:205–18 (Dec., 1963).
39. Walsh, W. H., 1960, *Philosophy of History*, New York.
40. Windelband, Wilhelm, 1958, *A History of Philosophy*, 2 vols., New York.
41. Wold, Herman, ed., 1964, *Econometric Model-Building: Essays on the Causal Chain Approach*, Amsterdam.

FACT AND THEORY IN ECONOMIC HISTORY

J. R. T. Hughes *

"I don't see that anyone save a sap-head can now think that he knows any history until he understands economics."　　　—EZRA POUND

It is customary that the audience stand up during the "Hallelujah Chorus" when Handel's *Messiah* is performed. This "social fact" may be observed and data can be collected each year on the recurrence of this phenomenon. Like the recurrence of industrial investment, changes in prices, unemployment and the like, the annual rise of the concert-hall audience must be explicable by analysis of some kind. What kind? Theoretical, historical, both or neither?

A historical analysis would soon enough produce the interesting tradition that Good King George II stood up in the London performance of 1743 in order better to see the source of the great sounds onstage.[1] The rules of decorum then prevailing required that all lower ranks stand up when His Majesty did. The tradition was continued. Why? The theorist, employing the general principles of dynamic-social-decision-making (or some such), could produce a suitable explanation why, when one man stands at the beginning of the chorus, the rest join. Perhaps also the dynamic principles of social-decision-making could explain, with the aid of

Source. EEH/Second Series, Vol. 3, No. 2. © Graduate Program in Economic History, University of Wisconsin, 1966.

* I am indebted to my colleague R. L. Basmann for two years of fascinating discussions regarding the logic and methods of history and science. Although much of what follows has withstood the weight of his criticisms, I assume responsibility for errors of fact or logic.

difference equations, the year-by-year recurrence of the phenomenon. But such analysis would not unearth the actions of King George, since his actions were a singular phenomenon not derivable from general principles.

So to know why people stand during the "Hallelujah Chorus" we need both historical and logical methods. Neither by itself will suffice. However, the *fact* that King George stood up and so did the audience can be discovered without reference to any general principles whatever, and the tendency for the audience to stand each year can doubtless be suitably explained without reference to King George. (Certainly the average highbrow, struggling suddenly to his feet as his neighbor rises, is unaware of his royal patrimony.)

Similar problems surround the study of economic phenomena that have actually occurred in the history of economic life. For, as in cultural history, not all knowledge generated in economic history needs a springboard in general principles [2] or "theory." The statements, "George II stood up in 1743," and "The crisis of 1857 had non-monetary origins," are both singular statements based upon observed factual evidence. On the other hand, any explanation of why the "real origins" of the 1857 crisis existed, and were important determinants of that crisis, involve the scholar in some resort to general principles since the facts, by themselves, explain nothing. How much theory and how much fact—both, neither, or either—ought there to be in that part of empirical economics we call economic history?

Around this question a great deal of discussion is currently centered. It has recently been argued by Robert Fogel that the separation between theoretical and factual intellectual enterprise in economic history dates from the rise of the German Historical School.[3] Doubtless the rise of that school gave a name and a certain respectability to studies in economics not rooted in received theory. But economics itself, like any science, has both a theoretical and an empirical base, and the duality of scholarly enterprise, I think, owes more to the peculiar problems of economic studies, the historical character of the evidence, the lack of laboratory technique and data, than to any particular school of thought within the discipline.*

* One notes with interest the lack of such problems in the current work of Vernon Smith on experimental economics. Freed from time and history, Smith, generating his own data in controlled laboratory situations, experiences virtually no problems of "theory and history." He confronts theory immediately with tests and the resulting data are used to further refine the logical structure he works with. V. L. Smith, "An Experimental Study of Competitive Market Behavior," *Journal of Political Economy,* Vol. LXX, April, 1962; "Effects of Market Organization on Competitive Equilibrium," *Quarterly Journal of Economics,* Vol. LXXVIII, May, 1964; "Experimental Auction Markets and the Walraisian Hypothesis," *Journal of Political Economy,* Vol. LXXIV, August, 1965.

The profession has long been beset by the same problems. Schmoller and the German Historical School are the most famous revolt against theoretical economics, but partly because they acquired a label. They weren't the first nor even the most important case of alienation between "fact" and "theory" people in economics.

Most of the classic controversies over the British currency were between "fact" and "theory" men, beginning with the Bank of England's suspension of specie payments (1797–1821). Henry Thornton, a most wise man and, for his time, no mean monetary theorist, attempted to amend, in *The Paper Credit* (1802), certain views concerning the internal circulation of money—views which descended through Hume and Smith to Ricardo.[4] On the basis of observation, experience and hunch, he wanted to reject the narrow view that the nation's money supply was simply a function of the balance of payments, and that *ad libitum* issues of paper money would merely drive an equal amount of specie out of the country, and, moreover, that therefore, Bank policy should be limited to issuing paper money "as if metallic,"—pound for pound (sterling) of gold deposited. He noted especially that credit was usually endangered by panic and internal drain. This could be best avoided if the Bank did not necessarily contract its issues of notes during an external drain.[5] The easy axioms of the narrow view, however, were picked up and refined by Ricardo in his writings, in his Pamphlet of 1810, and finally in his plan for a national bank.[6] Ricardo had a way with the logic of economics, and so *The High Price of Bullion* triumphed over *The Paper Credit* even though the latter is incomparably the more adequate piece of analysis. Knowledge of facts separated Thornton from Ricardo fundamentally, as it would their intellectual descendents. The differences were seemingly irreconcilable, not because Thornton knew no theory, but because he knew "how things worked," whereas Ricardo and his friends cared naught for facts and were extraordinarily persuasive. As Keynes noted, Ricardo had similarly bested Malthus over the possibility of deficient effective demand ". . . and Ricardo conquered England as completely as the Holy Inquisition conquered Spain." Bank policy based upon Ricardo's theories was a catalogue of needless disaster until the Germans caused the Bank Act of 1844 to be "suspended" for the last time in 1914. But we anticipate.

The issue of the bullion debates came up again in aggravated form following the crises of 1825 and 1836–37. These issues were again resolved in favor of the narrow view, this time on a long-term basis in the paragraphs of the Bank of England Act of 1844. Ricardo's posthumous army, led by Field Marshal Lord Overstone, overwhelmed Tooke and the undermanned legions of the Banking School.[7] Again it was "automatic" adjustment against "plain facts." Overstone, almost in Ricardo's words, argued that if the Bank of England's action contracted the money supply and raised interest rates, prices would fall, and the balance of payments would be aided in readjusting toward its "normal" equilibrium. In fact, the laws of the currency were as true as natural law in physical science.

> The great laws which determine the monetary equilibrium of the commercial world assign to this country a certain amount of money. No internal arrangements to which we may resort can alter or suspend the law . . . the monetary arrangements of this, as of every other country, must be subordinate to the great principles which regulate the monetary equilibrium of the world. Any attempt to resist or modify the result of these principles can result only in confusion and embarrassment.[8]

Thus Lord Overstone. Tooke, a long-time student of facts, a merchant (than which, in Ricardo's view, nothing could be more contemptible), could now swallow the dose in its purity. Like Lyndon Johnson, Tooke believed that, for the most part, interest rates were part of the cost of production, and attempts by the Bank of England to choke off economic activity by tightening up its credit would only raise prices so long as "other" factors made continued production profitable. Tooke (and later his friend Newmarch joined in the effort) insisted that interest rates and prices generally move in the same direction. Newmarch, like Thornton before him, argued that Bank-rate policy of the Ricardian kind only made commercial crises worse than they otherwise have been.[9] Such arguments were ignored, and have largely been ignored to the present time. Tight money policy by central banks in times of crisis become holy writ.

By mid-nineteenth century the split between "fact" and "theory" men was put on a regular basis, from M'culloch to Palgrave, but with some exceptions. In J. S. Mill's *Principles* some factual materials were used. Jevons was an indefatigable worker on facts. So was Marshall, and it was from his theoretic hands that Sir John Clapham received his apostolic blessing as an economic historian. Yet no synthesis was achieved in England, and to this day, like the Bank of England under the Act of 1844, the discipline of economics is divided into two departments. In English universities Economic History tends to exist in a world apart, as if advances in the logic of economics had no relevance at all for the study of factual evidence designated Economic History. (While I shall argue below for the importance of "non-theoretical" factual studies, the English extreme, separate departments of economic history, is not what I have in mind.)

The American Economic Association was not immune from the fact-theory split. As A. W. Coats has recently shown us, the problem appeared early in the history of the A.E.A. in the various forms of regionalism, social reform, institutionalism and empiricism opposed to the orthodoxy of the "eastern" economics departments.[10]

A curious variation was based upon the belief that by careful observation of the facts, theory itself could somehow become more directly reflective of observed facts: for example, Veblen, whose identification as an economist is usually questioned these days. The business cycle seems to have been especially productive of professional disaster for those trying to directly link up "fact" and "theory." Jevons, for all his virtuosity both in theoretical and empirical work, was led to his ultimate ruination by his addiction to his interpretation of the "facts." Professor H. L. Moore's elaborate statistical studies of the weather and its effects on business conditions may also be cited. It almost seems to have been safer to stick with clean, if irrelevant "theory," and well-documented, if unedifying "fact." [11]

In the long, long run the work of the men who concentrated on discovering and establishing "facts" has come out well indeed compared to the "theory" men even if, in the short run, the "theory" men usually had their day. One hears little of Overstone today, but Tooke's empirical work is still in use.[12] Porter's *Progress of the Nation* is still in use, but how many read his contemporary, James Mill, anymore? Jevon's prices are still used, but how many economists today actually know his theoretical work first hand? Recent experience is similar. When *Measuring Business Cycles* was first published, the theorists came out in full cry and Burns and Mitchell were much maligned for selecting, recording, and measuring the relevant statistical magnitudes without the explicit imposition of any given business-cycle theory (in fact, it is puzzling to imagine what, with the theory of the time, Burns and Mitchell might have done).[13] The National Bureau of Economic Research still remains, and so do its theoryless techniques of business cycle measurement. But whatever happened to "business cycle theory" anyhow? Is it in fact, like the dodo, extinct? Schumpeter's great work, imposing "theory" upon history and statistics, now gathers dust in the corner with Montaigne's *Essays*.

This background is provided to emphasize that the present upheaval [14] regarding the "new" economic history is a further incarnation of a fundamental and long-lasting conflict in the general field of economics. It seems to me that the modern fact-theory problems, so far as they involve economic history directly, may be traced to the Keynesian Revolution and the later development of "modern" microeconomics using mathematical techniques. We find, among others, that Taussig,[15] the early Viner,[16] H. D. White,[17] and Seymour Harris [18] seriously worked with both theoretical and historical materials in their efforts to understand economic phenomena. In our own time Milton Friedman,[19]

Charles Kindleberger [20] and others are still working occasionally with serious historical problems, but the effort among theoretically-minded economists is rare now. In the late 1930's just about at the maturity of the present senior economic historians (those recently retired or now near retirement), economic theory moved dramatically ahead as an intellectual exercise. First, the problem of swallowing Keynes and his interpreters made theoretical work terribly exciting—even, for a time, at the expense of the eternal verities derived from the works of Smith, Ricardo, Mill and Marshall. Theory suddenly had a point; it was a threat to the establishment in the university chairs—men who had trouble learning "the new economics"—and at the same time seemed to open vista after vista of profound new understanding of the real world. Then after the World War II hiatus, in the counter-reformation, Keynesian macroeconomic theory was overshadowed by the tremendous strides of new-style microeconomics, mathematical economics, activity analysis, operations research, etc. Throughout this period the generation of economic historians contemporaneous with the older, pre-Keynesian theorists, continued their work with ever-dwindling numbers of recruits from economics departments. The pre-Keynesian theorists were themselves largely ignored or swept aside.

By the early 1950's the profession of economic history was largely being recruited from the ranks of graduate students in "straight" history. The small number of ranking economic historians trained as economists age 45 to 65 is dramatic evidence of this history. By 1950 the major textbook used in undergraduate courses remained largely unchanged since 1924. The revolutionary changes in the logic of economic analysis had passed American economic history by.

But when the change came to economic history it seemed terribly radical because of the long hiatus. Young men who came to economic history from economics in the 1950's and early 1960's to look for the economist's equivalent of "laws of nature" in the historical record had their primary training in the "new" and the "new-old" economics. They seemed to understand little of the methods and motives of the old-time "fact" men in economic history, and went to work rewriting economic history, revising much of the older interpretation, but also pushing the old framework aside altogether and producing entirely new information by new methods, statistical techniques and data processing. The senior economic historians, even if they had known some old-time economic theory, seemed to comprehend little of the extensive "engineering" side of modern training in economics. As a result, entirely conservative "mainstream" methods of statistical analysis and data processing were viewed with apprehension and distrust by the older generation. A primary consequence of this was a shift in the balance of power within the economic history profession and some bad feeling at conventions.[21]

This brings us up to date. The new economic historians speak the language, not of the old economic historians primarily, but of the "new" and the "new-old" economics. Their dream of the ideal economic historian is a cross between Koopmans and Kuznets. Their evaluation of a man like Clapham is, at its kindest, that he is incomprehensible.

The internal arguments of members of this Young (and Not-So-Young) Turk movement, and their assault upon their elders and upon non-quantitative practitioners, is largely what the present uproar is all about. Will these economic historians, the intellectual children of modern economics, remain "true to the facts" and still succeed in "integrating fact and theory"—as the slogan goes? Many certainly think so, but the complaint is heard that progress is slow. My point is, that against this historical background, one can easily see that progress might be slow, and also might not even take place. But it is not because of Schmoller and the German Historical School. The problem is economics itself.

II

After these preliminaries, I want to raise the temperature a bit. Not only do I think that the new economic history might not succeed in integrating fact and theory in all aspects of historical studies, but I really don't think that any general case can be made of such a procedure. It does not follow that good and useful quantitative work can only be done if it is narrowly directed by theory. If I see a two-toed horse, need I have an explanation of it based upon "theory" for my observation to be of use to biology? In fact, look at biology and geology. Taxonomy alone made powerful contributions to those sciences and if Carl Linnaeus anticipated Darwin, he failed to inform posterity of this momentous fact. Important measuring work was done on the physical aspects of Stonehenge without theory of even practical hypothesis—measurements which, in the event, made it easy for a man with a hunch to find a hypothesis and a believable explanation of the purposes of the monument. It was both admirable and the better part of wisdom for R. J. C. Atkinson to concede as late as 1960 regarding "why" Stonehenge was built: "We do not know, and we shall probably never know." [22] In 1964 G. S. Hawkins demonstrated in *Nature,* after employing computer techniques, that Stonehenge is a kind of neolithic computer.[23]

Measurement without theory. The *Gegenschein* has been under careful observation for two centuries without the slightest notion of what it is; but the careful work of observation made it possible for a satellite's pass through a "neutral zone" to produce a hypothesis.[24] Similarly, we know a good deal from measurement about the Zodiacal Light, but we await the hypothesis to explain its causes and effects—if any. Kepler had no convincing idea why Mars moved about the sun in an ellipse. He favored the hypothesis based upon circular movements—the Copernican view. But Kepler's careful measurements contributed to a great hypothesis in Newton's mind.[25] Economics, too, is full of great work not based upon theory; look at Imlah and Schlote.

The measurement and study of phenomena is a root of science, as well as theoretical speculation. The same must be true of economics if it is to progress. Both kinds of activity are required. It is the wedding of fact and theory that produce understanding, but facts chosen specifically to fit the theory to be tested—the "imposition" of the theory—will yield no falsifiable, testable, results. The "hard" facts of economic life, which have been measured and duly recorded by economic historians, constitute a great achievement. If those facts are not in a form convenient for tests of theory, that is unfortunate but not surprising, *since phenomena occur without reference to theoretical speculation.* There has always, obviously, been the stellar parallax, but both observation and hypothesis were necessary in our own solar system before men began the centuries-long search which finally led W. Struve in 1837 to find parallactic motion (swinging motion) in observations of the giant star Vega.[26] Theory helps us understand phenomena, not the other way around.

If the object of science, including economics, is to "discover nature's laws," then the rules of the game should not include strictures about the origins of inquiry. If "science is measurement," then the springboard of measurement surely ought not to be restricted to "economic theory only." It is the good fortune of economics that research workers have always been motivated by the full spectrum of human curiosity. I have stressed theoryless measurement here a moment in order, initially, to loosen up our frame of reference. Let us now consider the uses of theory as part of the process of deduction.

III

The use of theory to illuminate "fact" and explain it in economics is more difficult than one might suppose at first sight. The major problems are terribly "messy." I consider there to be four major problems involved. The first two problems are (1) *colligation,* and (2) *the discovery of initial conditions.*

1 . COLLIGATION

Except for work such as that now being done by Smith and others in experimental economics, empirical economics is necessarily, and therefore
should consciously be, caught up in the historian's eternal dilemma—colligation—the necessity of viewing a given economic event as one in a
temporal sequence, not convincingly understandable except when that
event is considered along with its temporal antecedents.[27] Partial equilibrium analysis, at a given moment of time, tells us a good deal about
the contemporary forces producing a given phenomenon, but not how
that phenomenon came to exist from some previous coalescence of economic forces, or whether the phenomenon might be expected to recur.
Unless a fact is a random one, in economics there is a tendency for facts,
data, to be produced by the real world *as parts of economic processes.* If
price B is 101, that is a fact, and we assume that our logic of price formation will inform us why price B is what it is just now. But if price A was
100, then the price has risen and the question "Why is B what it is?" has
as part of its answer the observation that B exists because the conditions
which produced A no longer exist, but have changed so as to produce B.
There was a market analysis which explained A, and one or more of the
assumptions, postulates, statements of initial conditions, etc., must be
changed to explain B. When the economist does this, he has become a
historian, whether he likes it or not.

The careful historian usually handles the colligation problem by
some introductory statement setting the "tone" of the initial point of enquiry with a reference to what has gone before, wherever in time he begins his account. A masterful example of this art is found in Gibbon,
such that after only six paragraphs we read:

> Such was the state of the Roman frontiers, and such the maxims of
> Imperial policy, from the death of Augustus to Trajan.[28]

Chapman faced his colligation problem with essentially a 380-page
introduction.[29] Mantoux took 190 pages to warm to his subject.[30]

On themes more modest than the rise and fall of empires and whole
economic systems, less space may be needed for the problem. Yet it must
always be faced, and there are really no fixed rules for deciding where to
begin. Here judgment based upon background learning is simply required. Thomas Wilson, writing of the "farm problem" in the 1930's,[31]
realized that the problem had antecedents and went back to the great col-

lapse of farm prices in 1919 for his initial "cut-in" point. Yet the problem of insufficient internal demand relative to American farm capacity does not begin there, nor is that even a particularly important point in time. It is amusing to see J. K. Galbraith,[32] in spite of his great surgical skills, but possibly because of his deep knowledge of the problem, simply throwing up his hands and going back to the early 17th century—to "the beginning." A writer facing the question of Churchill's 1925 exchange-rate decision might ponder whether, as Sir Albert Feavearyear suggested,[33] the reign of King Offa of Mercia really is the logical place to trace the remote origin of "the ancient right standard of England."

Since there is no general rule, it is vitally important that the empirical worker be intelligent about his colligation problem. If "theory" helps in this effort, fine, but other considerations as simple as the death of a king, could be key factors in choosing a cut-in point, or a cut-out point. Econometric models involving time, like historical narratives, have a double problem, the justification of the initial starting point, and then the internal sequence of repercussions as changes in any of the variables produce all-around adjustments in the other variables of a system of simultaneous equations. "Colligation" here is a set of constants and functional relationships. Yet at the end, the final adjustment has essentially been produced by a sequence of "events," just as sure as the peace treaty following a war, or a great corporate amalgamation represent outcomes of historical linkages. After all, the Interstate Commerce Commission has meaning *only* in the light of its history, and a non-colligated account of the operations of the ICC would be a fairly mysterious narrative.

All this is doubtless a great bother to the economist anxious to get on with his analysis, yet adequate information requires that in work using data which have actually been generated by the economy, the colligation problem be met, just as the log of experiments in laboratory work is part of the information which guides current research under way. There is always a relevant history and a beginning point in empirical work which need careful delineation. The results depend upon it. Had Professor Morgenstern discovered the slowly developing "stability" of the gold points in the genesis of the nineteenth-century gold standard, he would not have been so alarmed at the wide variance of actual rates away from his mean gold points. He also might not have calculated his gold points the way he did.[34]

2. THE DISCOVERY OF INITIAL CONDITIONS

Closely associated with the problem of colligation is that of the discovery and statement of initial conditions. It is sometimes cynically said that "History is what the historian says it is." It is true that the historian chooses his facts, his unit of history, on the basis of instinct, plan or theory, and ignores the rest. Whether he is a good historian or not determines the quality of the act of selection. Second, the historian, understanding his colligation problem, must decide at which point in the stream of causation his "history" begins; whether in events $a \ldots n$, the study of event k might better begin at h or even g than merely at i. The economist is involved in precisely the same sorts of operations. When he decides, as he must, which variables he will ignore, he is "choosing his facts," and when he states his "given" circumstances in his statement of initial conditions, he is creating his "world." In an analysis of prices, he may have as an axiom that all utility surfaces are convex, and that is a "theoretic term." [35] But if he assumes that perfect competition exists for firms in his market, he is stating, as his initial conditions, that there are no barriers to entry and exit, that perfect knowledge exists, that no single firm can influence price, and so forth. By placing the relevant world of study in the universe of time and circumstance by act of exclusion (i.e., excluding both time and events around the few events in the given period of time in which events are thought to have occurred), the economist completes the historian's role.

This is more like history than it is like physical science. To the physicist many of the initial conditions of the experimental work are known from previous experiments, from knowledge of the role of the technology, the importance of the temperature of the laboratory, the character of the equipment, the fineness of the chemicals used, etc. The economist, on the other hand, "creates" these things. He chooses them for himself. His initial conditions are not given but must be actively discovered, since his laboratory is the economic world and that reality contains his initial conditions. His view of that reality largely determines how he will choose his set of initial conditions. When, for example, an economist begins an empirical analysis of the American automobile industry, with the statement that it is best considered to be a case of "perfect" competition, the statement has been informed by observation, faulty or not.

As an aside, the economist who believes that he is "free" from the historian's dilemma because history is irrelevant to economic analysis is not only reckless as an empiricist, but as a theorist as well—at least if his theory is supposed to be about something, since "observation includes thinking and relies on background knowledge." [36]

Schumpeter's long introduction to *Business Cycles* is certainly one of the most knowledgeable and sophisticated disquisitions in the literature concerning the fine art of discovery and statement of assumptions about reality—initial and background conditions—anterior to the use of theory and knowledge about that reality in order to understand "phenomena." It is thrice unfortunate that *Business Cycles* is now in oblivion: (i) the work is a mine of information about the history of modern capitalism; (ii) Schumpeter's great culture and erudition ought to be a model for the student; (iii) Schumpeter understood that scientific work, especially in economics, is usually difficult, that theories lead to "understanding" only through extensive falsifications of predictions.

Consider Schumpeter's defense of the use of the perfectly competitive equilibrium model:

> The importance of the case does not, of course, rest with the frequency of its occurrence in actual life. A system satisfying its conditions in all its parts has probably never existed.[37]

But such a set of simplifying assumptions about the economy

> . . . however abstract or remote from real life it may be, yet renders indispensable service in clearing ground for rigorous analysis.[38]

Schumpeter clearly saw his twofold problem, clearing the ground (by his statement of initial conditions), and rigorous analysis using theoretic notions on that cleared ground.

It is interesting to observe, time and again, Schumpeter's painstaking efforts to justify his simplifying assumptions about the real world. He was aware both that abstraction must be made *and* that the resulting assumptions should not be irrelevant to the world about which they are supposed to make *some* statement that is not meaningless. His effort to justify his classification of various economic realities, changes in tastes, population growth, money supply, etc., as endogenous and exogenous variables is a model of its kind.[39] Here again it is knowledge of reality and not just logic itself which dictates the proceedings.[40]

Once all this is done Schumpeter proceeds to the application of his purely theoretic assumptions. The result was supposed to have been his great masterpiece and a monument to the powers of economic analysis: its surprising failure resulted from the weakness of a theoretical structure that was unequal to the task. Economists were not convinced that the logic of the three-cycle scheme together with the simplifying assumptions "explained" business cycles.[41]

For all its failure, *Business Cycles* is a singular work. Schumpeter did not choose his reality on the basis of theory. There was a phenomenon to be explained, the business cycle; there was the set of hypotheses about its development, the three-cycle scheme; and there was the relationship of history to the theory in the long statement and justification of the simplifying assumptions which enabled a great deal of "price theory" to be useful as information inputs along with crude fact. The method Schumpeter followed leads us to our further questions regarding economic history and theory: (3) *the falsification of the protasis* and (4) *treatment of externalities.*

3. FALSIFICATIONS OF THE PROTASIS

The process of deduction has two parts, the *protasis* and the *apodosis*. The *apodosis* is the consequence of the conjunction of statements which is the *protasis*. In empirical economics the *protasis* includes that statement of initial conditions, b, conjoined with the set of assumptions, axioms, etc., which comprise the theoretical knowledge employed, Θ. It is asserted that the conjunction of b and Θ will make it possible to derive s, the final conditions, *apodosis,* outcome, or predicted result.[42]

The statement b of initial conditions contains (as we have seen in Schumpeter) the premises relating to matters of fact; e.g., if we say that an assumption of the argument is that perfect competition exists, we are asserting that as our view of world for the purpose of producing s, our prediction. Some of our assumptions might be entirely theoretic terms, necessary in the logical structure for its completion, but bearing no directly observable characteristics at all—for example, that all utility surfaces of our consumers are convex, or that the marginal utility of money declines for each. Our assumptions are mixed as between reality and unreality, no particular virtue attaches to either state of the assumptions *except in the context of producing s.*

This combination of assumptions about the world *we choose* (i.e., the statement b of initial conditions), together with the theoretical assumptions and statements Θ we use to produce our final conditions, s, encompasses the problems we discussed above in a particular way. Since "laws of nature" are hard to establish in economics, they are not commonly part of economic analysis, and in economic analysis theoretical constructions take the place of natural law in the *protasis* as it is usually formed in physical science.[43]

Thus neither part of the *protasis,* neither b nor Θ, can be taken from authority, but in economics both are chosen by the investigator himself. Hence the statement of initial conditions *b* must be both "realistic" enough to be relevant to the world which produced the data under examination, and yet be "abstract" or generalized enough to be amenable to combination with the set of theoretical assumptions and statements which comprise ⊖. If the prediction *s* fails to find suitable agreement with real-world data, then the *entire protasis,* and not just ⊖, the theory, has been falsified, and the entire *protasis* must be re-examined to see whether it was a defective statement of relevant initial conditions, or a misstep in the structure of the theory, or both to which the falsification of the predicted result can be attributed. In any case, the *entire protasis* has been falsified, and we cannot say which parts without examination. After all, a perfectly good theory might fail to predict if combined with inappropriate initial conditions (theory of monopoly behavior together with relevant initial conditions tested against data from a perfectly competitive industry).

The existence of production at prices below variable costs, long noted as a practice in steel production during cyclical downswings,[44] does not mean that something is "wrong" with the theory of the firm. It does mean that a *protasis* which includes an assumption of perfect competition in the statement of initial conditions has been falsified. Clearly entry and exit are not "perfect."

A different notion of the *protasis* is found several times in Oskar Morgenstern's monumental *International Financial Transactions and Business Cycles.*[45] This vast study is an attempt to measure evidences of the international transmission of cyclical impulses through transactions of a primarily financial nature. To do this, Morgenstern had to know "what to look at" in the way of data. If one chooses to ignore trade and payments connected with goods and services (as Morgenstern explicitly did), then the relevant points at which data arise are at adjustment points which are *assumed to exist* in the basic theoretical model of the international economy.

Such points are essentially arbitrage points. (i) If country A's payments with country B run to such a deficit that bills on B purchased in country A rise to a sufficient premium, *then* a point is reached where, given the costs of shipment, it pays to buy gold and export it to B. That effective rate of exchange is the *gold export point* and marks the extreme limit of depreciation of A's exchange against B so long as gold movements are free and mint pars exist. (ii) In a perfect market, one and only one price prevails. Given the costs of transferring funds, there should be no extensive or long-term interest differentials between members of the international market. In both cases, interest and exchange arbitrage, the adjustment mechanism is assumed to work in the absence of government interference and imperfections in the market. These conditions, in which such adjustments *could take place,* were widely believed to exist before 1914.[46]

Morgenstern's problem was initially to (i) mark off the gold points, within which cyclical variations of exchange rates could be traced, and (ii) find comparable interest rates whose variations against each other reflected basic cyclical forces. The actual data Morgenstern produced would leave in a state of near-shock an economist well-versed in the painless axioms of the classical theory. Even so experienced a practitioner as Morgenstern was seemingly ill-prepared for the barbaric imperfections of the "real" nineteenth-century world.

In short-term interest rates gaps between countries were surprisingly great and long-lasting:

> The persistence of wide gaps is a phenomenon that will occupy us still further, when the question will be raised whether they are compatible with the gold standard and the implicit close interaction of the various countries. The reader will notice that there are almost always very considerable differences and that this hardly conforms with the expectations one might obtain from the literature.[47]

From our viewpoint this world is upside down. We are not surprised that our *protasis* must be reworked after a prediction has been proven false. That indeed is how we understand the world. But we raise neither doubts about "the gold standard" nor theory alone. The gaps Morgenstern describes *did exist during what has been called the gold standard period.*

Wide fluctuations of exchange rates beyond presumed "gold points" were found to be even more shocking, were indeed "violations."

> A further study of violations, including the incredible phenomenon of exchange rates often and persistently beyond the gold points, enabled us to isolate periods of international financial tension.[48]

There is a problem of definition here. No exchange rate can go beyond the gold points by definition, the extremities of the rates *are* the gold points. It is assumed for convenience' sake in model building that there are stable gold points but this is no reason at all for the empirical researcher to make the same assumption about data generated from real-world transactions. It is a stated initial condition in the *protasis* that makes the gold points stable, not any condition in the world. The assumption that gold-point stability in the real world was a narrowly confined set of exchange-rate fluctuations has introduced a great deal of muddle into discussions of the gold standard.[49] Our point here is that a part of the *protasis* was an assumption of stability in the general factor-price equalization model. The absence of gold-point stability does not imply anything wrong with international trade theory or anything mysterious in the real world.

Long-term interest rates also scarcely fit any model which assumes a solidarity in international financial markets. Morgenstern again finds the difference "remarkable." [50] It is wholly unexpected. But *everything* is un-expected to *a priori* argument only. Only in conjunction with a statement of simplifying assumptions are the facts interesting and amenable to analysis and understanding. *Both* parts of the *protasis* provide our prediction. Morgenstern thus is mystified by interest differentials that don't disappear.

> . . . capital movements never closed the permanent gaps where they existed. This indicates a lack of response quite out of keeping *with traditional theory* [my italics], and we must therefore look for such reasonable arguments as will help to enlighten us about these permanent margins.[51]

This indeed is what ought to occur when the *protasis* is shown to be inadequate. But it is not the theory alone which fails to account for reality. It is theory *plus* the simplifying assumptions about that reality which have failed. Morgenstern finds that risk differences account for the differential. Studies of the background conditions, however, lead one far into a study of productivity differentials [52] wherein an explanation probably lies that is warranted by the evidence. It is not news, by the way, to the economic historian that permanent interest differentials existed, nor that gold-point stability was only a convenient simplifying assumption.[53]

There are, of course, many examples in the literature in which the entire *protasis* is viewed as "theory" and statements regarding theory are made directly from evidence, or about the world from theory alone. An example is Macesich's effort to impose the Ricardian price-specie flow model, in all its purity, upon the American economy of the 1830's.[54] As might be expected, he was soon in trouble. The large American current-account deficit of the period is difficult to reconcile with evidence of *net specie imports*. An appeal was made to the evidence of "exchange rates" (he used bill prices, we will return to this shortly), and except for 1837 these indicate an *excess supply* of sterling. Sales of American securities abroad were assumed to have produced the gold inflow in spite of the current-account deficit (which, *coeteris paribus,* might be associated with a gold outflow). We were then told that "changes in exchange rates conform to theoretical expectations." [55] Again, after explaining a specie outflow in 1839 in conjunction with a large current-account deficit and *no significant movement of "exchange rates,"* we were told that: "In general, specie movements conform with theoretical expectations." [56]

As it happens, the simplifying assumptions Macesich used are not sufficiently in concordance with the reality of the 1830's. The basic assumptions he made are: (i) stable bank reserves; (ii) bimetallism works just like the gold standard; (iii) stable gold points could be maintained with the existing communications (sailboats) system; (iv) communications between markets on both sides of the ocean could support solidarity in the price relationships of the "transatlantic market." These initial conditions are not in accord with the reality of the period.

But apart from that, a closer study of the "background conditions" would illuminate enough of current practices to indicate that prices of bills of exchange do not constitute "exchange rates," since bill prices include a discount for interest charges, and bill prices thus tend to vary *inversely* with interest-rate movements.[57] In point of fact, throughout the period under discussion pure exchange rates—interest discount removed show sterling at a strong premium in America (excess *demand* for sterling), something one would expect, given the balance of payments situation.[58] The sterling premium disappeared in the early 1840's when an American export surplus developed and sterling was in excess supply.

Hence, the conformity of Macesich's reality to his "theoretical expectations" is odd considering that he's got his facts upside down. Given the structure of the *protasis,* if the theory is internally consistent, his initial conditions would have to be exactly wrong.

Why there should have been a net inflow of coin and bullion from 1834 to 1838, when sterling was at a premium, remains a mystery. Perhaps foreign investment is part of the answer. The entire *protasis* put together by Macesich is disconfirmed and, as a result, needs to be thought out again. As for "theoretical expectation"—that, in our view, does not exist apart from the stated initial conditions. Theory must be "about something." Obviously the bullion and exchange-rate movements of the 1830's can be explained, but by 1835 Ricardo had been dead a decade, and anyway, he knew nothing of American conditions. Fresh work is needed.

In neither of the last two cases we have used by way of illustration is the falsification of the *protasis* ground for not accepting "theory," as a narrow predictivist might urge us to do. Instead, a more diligent search for relevant initial conditions is called for.

Finally, let it be noted again that falsification increases our knowledge. The Morgenstern findings are especially suggestive of this. Perfect confirmation of the *protasis* might merely indicate coincidence, or that the *protasis* is too general, and can be used to predict too wide a range of events to be meaningful. We gain knowledge by knowing the specific circumstances under which our *apodosis* is not in agreement with warranted fact. Morgenstern's gold-point "violations" constituted new information of the first rank when so many economists believed in perfect gold-point stability. We noted earlier a similar example of the importance of falsification in evidence that iron and steel firms continued to work in depressions when their variable costs were *not* covered (borrowing from banks to pay wages). An enquiry into the components of the simplifying assumption of perfect competition and its non-concordance with reality yielded vital new information, especially about the trade cycle.[59]

To do any work of this kind correctly calls for information which comes not from "integrating theory and history," as some "new" economic historians urge us to do, but rather from critically analyzing factual information derived from historical research *and* from understanding the nature of simplifying assumptions. I think this is *not* what some of the new economic historians are encouraging, and that it is unfortunate, both for economics and economic history. Only from rigorously constructed work of this kind will we understand both the annual rise of the *Messiah* audience *and* its royal origins. Economic history deserves no less an attempt to find the truth than does cultural history.

4 . THE PROBLEM OF EXTERNALITIES

Finally, attempts to find uniformities in economic behavior over time are continually sand-bagged by autonomous or "external" occurrences. These externalities—whether they be obvious and easily identified, like wars and harvest failures, or are more difficult to uncover—are non-systematic disruptions of normal economic life; nevertheless, they are felt and must somehow be handled in colligated analyses like economic histories and econometric models. As Pirenne put it:

> An unforseen event is always followed by a catastrophe in proportion to its importance. It flings itself, so to speak, across the current of historic life, interrupting the series of causes and effects of which this current is constituted, damming them up . . . and by the unexpected repercussions overturning the natural order of things.[60]

Returning to part 1 of this section, if A moved to B because of a Presidential order activated by some state agency, and none of the "technical" relationships changed initially, the order and its consequences become a part of the empirical economist's "bag of tools" if he still wants to discuss the real world relevantly. Both the historian and the empirical economist handle the problem by suitable adjustments. They must do so in order to weave the Presidential order in period B into their thinking —the results of the Presidential order will already be in the data—so that the handling of the colligation problem will not be accidentally exclusive of relevant fact. In a future period, C, the results of the Presidential order, an externality when it first appeared, might be hardened into a fact of economic life to be treated in the statement of initial conditions. Hence there is much more to the construction of the *protasis* than a merely *a priori* formulation of theoretic assumptions.

The problem, therefore, if one wants to understand the sequence of actual phenomena over time, is further complicated by an additional issue which *does not* depend for its solution upon "integrating theory and history," but rather upon very carefully worked out historical inference.

However trivially obvious this would be to a historian, its importance is not always recognized in economics.[61] Also, Schumpeter's defense of the usual procedure in economic analysis is interesting.

> Hence we arrive at the very important concept of factors acting from without (let us call them External Factors), which it stands to reason we must try to abstract from when working out an explanation of the causation of economic fluctuations properly so called, that is, of those economic changes which are inherent in the working of the economic organism itself.[62]

Taken at face value, Schumpeter's position is illogical since, as any economic historian should know, and as Pirenne emphasized, there *are* reactions which set permanent change in the stream of economic life due to external causes (Schumpeter agreed that his assumption would limit him somewhat to the surface of things).[63] Evidence of the changing slope of the consumption function after World War II is surely a measure of changing attitudes toward spending and saving due to an "externally" produced period of high earnings and liquidity which somehow came to be accepted as normal.[64] In the current jargon of economics there was a "ratchet effect" of wartime prosperity which was reinforced in the postwar period by high-level spending from wealth and earned income. The failure to recognize such factors caused an earlier generation of American economists enormous embarrassment when the depression of 1946–47 failed to materialize.

Yet Schumpeter, too, has a valid point, in that, as he emphasizes, there *are* regularities which theory can help to elucidate, and these regularities cannot be understood unless they are studied mainly in isolation from all external events. The "Principle of Causality" [65] surely ought to stimulate economists, as well as other scientists, to try to discover isolated systems of events whose initial conditions are repeatable.

This is a great problem yet to be solved in economics. For the historian, using the marvelously flexible techniques of a verbal language, the problem is not a barrier to understanding. Economists, however, utilizing the more formal equipment of mathematics, have a problem here. I cannot believe that a "new" economic historian, *looking for facts on the basis of existing economic theory,* can conceivably be of much assistance here. In fact, the economic historian's contribution to the solution of the general problem of externalities will increase as he establishes, without reference to theory, the specific effects of external economic disturbances.

CONCLUDING REMARKS

In this essay I have *not* said that theory is of no use in economic history. I have said that historical investigation should not be strictly limited by theoretical information. The distinction is not a very subtle one, and I hope it does not cause misunderstanding. I agree wholeheartedly that theory helps us to understand and explain economic phenomena. But I also believe that we advance knowledge not by theory alone. There is a big difference between research which is stimulated by theoretical questions and research that is limited by them.

Much has been done in recent years to aid the understanding of economic processes by empirical research in economic history which utilizes recent advances in the training of economists. Much could be lost, however, if the "new" economic historian failed to mind the dictum that in the end, the historian must remain true to the facts. This is not an excuse for unimaginative work in economic history, work which is not at all informed by theoretical insight. But it is a constraint placed by expectations of non-historians upon historians that they, like others, should try to pursue truth for its own sake. "No holds barred' as a rule of technique is a good rule in the pursuit of truth. Clio is unkind to those who confuse ends and means in the pursuit of historical understanding.

Purdue University

NOTES

1. Herbert Weinstock, *Handel* (2nd ed.; New York, 1959), p. 253.

2. Professor Douglass North seems to be calling for such universal reliance upon economic theory as the springboard to empirical research. *American Economic Review,* Papers and Proceedings, 55 (No. 2): *passim,* (May, 1965).

3. *Ibid.,* esp. pp. 94–95.

4. A concise treatment of this classical literature is found in two essays by J. K. Horsefield, "The Duties of a Banker, I, The Eighteenth Century View," and "The

Duties of a Banker, II, The Effects of Inconvertibility," printed in T. S. Ashton and R. S. Sayers (editors), *Papers in English Monetary History* (Oxford, 1953). The early descent of the doctrine of automatic adjustment of paper currency under gold payments is traced from Hume onwards, pp. 4–7.

5. *An Enquiry into the Nature and Effects of the Paper Credit of Great Britain* (New York, 1939), pp. 123–128. Also Horsefield, *op. cit.*, II, pp. 23–29, on Thornton.

6. Ricardo published three letters to the *Morning Chronicle* in 1810 as a pamphlet, *The High Price of Bullion: a Proof of the Depreciation of Bank Notes* in 1810 developing his view, in accord with Smith and earlier writers (above) that notes merely displace coin, and in his *Plan For the Establishment of a National Bank* (1824, posthumous) his view appeared in its boldest form.

The Bank of England performs two operations of banking, which are quite distinct, and have no necessary connection with each other: it issues a paper currency as a substitute for a metallic one; and it advances money in the way of loan, to merchants and others. That these two operations of banking have no necessary connection, will appear obvious from this—that they might be carried on by two separate bodies, without the slightest loss of advantage, either to the country or to merchants who receive accommodation from such loans (p. 1).

The Bank's policy need not exist, apart from exchange notes for gold, and otherwise acting as an ordinary commercial bank, restricting its loans if its own resources declined through a bullion drain.

7. See J. K. Horsefield, "The Origin of the Bank Charter Act of 1844," reprinted in Ashton and Sayers, *op. cit.;* also my own treatment in *Fluctuations in Trade, Industry and Finance* (Oxford, 1960), pp. 228–236 and the sources cited there.

8. *Ibid.*, p. 231.

9. Sir Albert Feavearyear, *The Pound Sterling* (2nd ed.; Oxford, 1963), p. 266. Newmarch's view was put forward on the basis of the facts of changes in prices, interest rates and the volume of bills of exchange in his well-known paper ". . . The Magnitude and Fluctuations of the Amount of Bills of Exchange . . . ," *Journal of the Statistical Society,* Vol. XIV, 1851.

10. A. W. Coats, "The First Two Decades of the American Economic Association," *American Economic Review,* 50:555–74 (Sept., 1960); "The Political Economy Club," *ibid.,* 51:624–37 (Sept., 1961); "The American Economic Association, 1904–29," *ibid.,* 54:261–84 (June, 1964).

11. To the reader used to modern empirical work, Moore's early efforts show striking care and method. The oblivion into which that work has fallen might be a sombre prospect for the empirical worker.

12. His price series were used by Jevons in the construction of his first index. The factual materials in the volumes of *The History of Prices* underpinned Clapham's narrative up to the year 1856, and thus much of modern historiography. See Clapham's tribute, *An Economic History of Modern Britain* (Cambridge, 1932), II, p. 366, n. 3.

13. For example, Tjalling Koopmans, "Measurement Without Theory," *Review of Economic Statistics,* 29:162 (August, 1947), ". . . utilization of the concepts and hypotheses of economic theory . . . as a part of the *process of observation and measurement* promises to be a shorter road, perhaps even the only possible road, to an understanding of cyclical fluctuations." (His italics.) Koopmans can be interpreted as favoring the limitation of relevant data by the line of theory used, only Ptolemaic data for Ptolemaic astronomers and Copernican data for Copernican astronomers. Obviously he can't have meant such an interpretation, but authors have no control over the uses of their printed views. So far, the road suggested, as a *combination* of the

Kepler and Newton "stages" of research into celestial mechanics applied to economics, has apparently been no road at all.

14. A great deal indeed has now appeared regarding the "new" economic history. For example: L. E. Davis, J. R. T. Hughes and Stanley Reiter, "Aspects of Quantitative Research in Economic History," *Journal of Economic History*, 20:539–47 (Dec., 1960); Douglass North, "Quantitative Research in American Economic History," *American Economic Review*, 53:128–30 (March, 1963); G. C. S. Murphy, "The 'New' History," *Explorations in Entrepreneurial History*, 2nd Ser., 2:132–146 (Winter, 1965); the entire Discussion and Papers, "Economic History: Its Contribution to Economic Education, Research, and Policy," *American Economic Review*, Papers and Proceedings, 55:86–118 (May, 1965).

15. F. W. Taussig, *The Tariff History of the United States* (New York, 1888).

16. Jacob Viner, *Canada's Balance of International Indebtedness* (Cambridge, Mass., 1924).

17. H. D. White, *The French International Accounts, 1880–1913* (Cambridge, Mass., 1933).

18. Seymour Harris, *The Assignats* (Cambridge, Mass., 1930).

19. His students appear as men with historical interests. See *Studies in the Quantity Theory of Money* (Chicago, Ill., 1956). Friedman has recently made his entry as an economic historian with Anna J. Schwartz in *A Monetary History of the United States* (New York, 1963).

20. In spite of his disclaimers, one is bound to consider his *Economic Growth in France and Britain 1851–1950* (Cambridge, Mass., 1964), as economic history.

21. The subjective character of these observations ought to be obvious to the reader. They are based upon my own observations and experiences after a decade as an economist and economic historian, reading, teaching, observing the annual convention jousting, and talking with survivors. Clearly I can claim no irrefutable authority or logic for these views. If the reader disagrees with me, I ask his indulgence since this personal interlude is, I think, important as a preliminary to what follows.

22. R. J. C. Atkinson, *Stonehenge* (London, 1960, Pelican edition), p. 168.

23. Walter Sullivan, "Stonehenge Study," *New York Times*, June 21, 1964, Sec. IV, p. 7; Gerald S. Hawkins, "Stonehenge: A Neolithic Computer," *Nature*, 202:1258–1261 (June 27, 1964).

24. *New York Times*, December 16, 1964.

25. Stephen Toulmin, *Foresight and Understanding* (New York, 1961), pp. 18–43. Koopmans, *loc. cit.*, who states clearly the irrelevance of Kepler's Copernican hypotheses to his great discovery of the ellipse of Mars, and the importance of that unadorned set of facts to Newton, nevertheless urges that economists speed up the advance of economic science by merging Keplerian fact-finding "stage" with Newtonian theorizing "stage." Yet Kepler was attempting to merge his own stage with that of Nicolaus Copernicus, and the advance Kepler made was not due to the aid of his hypothesis, but rather, in spite of it. To Kepler the ellipse of Mars was "just one more cartload of dung" which was needed to make sense of his own ideas. Toulmin, *op. cit.*, p. 33.

26. Sir James Jeans, *The Universe Around Us* (Cambridge, 1960), p. 27. Actually F. W. Bessel is credited with first *successfully* measuring the parallax in 61 Cygni in 1838. Struve's calculations using Vega were considered to be excessively inaccurate.

27. W. H. Walsh, *Philosophy of History* (New York, 1960), pp. 59–64.

28. Edward Gibbon, *The Decline and Fall of the Roman Empire* (New York, Modern Library edition), I, p. 5.

29. *Op. cit.*, Vol. 1, the first eight chapters.

30. Paul Mantoux, *The Industrial Revolution in the Eighteenth Century* (London, 1928), all of Part I.

31. *Fluctuations in Income and Employment* (3rd ed., New York, 1949), p. 160.

32. *American Capitalism, The Concept of Countervailing Power* (Boston, Mass., 1952), Ch. xi.

33. *Op. cit.*, p. 7.

34. This episode is treated in L. E. Davis and J. R. T. Hughes, "A Dollar-Sterling Exchange 1803–1895," *The Economic History Review*, 2nd Ser., 13:52–78 (August, 1960).

35. The usefulness and place of theoretic terms is discussed by Ernest Nagel in his adventure into the world of economists; "Assumptions in Economic Theory," *American Economic Review*, Papers and Proceedings, Vol. LII, No. 2 (May, 1963), pp. 212–213.

36. C. F. Pressley, "Laws and Theories in the Physical Sciences," *Philosophy of Science* (New York, 1960), p. 207. The quote is from Mackie.

37. *Business Cycles, A Theoretical, Historical and Statistical Analysis of the Capitalist Process* (New York, 1939), I, p. 46, n. 2.

38. *Ibid.*, I, p. 68.

39. *Ibid.*, I, pp. 72–129.

40. Schumpeter was the picture of lucid methodological organization compared to the disarray into which the economics profession has fallen since Milton Friedman's initial foray into "predictivism" and the subsequent discussion. Samuelson describes Ernest Nagel's "defense" of Friedman as "an attempt to save Friedman from himself." The discussion thus generated continues and generates at least as much heat as light. Nagel, *loc. cit.*, *passim*, and Samuelson's discussion, pp. 231–236; followed by Fritz Machlup, "Professor Samuelson on Theory and Realism," and Samuelson's "Reply," *American Economic Review*, 54:733–739 (September, 1964). Some of the central issues in this discussion are given a full airing in Jack Melitz, "Friedman and Machlup on the Significance of Testing Economic Assumptions," *Journal of Political Economy*, 73:37–60 (Feb., 1965). For the economic historian much of this entire discussion will seem sterile since economic historians actually do work with data *and other* historical materials regularly and the issue is not purely academic. My own preferences regarding the problems of separating simplifying and theoretical assumptions are given in footnote 42 below. If one is studying, say, the growth of a steel industry and associated economic phenomena, and one "assumes" the presence of coalfields, the existence or nonexistence of such fields is of some importance. If one assumes that the industry is monopolistic, whether this be in fact so is important.

41. The exception is perhaps Rendigs Fels, *American Business Cycles* (Chapel Hill, N.C., 1959).

42. Pressley, *op. cit.*, *passim*, R. L. Basmann, "On Predictive Testing of a Simultaneous Equation Model: The Retail Market for Food in the U.S.," Institute for Quantitative Research in Economics and Management, Paper 78, Krannert Graduate School, Purdue University, pp. 1–22. Basmann also touches on this matter in "The Role of the Economic Historian in the Predictive Testing of Proffered 'Economic Laws'," *Explorations in Entrepreneurial History*, 2nd Ser., 2:159–186 (Spring/Summer, 1965).

43. Pressley, *op. cit.*, p. 210.

44. Duncan Burn, *The Economic History of Steelmaking 1867–1939* (Cambridge, 1961), pp. 35–36. Also: Hughes, *op. cit.*, pp. 180–181; R. H. Campbell, "Fluctuations in Stocks," *Oxford Economic Papers*, New Series, 9:50–55 (Feb., 1957), for Scottish practice; D. H. Robertson, *A Study of Industrial Fluctuations* (London, 1948 reprint), p. 33. In the instances cited the existence of time in the "real world," ability

to produce for inventories, excessive cost of rebuilding furnaces if output stops even though average revenue is less than average variable cost, the relative financial strength of the firms involved, together with financial barriers to entry into the industry, all serve to destroy the usefulness of usual stated initial condition of perfect competition in the iron and steel industries in the cyclical downswing.

45. Princeton University Press, for the National Bureau of Economic Research, 1959.

46. Paul Einzig, *The History of Foreign Exchange* (London, 1962), Ch. 15, esp. pp. 172–173 on this point.

47. Morgenstern, *op. cit.*, p. 157.

48. *Ibid.*, p. 276.

49. Davis and Hughes, *op. cit.*, pp. 60–64.

50. Morgenstern, *op. cit.*, p. 470.

51. *Ibid.*, p. 161.

52. A recent attempt to explain long-term productivity differentials between the United States and the United Kingdom by an economic historian is, H. J. Habakkuk, *American and British Technology in the 19th Century* (Cambridge, 1962). A penetrating critique of this work is David Landes, "Factor Costs and Demand; Determinants of Economic Growth," *Business History*, Vol. VII, No. 1 (Jan., 1965).

53. A straightforward discussion of gold-point stability as a slowly-developing characteristic of the pre-1914 financial system may be found in Margaret G. Myers, *The New York Money Market* (New York, 1931), pp. 341–344. The long-lasting interest differential was part of the understood conditions of nineteenth-century finance. See tables in Sidney Homer, *A History of Interest Rates* (New Brunswick, N.J., 1963), Ch. XIII and XVI, comparable years and maturities.

54. George Macesich, "Sources of Monetary Disturbances in the United States 1834–1845," *Journal of Economic History*, 20:407–426 (Sept., 1960).

55. *Ibid.*, p. 416.

56. *Ibid.*, p. 417.

57. Davis and Hughes, *op. cit.*, pp. 53–56 for a discussion of the adjustments that are necessary to correct the bill prices in order to "free" them of the interest discount and other anomalies, and extract from them a pure rate of exchange.

58. *Ibid.*, p. 72, Table A-2. Compare with the chart given by Macesich in the relevant period, *op. cit.*, p. 415.

59. See footnote 44 above.

60. Henri Pirenne, *A History of Europe from the Invasions to the XVI Century* (New York, 1956), p. 50. Pirenne is here referring to the long-term impact of the Moslem invasions upon the course of European history.

61. See Basmann, "On Predictive Testing," *op. cit.*, pp. 57–59 for comment on current practice, and in particular, the well-known test by Carl Christ of L. R. Klein's econometric model of the United States. The model was based upon 1921–47, but the test used only the two years 1946–47 for data, as if World War II and its aftermath would have no important effects upon the structure of the economy.

62. *Op. cit.*, Vol. I, p. 7.

63. *Ibid.*, p. 7, n. 2.

64. See the data and summary of the discussion in R. A. Gordon, *Business Fluctuations* (2nd ed.; New York, 1961), pp. 98–105. The Korean War also had at least short-run effects upon the community's consumption habits.

65. Philipp Frank, *Philosophy of Science* (Englewood Cliffs, N.J., 1962), Ch. 12, esp. pp. 284–285.

"AND IT WILL NEVER
BE LITERATURE"*
THE NEW ECONOMIC HISTORY:
A CRITIQUE

Lance E. Davis

I. INTRODUCTION

The term "new economic history" was coined by my ex-colleague, J. R. T.
Hughes, and in the words of the typical British female detective story-
writer, "if he had known then what he knows now," I am sure he would
not have done it. Any discipline (and that includes economic history)
progresses only if substantive work is done, and the controversy over the
"new" history has certainly diverted resources away from that end. The
young (or perhaps not so young) Turks have latched onto the term and
proclaimed that their work is "new"; and their elder (or, perhaps, "traditional" might be a better word) counterparts have been equally definite
in asserting that the work is not new and/or not history. Claims of these
sorts act on any profession like a young boy standing on a corner in a
slum area yelling, "Fight, fight." Economic historians, both new and traditional, have dropped whatever they were doing and "come a running."
As a result, the past few years have seen a transfer of energies from serious work to methodology; and I, for one, cannot think of a better way to
kill any profession. Although I personally believe that the "new" history

Source. EEH/Second Series, Vol. 6, No. 1. © Graduate Program in Economic History,
University of Wisconsin, 1968.
　　*This paper by Lance Davis and the one that follows by Fritz Redlich with com-
ments by George Green were originally delivered to the Pacific Coast Branch, American
Historical Association, August 29, 1967.

is both new (if you will accept as a definition of new—outside the mainstream rather than without antecedents) and history (if you will include as history anything that contributes to our understanding of the past), I think the argument is quite sterile, and I would much prefer to see the "new" discipline judged on its substantive contributions.

Given these reservations, I would like to narrow my comments on this twentieth-century *Methodenstreit* to three questions: How does the "new" economic history relate to the field of economic history as a whole? Does the dependence of the new history on the hypothetical alternative differentiate it from the more traditional? And finally, have some of the models chosen by the "new" historians clouded rather than cleared our view of the past?

II. THE SCOPE OF THE ''NEW'' HISTORY

If the "new" discipline is defined as that portion of history that relies on the use of explicit models, it can never encompass more than the theories that underlie those models. If one argues that the models can be drawn from any of the social sciences, then the "new" history would encompass all the areas about which we can make scientific statements. Even that, however, is a relatively narrow area (although one that is likely to expand as social and political theories become more operational). If, on the other hand, the term is narrowed to those questions amenable to economic analysis (and this definition would cover almost all of the work in the new history to date), the area is quite small indeed.

Although the distinction is somewhat artificial, consider four classes of historical questions: (1) those that can be dealt with within the framework of existing economic theory, (2) those that are amenable to analysis, but by some other than economic theory, (3) those that cannot be answered within the framework of existing theory but might in the future be amenable to analysis by theory drawn from one of the social sciences, and (4) those that involve several disciplines and depend therefore on the existence of some "unified field theory" in the social sciences. Questions of types (1) and (2) can be treated in a scientific manner by the "new" history. Questions of types (3) and (4) are outside the "new" methodology. The latter can be examined by historians, events can be described, certain assertions of a non-scientific nature can be made, and these descriptions and assertions may be useful in themselves and/or they may suggest modifications in existing theory or new theories that will help explain similar constellations of events in the future.

To understand better the limits of the "new" discipline, let us look at the history of the Tennessee Valley Authority.[1] Because it presents a mix of social, economic, political, and welfare questions, as well as problems of both a static and dynamic nature, the definitive history of that organization has yet to be written. This paper will not attempt to write such a history, but it will attempt to use the experience of the Authority as a case study in the limits and potentialities of the "new" history. The TVA is a natural subject for historical inquiry, and the complexes of that socio-politico-economic organism make its development a natural seting within which to examine what the "new" history can and cannot do.

The outlines of the history of the TVA are well known: the early attempts at the improvement of navigation on the river, the first dams begun by the Corps of Engineers during World War I, the nitrate plants of the same period, the debates over the sale of the facilities to the private sector that occupied the twenties, the decision to expand the operation under public control during the early 1930's, the legal assaults on federal power by the private utilities during the 1940's, and finally, the completed complex of flood control devices, navigational aids, recreational facilities, and electric power generation stations.[2] Here our interest in the TVA is limited to some examples of questions to which the techniques of the new history might be applied and some that the current state of theory puts outside the "new" history.

Much of the best of the "new" economic history has been concerned with questions of the rate of return or the social savings engendered by particular investment policies. Similar techniques could be brought to bear on the question of the contribution of the TVA. Professor Robert Fogel explicitly introduced the concept of social savings to economic history in his attempt to assess the contribution of the Union Pacific Railroad to the American economy.[3] He noted that all profits do not accrue to the decision-making unit and wanted to measure the total (private plus social) return of the government's decision to underwrite the construction of the UP. Although his measure of total returns was at best a partial one, his conclusion (that the rates were very high) appears to be well-substantiated. More recently, Fogel, Albert Fishlow, and Stanley Lebergott have all employed a concept of social savings in their attempts to assess the total contribution of the railroads to economic growth. The controversy among the three points up the real strengths of the "new" economic history. Fogel attempts to contrast the actual cost of shipping agricultural products in 1890 with the hypothetical cost in a world without railroads, and he concludes that the social savings of the railroads, while not insignificant, were not as high as others had implied.[4] Fishlow's model is similar but he concludes that while the social savings were fairly small in 1859, at a later date (1890, for example) they must have been quite high—as high, perhaps, as earlier writers had suggested.[5] Finally, Lebergott has argued that these attempts to measure total savings are doomed by the lack of adequate theory on which to base a counter-factual measurement, and he instead attempts to estimate the potential profitability of railroads as seen by an ante-bellum investor.[6] His conclusion (based on a model of investment choice) is that the railroads would have appeared very profitable when compared with a technology based on canals and wagons. Similar techniques could be applied to the TVA.

The casual reader may be a bit disturbed by the claim that this debate over the contribution of the railroads represents the best of the "new" history, or that, if it does, the "new" history is worth discussing. How useful can any discipline be if three authors using very similar operational concepts can conclude (1) that railroads were not indispensable in 1890, (2) that they were not indispensable in 1859 but were in 1890, and (3) that they were indispensable even before 1859? The answer lies in the nature of the models selected and in each author's view of the relevant alternative. Thus, while Fishlow and Fogel compare "actual" trade with hypothetical trade, Lebergott compares capacity trade with railroads (*i.e.,* he assumes full capacity utilization) with capacity no rail trade. Again, while Fogel is willing to build new canals, Fishlow is not; and Lebergott does not want to assume any secondary and tertiary changes. Disagreement, certainly, but in each case the reader is made aware of what has been done and what has been assumed. It is this explicit unveiling of hypotheses that is the strength of the new economic history. If the "new" historians were to turn their attention to the TVA, the effort might well yield several quite different estimates of the social returns; however, each would be accompanied by an explicit statement of the assumptions on which it rests. Progress can come not only from discovering new "truths," but also from providing a basis for meaningful dialogue. Such work is not figmentary history.

In a similar vein, Zvi Griliches has produced an excellent study on the social returns on the investment in research and development in hybrid corn during the early twentieth century.[7] Griliches combines his data with an explicit model of the rate of return and with some educated guesses about the relevant elasticities and discovers that the social rate of return from this investment was an incredibly high 700 per cent. A similar model could certainly be built to examine the expenditures on the TVA, and, in fact, Griliches explicitly shows the relationship between his rate of return, and the cost-benefit ratio frequently employed by the Corps of Engineers in their economic feasibility studies. Once again, however, it is clear that other models based on other assumptions could yield quite different conclusions.[8] It is equally clear that even if all of these studies indicated a rate of return in excess of that which could have been earned elsewhere, that conclusion is not equivalent to the argument that general welfare has been increased (or vice versa) by the TVA.

A good deal of the controversy surrounding the TVA turns on the relative efficiency of the government power generation facilities versus those owned by private industry. This question again ought to be amenable to analysis by the techniques of the "new" economic history. Economists utilize a number of logical constructs, and among these the production function is one of the most common. Moreover, a great deal of empirical work in agricultural economics and engineering economy involves estimation of the parameters of particular production functions under certain specific assumptions. Given a number of plants and a set of theoretical assumptions, it is possible to construct a function relating inputs to outputs for a "typical" firm. If some firms use fewer units of input per unit of output, it can be argued that these firms are relatively more efficient. Robert Fogel has adopted a similar technique in his study of the quality of public land alienated under the Homestead Act. Utilizing a sample of the farms drawn from the manuscript census, he constructs a production function for an "average" farm. He then tests to determine if the form of land alienation contributes to the "efficiency" of an individual farm (that is, he looks to see if the inclusion of a variable representing the form of alienation contributes significantly to the "explanation" of the observed data). Fogel is, of course, assuming that all farms are employing the same technology, that the quality of management is uniformly distributed across farms, and that differences in productivities reflect differences in the qualities of the soil. In the case of the TVA, one would assume that the technologies are identical, that there are no private-public locational differentials, and that productivity differences reflect managerial skill. Although both Fogel's work and the proposed TVA study can yield suggestive results, they cannot ever produce *certain* results. The conclusions will always depend on the assumptions of the particular model employed, and it will never be possible to compare the generation facilities of Wheeler Dam operating under public and under private management with nothing else having changed.

Since the depression of the thirties and the anti-depression policy of the Federal Government are a subject of concern to historians, one might be interested in the impact of TVA spending on the short-run level of income both in the region served by the Authority and in the rest of the country. E. Cary Brown in his classic study of fiscal policy in the thirties has shown the power of a relatively simple Keynesian model in analyzing government policy in a historical situation.[9] Brown has shown that (contrary to the well-established view) one can hardly talk about a conscious economic policy aimed at achieving full employment (in fact, the size of the government sector relative to the total economy changes hardly at all over the period). Moreover, his work indicates that, whatever actual economic effects federal legislation did have, they tended to be the unconscious (and at times unwanted) results of laws passed not for economic but for social and political reasons. With little modification, one could use Brown's model to examine the impact of the TVA on the aggregate level of activity, and with some change a similar model could yield estimates of the impact on the region's economy. Once again, however, since the TVA did exist, it is not possible to "know" for certain what an economy without the TVA would be like.

From the short-run impact on the region to the role of the TVA in the region's growth is a logical step; and regional development is another subject to which the new economic history has made substantial contributions. The more we learn about the American economy in the nineteenth century, the more we realize that there was no *American* economy. Instead, there appears to have been a number of regional economic units only gradually linked together by expanding transport and communication systems. The work of Douglass North on the ante-bellum economy makes this point quite clear.[10] However, North's own model is not well-specified and, as a result, it is at times difficult to follow his argument.[11] Despite the lack of adequate specification, the type of regional analysis that he suggests appears particularly appropriate for examining the impact of a particular disturbance (in this case the TVA) on the economy of the upper South. To accomplish this end, however, a more formal model than North's would almost certainly be required; and some form of a regional input-output model appears appropriate. The new history has produced two successful applications of the Leontief technique to historical situations. John Meyer has employed an input-output model in his examination of the effect of a retardation in the rate of growth of the foreign sector on the British economy in the late nineteenth century.[12] The model allows him to measure both the direct and indirect effects of the decline in the rate of growth, and he shows that the total effects of that fall are sufficient to account for the lag in aggregate British growth. Again, William Whitney has used a similar model to examine the impact of changes in the tariff level on the growth of American manufacturers in the same period.[13] The work on regional models has been less rewarding, but the theory has been worked out. Moreover, the attempt by Davis, Quirk, and Saposnik to simulate the Northean world (while extremely naive and yielding hardly earthshaking results) suggests that it is possible to apply these regional techniques to historical situations.[14] Moreover, the work of Walter Isard on Philadelphia indicates that for the recent past at least the data problem is not insuperable.[15] Once again, however, the results would be a comparison of the Tennessee Valley in the period 1930–1960 with and without the TVA.

Not all questions, however, need be strictly in the area of economic history. It is impossible to talk about the decision to launch the TVA without reference to politics, and every assessment of the value of the Authority involves not only economic variables but political and social ones as well. Throughout much of the thirties, for example, there was continual discussion between the Authority and Congress about the size and timing of expenditures. To analyze these developments, economic analysis is not always relevant and almost always not sufficient. However, some of the work done by Otto Davis and others on non-market decision-making might provide the necessary theoretical models.[16] Again, a historian could well be interested in the sources of legislative support for the Authority, and recent work in political science has made it possible to build empirical models of the voting behavior of political parties (or other coalitions).[17] Techniques of this sort have already made substantial contributions to our understanding of party structure in both U.S. and English history.[18] Moreover, since there appears to have been a substantial change in Congressional attitude over the decades preceding the depression, it might be interesting to examine the history of bloc and party in their response to TVA related legislation as far back as World War I. Finally, although operational theory in sociology is even more primitive than the theories of political and administrative sciences, that field too yields certain theoretical propositions that appear to be of value in writing the history of the TVA. No evaluation of the Authority could be complete without some discussion of the social changes that have been produced, and in that area some of the work utilizing models like ecological correlation might make it possible to understand changes in social structure and mobility.[19]

It would be "a nice thing" to be able to assert that today's theory is adequate to deal with all the problems that historians must face. Unfortunately, not only are political and social theory inadequate, but even economic theory cannot be brought to bear on some of the most pressing problems. How, for example, can one discuss the history of the Authority during the 1930's without reference to the famous feud between Chairman Arthur Morgan and board members David Lilienthal and Harcourt Morgan? Clearly the "civil war" seriously disrupted the organization and had important overtones for the future direction of the Authority; however, the dispute at least was partly the result of personality conflicts. Although economic theory can be usefully brought to bear on many situations, it does not help explain the particular actions of particular individuals. Nor can theory provide much help in answering the question, "Is the nation better off with the TVA?" hardly an unimportant question.

The "new" history may provide estimates of the increases (if any) in personal income that have come from the project, and, perhaps, even some suggestions as to how these income changes were distributed. Assuming for the moment that the changes were positive and large and the redistribution in the direction of greater equality, these findings still do not imply an increase in general welfare. Work in economic theory has shown that statements involving interpersonal comparisons can be made only under very restrictive sets of assumptions. While such results may well warn the economic historian to be careful in making welfare judgments, they do not help the historian who would like to be able to assess the total contribution of the Authority. Similarly, much of economic theory is static, but history by its very nature is dynamic, and our dynamic theory is woefully inadequate. Moreover, not only is the theory inadequate, but what we do have suggests that ofttimes static theory (the best set of tools in the economic workshop) may provide misleading dynamic results.[20] Recent work, for example, has shown that it is possible for short-run optimization procedures to lead the economy off the long-run optimum growth path. As a result, the "new" history can contribute considerably less than one might hope to our understanding of the relationship between the TVA and the growth of the American economy. It has provided the basis for a few halting steps toward a dynamic theory, but it has not produced a usable theory, and it is the historian who must suffer.[21] Finally, almost all the theory that we do have is highly compartmentalized: we have economic theory, social theory, and political theory, but we don't have a "unified field theory" for the social sciences. As a result, while the application of theory to history has yielded significant (but narrow) results, it has not been able to push into the border areas relating one discipline to another, and it is in this area that many important problems lie. As Professor Redlich has pointed out, economics has (perhaps unfortunately) not become more social (to say nothing of more philosophical). This failure is apparent from any reading of the literature in economic development, and it is at least equally vexing to the economic historian.

In summary then, as dismal as it may be, if a "new" historian were writing about the TVA, he would be unable to explain particular actions of individuals, he would be unable to demonstrate that the TVA has been a "good" thing, he would be unable to prove that the Authority's policies have resulted in more rapid economic growth, and he would be unable to explore the interrelationships between the economic activities of the TVA and the social and political behavior that underlay and were produced by them. While the new history might well provide substantial insights into certain aspects of the Authority, clearly there is still considerable room for the gifted insights and interpretations of the traditional historian.

III. THE COUNTERFACTUAL

The foregoing discussion of the "new" history should have indicated how sensitive its findings are to the nature of the hypothetical alternatives drawn. No aspect of the methodology of the "new" economic history has generated more fire (but perhaps less light) than its practitioners' insistence on the explicit use of the counterfactual (or contrapositive or hypothetical alternative). To many "traditional" historians, counterfactual history is anti-history or non-history, but these same historians continually employ implicit counterfactual arguments. The difference between the old and the new is in the *explicit* use of the contrapositive, not in the innovation of the counterfactual argument.

In a recent article my co-speaker, Professor Redlich, has divided all of the new history into three parts: Class I, those "new" historians who are really old historians and write real history (he includes me in this category); Class II, the "theoretical" new historians who are primarily concerned with hypothesis testing and write near history (in this group he puts, for example, Douglass North); and Class III, the "counterfactual" historians who depend on "figments" and who do not write history at all (and here he places Fogel and Meyer and Conrad).[22] The difficulty with this triparte division lies not alone in its artificiality (the counterfactual is used in some form by all three groups) but, more important, in its suggestion that the best of the "new" historians are those who do not make explicit use of the counterfactual and that the worst are those who do. In fact, most "new" historians would argue that the reverse is true.

It is certainly possible to describe objects or events without reference to any counterfactual world. Historians can talk about American immigrants in terms of their age and sex composition, about frontier banks in terms of their capital and loans, or about ante-bellum plantations in terms of their work force, acreage, and output. To this extent, therefore, it is possible to write "non-figmentary" history. Few historians (new or traditional) would, I think, be willing to limit themselves to pure description. Instead, most would argue that the unique contribution of the historian lies in his ability to understand sequences of events (*i.e.*, to interpret causal relationships). Any step in this direction, however, leads necessarily to the use (implicit or explicit) of a counterfactual argument. Take, for example, the work of Professor Harry Scheiber, one of the young critics of the "new" history. In a recent article he has described settlement in the northwestern corner of Ohio.[23] To the extent that his work is limited to that description, he has no need for a contrapositive argument. But to the extent that his work is so limited, so is his contribution. In fact, the importance of Scheiber's work (since others had already described settlement in similar terms) lies in his analysis of the causes of the particular pattern of settlement. Scheiber argues that settlement was much slower than one would have expected and that the explanation for the delay lay not, as others have implied, in the physical characteristics of the area, but in the particular land policy that led to large purchases by "speculators."[24] Scheiber's arguments are compelling, and I, for one, am convinced; but his argument by its very nature is a contrapositive one. Scheiber implicitly (by using terms like "slower") compares a situation that was (the actual distribution of the land) with one that never was (a land distribution policy designed to get the land quickly into the hands of the farmer). Moreover, he goes on to assert something about the character of that "never, never land" (*i.e.*, he argues that the experience of five nearby counties in Indiana can be used as a proxy for Ohio with a different land policy), and finally he concludes that in some sense the economy was made "worse off" by the particular system of land distribution that was employed. This explanation is not meant as a criticism of Scheiber's work (his article is a very good one) but to show that he has written counterfactual history. There is, in fact, no way that cause and effect can be discussed without comparing the observed with the hypothetical.

Granted then that counterfactual arguments are a part of all but purely descriptive history, can we ever be certain about the nature of the contrapositive world that we postulate? Its character will always depend on the implications of the model that we choose. Although Robert Fogel's name is anathema to some historians, the social savings controversy, as we have seen, nicely illustrates the question of the relevant counterfactual. What the controversy indicates is that there is no "correct" counterfactual. The one you choose depends on the model you select. What Fogel, Fishlow, and Lebergott have done is to make their models explicit, and this is the strength of the new discipline. There is a basis for a dialogue with both point and focus. Differences certainly, but no question about the nature of these differences. Fogel, Fishlow, and Lebergott all know where they stand and so, more importantly, do their readers.

But what of the other two categories of the "new" history to which Professor Redlich alludes? Redlich places the work of Douglass North on the regional growth of the ante-bellum economy in Class II (near history). Does North not employ the technique of figmentary history? North uses a theoretical model that relates shifts in the foreign demand for cotton to both secular and cyclical changes in income in the United States. From this model he concludes that the dependence of the South on cotton caused income growth in that area to lag and that the growth of income in the West can be attributed to the secondary effects of the foreign demand for cotton coupled with that region's ability to isolate itself from world markets. Certainly, his argument contains an implicit counterfactual world without cotton and interregional trade, with higher tariffs, with a different distribution of income, and, perhaps, with a host of other characteristics as well. In fact, the most serious criticism of North's work turns on his failure to specify his model and the resulting inability to formulate adequately the nature of the relevant counterfactual. Without that counterfactual it is not possible to test his model in any meaningful fashion.[25]

Finally, in Class I (real history) Redlich cites with approval the work of certain of the new economic historians whose method, he argues, depends on neither theory nor counterfactuals. Take as example of Class I history my work on the evolution of the capital markets in the U.S.[26] Far from denying models and counterfactuals, the work depends on them, and serious criticism can be raised over my failure to specify them adequately. The model assumes that initially markets were essentially local, and there was no mechanism capable of sustaining arbitrage. As a result, there was no force producing capital transfers and no move to equilibrate interest rates between the markets. It further assumes that, over time, certain institutional innovations made regional arbitrage possible, caused capital to flow from low to high interest areas, and eliminated (or at least reduced) the interest differentials. Implicit in this theory is a counterfactual world without such financial innovations. Clearly a myriad of other theories (not based on a lagged supply model) could be called on to explain this constellation of events, and, in fact, Professor Stigler has suggested a single market model that he feels is more relevant.[27] Ultimately certain tests can be brought to bear on the issues and some of the questions between Stigler and myself can perhaps be resolved, but certainly the discussion of the evolution of the capital market is theoretical history, and the nature of the counterfactual is relevant.

Professor Redlich is correct in arguing that Class I is the nearest to traditional history and Class III the furthest removed. He is, however, incorrect in inferring that it is the existence or absence of the counterfactual that provides the basis for this comparison. All three classes contain counterfactual arguments. The differences lie in the degree to which the theories have been specified. The weakness of traditional history (and of Class I and, to a lesser extent, Class II "new" history) lies in the lack of explicit models from which explicit counterfactuals can be deduced. The strength of the type of work typified by Fogel, Fishlow, and Lebergott lies in the complete specification of the model. Each of the three has suggested a different standard against which to measure the contributions of the railroads. Another example of the power of the "new" history is produced by Conrad and Meyer's work on the profitability of slavery. Not everyone agrees with their conclusions, but their model is specified, their counterfactual is explicitly drawn, and their critics know what assumptions they have made and how their evidence relates to their conclusions. Criticism has, therefore, been directed towards building models based on alternative sets of assumptions and on examining their evidence at the crucial points.[28] Agreement and certainty are, like motherhood, a "good thing," but an explicit statement of the basis for disagreement also represents progress. On the TV show "To Tell the Truth" resolution occurs when the Master of Ceremonies says, "Will the real Ignantz Jastro please stand up?" The "real" counterfactual will never be so easily identified (after all, it does not exist), but meaningful discussions leading to better understanding can come when the basis for the choice of counterfactual and the characteristics of that contrapositive are known. The five Indiana counties may or may not provide an adequate proxy for Scheiber's northwest Ohio sans speculation, but unless the reader is aware of the theoretical model used, he has no basis for deciding if the proxy is relevant.

IV. THEORY, THE SIREN LURE

While the "new" economic history has been frequently criticized for what it has done right, it has been far less frequently criticized for what it has done wrong. No impartial survey of the discipline could fail to turn up examples of scholarship that would not be tolerated in any undergraduate history department in the country, not could it fail to indicate the subject bias that appears to reflect the ease of access of sources far more than the importance of subjects themselves. The most pernicious failure, however, lies in the formulation and application of irrelevant models to history. As long as one is interested solely in the mathematics of an argument, its elegance and cleverness are important, but its applicability is not. If, however, one wants to employ a model to explain some aspect of reality, the latter quality assumes prime importance. Some of the "new" historians have failed to understand this point, or if they do understand they have chosen to ignore it. It is, however, in this area that the traditional historian, although undoubtedly aggrieved by what he must realize is a twisting of the past into unrecognizable shapes, is least capable of formulating a relevant objection. Theory *can* be useful in understanding history; it does not, however, follow that all theory is useful. A particular theory (no more logically valid than any of an infinite number of other theories) can aid the understanding of the past only if it has some relevance to the conditions it is attempting to explain. While this proposition may seem eminently sensible and so obvious that it is not worth discussing, it has been ignored by some of the "new" economic historians. Here, then, is real "figmentary history."

Paul David, in his extremely facile analysis of the innovation of the reaper, develops the concept of a threshold farm size (*i.e.,* a minimum size below which the farmer would find it more profitable to harvest by hand than by machine).[29] He produces a model that allows him to estimate the threshold, notes that many farms moved above that level during the 1850's, argues that the increase in wheat prices caused that increase in farm size, and concludes that it was in this manner that the increase in demand for wheat speeded the process of reaper innovation. Here we have a theoretical argument about an historical process. The model is logically valid, but the question remains: Does the model help us to understand the process of innovation? David's model applies to a world where the services of a reaper are indivisible; and the conclusions would not necessarily hold if such services were not indivisible. It is obvious that the reaper is mechanically indivisible at least within the limits of an 1850 technology). The argument, however, does not rest on the indivisibility of the machine, but on the indivisibility of the services of that machine. The evidence on that point is less clear. Today, for example, such divisibility of services is achieved both through the cooperative purchases of reapers and through the growth of firms specializing in reaping. Did similar institutions exist in the 1850's? The evidence suggests that they did. In the words of Allan Bogue: "I gave this problem to a graduate student one morning at eight o'clock and he was back in my office by ten with a long list of cooperative purchases."[30] While David's model is extremely clever, it is doubtful that it can be directly applied to the American economy in the 1850's (*i.e.,* it has little historical reality). If David wishes to use the model as an explanation of the process of innovation, he must show either that Bogue's evidence is wrong, or that in some regions there were legal or other institutional barriers to cooperative ventures or the growth of reaping firms. In the absence of this additional evidence, it can scarcely be argued that the model has made a substantial contribution to our understanding of the process of innovation.

Similarly, Peter Temin has employed a *very* formal model in an attempt to resolve the questions raised by Rothbart, Habakkuk, and others about the nature of technology in Great Britain and the United States in the nineteenth century.[31] His model is logically impeccable, and he derives some very strong (not to say, very strange) conclusions about the nature of innovation in the United States and about the nature of the U.S. economy itself. For example, he argues that innovations tended not to be labor-saving and capital-using, but capital-saving and labor-using and that real wages in the U.S. were lower than real wages in the U.K. Since these conclusions are at odds with most of the received doctrine about American development, the work (if it is correct) represents a major revision of economic history. The evidence, however, appears to belie these conclusions, and even Temin is obliged to try to explain this variance. He argues, for example, that while the U.S. appears to have utilized a great deal of capital, it was not very good capital. The problem, however, may not lie in the evidence but in the model which Temin has chosen. While his conclusions are strong, so are his assumptions; and not only are they very strong, but they postulate a world which is quite unlike any that we have ever known. While simplified models are the stock in trade of every economist, oversimplification can lead to lack of explanation. Occam's razor, after all, can help us choose between models only if both predict equally well. In Temin's case, although his general model postulates the traditional three factors of production, only two (labor and capital) are used in manufacturing and only two (land and labor) are used in agriculture. Every historian recognizes that agriculture does use capital and, if one is willing to broaden the definition of land to include raw materials, that manufacturing uses land. If Temin's model is reformulated with these additions, it is possible to conclude that innovations would be labor saving and that real wages would be higher in the U.S.[32] Theory is important—the explicit use of theory is the contribution of the new economic history—but *no* economic historian (be he old or new) should allow himself to be so completely seduced by the logic of theory that he forgets the facts. Theory can help us order and understand facts, but the facts can also suggest that certain theories are inappropriate as explanatory devices.

V. SUMMARY

What then is the current state of the "new" economic history? It has produced some substantial results, but it is certainly not free from criticism. Its critics have, however, frequently misunderstood its methodology; and, as a result, many of their barbs have been aimed at its strengths rather than at its weaknesses. A decade of work within the new framework has produced some substantial revisions of our understanding of historical relations. Some aspects of theory have been modified to make them more useful, and a great deal of meaningful debate has been conducted on issues which are still unresolved. It may not be literature; it's certainly not without problems; but the new history has made a substantial contribution to both history and theory.

Purdue University

NOTES

1. The focus on the TVA was suggested by Professor H. Scheiber at the recent OAH meeting. See H. Scheiber, "Lance Davis and the 'New Economic History.'"

2. The historical evidence on the TVA has been taken from W. Droze, *High Dams and Slack Water* (Baton Rouge, La., 1958), D. Lilienthal, *TVA Democracy on the March* (New York, 1953), and P. Habbard, *Origins of the TVA* (Nashville, Tenn., 1961).

3. R. Fogel, *The Union Pacific Railroad: A Case of Premature Enterprise* (Baltimore, Md., 1960).

4. R. Fogel, *Railroads and Economic Growth, Essays in Econometric History* (Baltimore, Md., 1964).

5. A. Fishlow, *American Railroads and the Transformation of the Ante-Bellum Economy* (Cambridge, Mass., 1965). Fishlow's product coverage is greater than Fogel's; he permits less adjustment in his counterfactual world, and he is more concerned with actual trade flows.

6. S. Lebergott, "United States Transport Advance and Externalities," *Journal of Economic History*, December, 1966.

7. Zvi Griliches, "Research Costs and Social Returns: Hybrid Corn and Related Innovations," *Journal of Political Economy*, 1961.

8. For example, even in Griliches' work an inclusion of the early (*i.e.*, 1876–1902) expenditures on research drastically reduces the social return. See D. Beebe, "The Rate of Return in Hybrid Corn Research 1876–1965," unpublished manuscript.

9. E. Cary Brown, "Fiscal Policy in the '30's, a Reappraisal," *American Economic Review*, 1956.

10. But we should bear in mind that much of traditional history is also written within the framework of regional development. Perhaps, then, North's real contribu-

tion was to convince the "new" historians that more complicated models are necessary.

11. Douglass North, *The Economic Growth of the United States 1790–1860* (New York, 1961).

12. J. Meyer, "An Input-Output Approach to Evaluating British Industrial Production in the 19th Century," in J. Meyer and A. Conrad, *The Economics of Slavery* (Chicago, 1964).

13. W. Whitney, "The Structure of the American Economy in the Late 19th Century, An Exercise in Historical Input-Output Analysis," a paper presented at the Fifth Purdue Conference on the Application of Economic Theory and Quantitative Techniques to Economic History, 1965.

14. L. Davis, J. Quirk, and R. Saposnik, "A Simulation Model of the Northean World," a paper given at the Second Purdue Conference on the A of ET and QT to EH, 1962.

15. W. Isard, "An Interregional Interindustry Model for the Philadelphia Metropolis," paper presented to the First World Econometric Conference, Rome, 1965.

16. O. Davis, M. Dempster, and A. Wiloavsky, "A Theory of the Budgeting Process," *American Political Science Reviews*, 1966, and Davis, Dempster and Wiloavsky, "On the Process of Budgeting: An Empirical Study of Congressional Appropriation," in G. Tullock (ed.), *Papers on Non-Market Decision Making* (Charlottesville, Va., 1966).

17. L. Guttman, "The Basis for Scalogram Analysis," in Stauffer (ed.), *Measurement and Prediction,* Volume 4 in *Studies in Social Psychology During World War II* (Princeton, N.J., 1949).

18. See, for example, A. Bogue, "Bloc, Party, and the Senators of the First Civil War Congress," paper delivered to the OAH 1967 and W. Adellotte, "The Conservative and Radical Interpretations of Early Victorian Social Legislation," paper presented at the Seventh Purdue Conference on the A of ET and QT to EH, 1967.

19. For example, it might be interesting to see if the Valley becomes "dissimilar" from the surrounding area in terms of certain social factors after the completion of the Authority's major programs. For a discussion of ecological correlation, see L. Goodman, "Some Alternatives to Ecological Correlation," *American Journal of Sociology,* 1959.

20. This point was made long ago by Schumpeter who argued that while monopolies might distort the allocation of resources in the short run, they might also underwrite a more rapid rate of growth than that engendered by competitive firms. See J. Schumpeter, *Capitalism, Socialism, and Democracy* (New York, 1950).

21. For example, Richard Easterlin has reached into the American past to provide a model of "long swings" where demographic changes provide the exogenous stimuli to the economic model. Dorothy Brady has turned traditional price studies inside out by systematically investigating changes in the cross-section of prices as a first step toward an understanding of the relationship between technological change, demand, and economies and diseconomies of scale. In a similar vein, several studies have examined the relationship between changes in economic institutions (institutions usually assumed fixed in economic theory) and economic growth. Douglass North has shown that it was not technological change in ship design but institutional adaptations in policing methods and market organization that underwrote the decline in shipping rates in the eighteenth and nineteenth centuries. Lance Davis and J. R. T. Hughes have argued that it is misleading to assume that the "gold standard" operated in the classic manner before the last quarter of the nineteenth century, and that in

earlier years that institution was undergoing continual change. Davis has shown that in both the United States and England the development of a national capital market depended on the innovation of new, and the adaptation of old, financial institutions to meet the demands of new industries and new regions.

R. A. Easterlin, "Economic-Demographic Interactions and Long Swings in Economic Growth," *American Economic Review*, December, 1966. Dorothy Brady, "Relative Prices in the Nineteenth Century," *Journal of Economic History*, June, 1964. D. C. North, "Determinants of Productivity in Ocean Shipping," paper given to the International Historical Society, Vienna, 1965. L. Davis, "Capital Immobilities, Institutional Adaptation, and Financial Development: The United States and England, an International Comparison," paper given to the International Econometric Conference, Rome, 1965, and "The Investment Market 1870–1914: The Evolution of a National Market," *Journal of Economic History*, September, 1965.

22. F. Redlich, "New and Traditional Approaches to Economic History and Their Interdependence," *Journal of Economic History*, 1965.

23. H. Scheiber, "State Policy and the Public Domain: The Ohio Canal Lands," *Journal of Economic History*, 1965.

24. Scheiber never defines the term "speculator," but it appears that he means sales to persons who themselves did not farm the land.

25. At the simplest level, although North himself talks of a world with only some five or six commodities, a minimum of thirty-six are implicit, and since there are at least three regions, the minimum number of commodities that must be treated are one hundred eight (3 x 36).

26. L. Davis, "Capital Immobilities and Finance Capitalism," *Explorations of Entrepreneurial History*, 2nd Series, 1963; "The Investment Market, 1870–1914: The Evolution of a National Market," *Journal of Economic History*, 1965; "The Capital Markets and Industrial Concentration: The U.S. and U.K., a Comparative Study," *Economic History Review*, 1966.

27. G. Stigler, "Imperfections in the Capital Market," unpublished manuscript.

28. A. H. Conrad and J. R. Meyer, "The Economics of Slavery in the Ante-Bellum South," *Journal of Political Economy*, 1958. For an example of alternative models see Y. Yasuba, "The Profitability and Viability of Plantation Slavery in the United States," *Economics Studies Quarterly*, 1961, or R. Sutch, "The Profitability of Ante-Bellum Slavery—Revisited," *Southern Economic Journal*, 1965. For the questions of evidence see E. Genovese, "Food Costs of Slaves and the Profitability of Slavery in the Ante-Bellum South," paper given at the 3rd Purdue meeting on the A of ET and QM to EH, 1963, or E. Sarayder, "A Note on the Profitability of Ante-Bellum Slavery," *Southern Economic Journal*, 1964.

29. P. David, "The Mechanization of Reaping in the Ante-Bellum Midwest," in H. Rosovsky (ed.), *Industrialization in Two Systems* (New York, 1966).

30. Bogue notes that no other graduate student could have found the evidence so quickly; this one was particularly well acquainted with the McCormick papers.

31. P. Temin, "Labor Scarcity and the Problems of American Industrial Efficiency in the 1850's," *Journal of Economic History*, September, 1966.

32. Temin's work has been criticized along these lines by E. Ames and N. Rosenberg, "The Enfield Arsenal in Theory and History," *Krannert Institute Paper No. 153,* and R. Fogel, "The Specification Problem in Economic History" (revised), *Journal of Economic History* (forthcoming).

POTENTIALITIES AND PITFALLS IN ECONOMIC HISTORY

Fritz Redlich

I

If we wish to understand the potentialities and pitfalls in economic history, we have to start by recognizing that every approach to the social sciences and humanities is determined by *Weltanschauung,* and by *Weltanschauung* we mean a consistent outlook on the world which can neither be proved nor disproved. Disregarding here the historical past, we find that at this moment there exist only two that are relevant for the scholar, Positivism and anti-Positivism. While one of the two is behind every research in the social sciences and humanities, it is not implied that *Weltanschauung* determines unilaterally the path to any particular research job to the exclusion of any other. We shall see that as we go along. Moreover, individual scholars can be more or less radical in drawing the consequences of their *Weltanschauung* which, however, sets definite limits. Eclecticism certainly represents no way out. It is beset with a great many pitfalls, since the consistence of any eclectic presentation necessarily equals nil.

In view of the tremendous success of science in the nineteenth and twentieth centuries, it is not surprising that recently economic and social historians adopted "scientific" methods that went hand in hand with their adoption of Positivism as their *Weltanschauung.* Now for the scientist proper, nothing matters that cannot be counted, weighed, or measured. Consequently for any scholar outside of the natural sciences who adopts the "scientific" method, measurement becomes an overwhelming interest. The effect of this emphasis on economic history will be shown

Source. EEH/Second Series, Vol. 6, No. 1. © Graduate Program in Economic History, University of Wisconsin, 1968.

shortly when we discuss the quantitative approach. But the quantitative method is not the only one that the positivistically oriented student of human affairs and the social and economic historian can use. Falling into the research category that one has come to call "qualitative," this second procedure can be characterized as factual or empiricistic. Instead of stressing figures, the scholar emphasizes facts, facts for their own sake. If a historian, he has in this case in principle only one arrow in his quiver, *i.e.*, he has only one question to ask, namely what happened and when, and he presents his findings by narration lined up according to chronology. Combinations of both the qualitative factual and the simple quantitative approaches are common in the earlier literature on economic and social history.

The underpinning of economic and social history by the *Weltanschauung* of Positivism can be traced back to the middle of the nineteenth century. Qualitative Empiricism then came to dominate European historiography for several decades; it reached the United States somewhat later. This dominance found expression in the prevailing interest of historians in editing sources with footnotes attached, and I have found in the contemporary literature expressions of the idea that a historian could not go further than that, if he wanted to remain within the boundaries of genuine scholarship. On the other hand, Henry Thomas Buckle's famous and awful book, *History of Civilization in England,* contributed to ushering in the era of quantitative economic history.

In contrast, if the scholar interested in human affairs or the economic and social historian is a non-Positivist by *Weltanschauung,* he will choose a different approach, called humanistic or hermeneutic. The former term stresses the fact that the man concerned is interested in human beings, their role in history, their goals, values, and actions, which he tries to understand; rather than in facts and figures, which are merely registered by the Empiricist. The latter term (hermeneutic) emphasizes the method which is applied in non-Positivistic research. The method is interpretation, the beginnings of which go back to the period of the Renaissance and Reformation, when it was originally developed in the field of Bible interpretation.

Professor John Higham [1] characterized the two possible approaches in a somewhat different way. According to him the "scientific" approach aims at "logical systematization of knowledge," the result being verifiable and amendable by further observation. It seeks "analytical generality" and abstracts what is measurable in whatever subjects are thus studied. In contrast the humanistic approach tries to "preserve the complexity of reality," catching it by "expressive rather than technically precise language." It aims at totality rather than at its "dissection."

It seems difficult for scientists proper, typical social scientists, and positivistically oriented economic and social historians to see that the humanistic approach to this field is just as viable and necessary as the "scientific." Both taken together open up the field in its entirety. Especially younger men, enthusiastic about the results of their "scientific" studies and carried away by present-day scholarly fashion, are inclined to overlook the Janus face of investigations of human affairs and specifically of social and economic history. It is all the more valuable that Hermann Weyl, one of the outstanding mathematicians and philosophers of our time, has pointed to this and written: "Scientists would be wrong to ignore the fact that theoretical construction is not the only approach to the phenomenon of life; another way, that of understanding from within (interpretation), is [also] open to us." [2]

II

The next step in our argument is predicated on the question: Which role does theory play in research on economic and social history? Dyed-in-the-wool empiricists deny that theory has any legitimate place in the writing of history. But I would guess that a majority of present-day economic historians, both old and young, would answer otherwise. On this point both positivistically and humanistically oriented modern economic and social historians agree. By the introduction of theory into pertinent research, both quantitative and qualitative economic and social history become *analytical* quantitative or qualitative economic and social history as opposed to the corresponding strictly narrative varieties. In other words, these two analytical approaches parallel on a new level those described in the preceding section of this paper.

When I spoke earlier of the empiricistic way as having only one question to ask, I added the qualifying phrase "in principle." As a matter of fact, many traditionally inclined historians, who are dead set against the use of theory in history, supplement the question of what happened and when by asking "why." Yet what those historians do not realize is that any answer to the question "why" is based on some kind of theory or philosophy. This kind of theory or philosophy the Empiricist has usually absorbed somehow because it is traditional or fashionable or at least seems to him to make sense. In each historical period primitive theories and popular philosophies are in the air. It is really undeniable that no answer to the question "why" in history is possible without recourse to theory or philosophy. Therefore our colleague, the economic historian Rondo Cameron, has stated perfectly correctly that, if a historian does not want to remain strictly within the boundaries of Empiricism, his choice is not between theory or no theory but between professional or primitive laymen's theories.

It appears impossible to me that one can argue about the necessity of using theory in the writing of economic and social history; the only question is how theory is to be used. In this respect there will be by necessity a difference between the Positivistic social "scientist" and the Humanist. My own approach, that of the Humanist, consists, on the one hand, in using theory in framing concepts on which I base the historical questions to be answered, while I do answer those questions by traditional historical methods. On the other hand, I use theoretical models as flashlights to illumine dark corners of our knowledge in economic and social history. That is to say, theory appears on two levels in my work. On the second level I *compare* what I found by the application of historical methods with the model or models I have applied in the conceptualization of the historical problem. The closeness to or deviation from such models helps to answer the proposed question and to understand the problem that is to be elucidated.

The quantitative analytical historian uses theory in a different way. He lets it permeate his presentation more than it does mine, which is methodologically hermeneutic, that is, geared to interpretation. Theoretical models establishing correlations are used by such historians to find unknown quantities. But if one uses this method, one has to keep in mind that in reality a correlation established in the model may be so overlaid by other causal factors that the looked-for unknown becomes misrepresented by over-reliance on the model. For this reason it might remain unknowable. There is a pitfall to be avoided. The modern analytical-quantitative economic historian is also inclined to introduce assumptions into his presentation. I shall speak about this later.

Here I want to point out that there are various kinds of theoretical models which can be used in research on economic and social history. First, there are strictly historical models, of which I cite but one, namely town economy. Something like this does not nor did it exist in reality. What did exist in historical reality is, for example, the economy of the town of Basel in the sixteenth century. The problem that there is a gradual approximation of the model to reality will not be discussed here, except to draw your attention to such steps in the approximation to reality as town economy, medieval town economy, German medieval town economy, German medieval town economy in the sixteenth century, and finally the town economy of Basel in the sixteenth century.

Second, there are the models forged by the social sciences that present certain problems to the economic and social historian who wishes to use them. In my opinion and according to my experience, the Humanist can almost never use them just as they come out of the workshop of the social scientist. He has to remodel them for the purpose on hand. As I observe the work of quantitative analytical economic historians it appears to me that they use economic models pretty much unchanged.

But there is still another problem connected with the use of models in research on economic history, which I can only touch upon. The Humanist aims at dealing with the totality of the problem involved. Therefore he is inclined to use models made available by any one of the social sciences; as they fit his research goal. If you know the work of Thomas C. Cochran, you know that he widely uses sociological models, which I also found very helpful in some research, while in others, for example my banking research, I have used economic models. Quantitative economic historians have usually restricted themselves to the use of economic models, as will be explained later.

III

We have now arrived at the following schema. There are two main approaches to economic and social history, the Humanistic and the Positivistic ones. The former is necessarily qualitative but can be either narrative or analytical; the latter can be either qualitative or quantitative. The quantitative approach, in turn, can be narrative or analytical according to the role which theory plays in the execution of a particular research job.

The question then is: How does what has come to be labeled "the new economic history" tie into this schema? Before we answer this question it must be understood that we deal here with a generation phenomenon. The so-called "new economic history" is in fact the approach of men born between about 1920 and 1930 who came into the field of economic history from economics rather than from history. Their rigorous economic training and their familiarity with mathematical statistics are reflected in their approach. They have rallied around the banner or rather battle cry, "the new economic history." To be sure, the following group of coevals, a phrase standing for the alternative, "historical generation," has already joined the older one and is developing the field. Second, it would be an error to identify the so-called "new economic history" with quantitative economic history pure and simple. Masterly performances in this area can be found as early as the nineteenth century. We come closer to an understanding of the movement when looking at it as analytical quantitative economic history. But again that is not enough; for analytical quantitative economic history as such can at least be traced back to the international historical price research of the 1920's. Actually and thirdly, in developing analytical quantitative economic history the exponents of the movement endowed it with some specific characteristics; namely, on the one hand with the specialization on the purely economic aspects of economic history and on macro-economic topics and, on the other, with the use of highly sophisticated economic theory using mathematical symbols and mathematical arguments. But fourth, there is nothing like *"the* new economic history." In fact as to details its exponents practice quite different approaches within the framework mentioned above, and I have observed that they may even differ quite angrily among themselves.

We can look at the products of their endeavors from various points of view. We can, for example, see the results against the background of earlier findings. Some of the products are genuinely new and could not have been reached by older and traditional methods. I am thinking of various studies by different authors on the development of productivity in shipping, or wheat growing, or other fields. Or I might mention, following a report by Professor R. W. Fogel analytical quantitative studies on the growth of particular industries or the diffusion of technology.[3] Again I would refer to the investigation of Lance Davis which proved that the gold-point mechanism did not operate in the foreign exchange markets in the first half of the nineteenth century. A second group of studies has brought out, by refined quantitative methods, that certain historical facts long considered as undeniable are actually what they were held to be. I am reluctant to approve the expenditure of money, time, and effort to demonstrate in detail what has been known before. But one can give the students in question the benefit of the doubt and appreciate the value of having arrived at identical results by different methods. A third group of "new" economic historians, about which we shall speak shortly, produces what I cannot accept as economic history at all.

Looking at the products of the modern analytical quantitative economic historians from another angle, we find what can be characterized as data processing jobs. At least one is an extensive macro-economic analysis of American economic development by refined statistical methods. A third, as I must repeat, is in my opinion not history at all.

IV

In an earlier section of this paper I asked about the role of theory in research in economic and social history. This question is now to be paralleled by another: What is the role of assumptions in such research? While I could answer the former query without reluctance in the affirmative, the parallel problem is a rather tough one. I have pointed out above that any answer to the question "why" is based on theory or philosophy, and this holds true also of any interpretation that the analytical historian proposes. These statements imply that assumptions cannot be avoided in historical research unless one wants to remain strictly within the limits of empiricistic research, be it qualitative or quantitative. In research on human affairs causal relationships are assumed but never provable, so that answers to questions about the "why" contain hidden assumptions.

But it is one matter to use an assumption as to causal relationship, an assumption that one is convinced is correct, or to make a simple conjecture without far-reaching consequences for the presentation, as a whole. It is another matter to base a train of essential mathematical-statistical operations for historical ends on a mere assumption and even on one that is known to be incorrect, such as are called counterfactual assumptions or figments. As a matter of fact, the introduction of counterfactual assumptions (figments) into research on the economic past is what some of the so-called "new" economic historians practice, and that, in turn, means research on what would have happened if something had happened that did not happen.

It has been generally accepted by historians in the past that the question of what would have happened "if," is non-permissible. It leads nowhere to ask what would have happened if Napoleon had been the victor at Waterloo or what would have happened if King Henry IV of France had not been murdered while he was preparing an invasion of Germany. Those who believe that history is an open-ended process know that in such cases the historical process would have been different; in contrast, determinists in history will say that the ultimate outcome would not have been any different anyway. Incidentally, this is a good example of how *Weltanschauung* determines historiography.

It appears to me that there is no reason whatsoever to exempt economic and social history from the rule valid for history as a whole, namely, that historical research deals with the past that was and not with the past that might have been. Moreover I cannot see how one can know in exact quantitative terms, even to two decimals (why not five?), something that actually never happened. The result of such investigations is for me "as if" history, quasi-history, fictitious history—that is, not really history at all. The future alone can decide if this kind of work, which in fact demands high caliber reasoning, will become part and parcel of scholarly endeavors and, if so, how it will be classified. If it were to become classified as history, the subject "history" would have to be redefined, and, if I see the matter correctly, genuine historians are in no mood to do that. If research on historical material with the help of assumptions is more than a fad, I would classify it as model building, that is, tool production for purposes of realistic empirical research. Its usefulness to that end would justify the effort. The potential usefulness of figments in *social science* as opposed to historical research is established.

v

In the following section I plan to change the approach and to look at the work of those scholars, who from now on will be called "counterfactualists," from a more sophisticated methodological and epistemological point of view. I shall explain at some length my refusal to consider research based on counterfactual assumptions as genuinely historical research. But I do not want to be misunderstood. I do not take a stand against this kind of research per se, nor do I consider it worthless; I only want to have it recognized as part and parcel of the social sciences and to stress its tool character as far as history is concerned.

In his most recently published, although not his most recently conceived paper, Robert W. Fogel has shown an unwillingness to recognize the difference between nonfactual and counterfactual, the difference paralleling that made in an earlier paper of mine between hypothesis and figment.[4] Needless to say, every hypothesis is nonfactual by character, otherwise it would not be a hypothesis. But not every hypothesis has a counterfactual assumption at its basis that makes it *ipso facto* a figment. The lack of a distinction between the two different logical categories comes out with clarity in Fogel's paper.[5]

Fogel tries to make his point, namely, that it is common practice among traditional economic historians to make implied counterfactual statements, by referring to an article of Eugene Genovese entitled, "The Significance of the Slave Plantation for Southern Economic Development." In this paper Genovese holds that the low level of manufacturing in the ante-bellum South was due to the inefficiency of southern demand for manufactured goods. Fogel goes on: "While Genovese appears to rest his case on what was rather than on *what might have been* [italics mine], his argument is crucially dependent on a series of implicit . . . statements and a series of theoretical assumptions." The word left out in this quotation is the moot word "counterfactual." What in my opinion belongs here is the word "nonfactual," for all Fogel shows is that whenever a theorem is used by an economic historian to explain a causal relationship, this relationship can be expressed positively or negatively. However it is expressed, it implies the logical opposite as a conditional. Or expressed metaphorically, every medal has necessarily a reverse. In this particular case, saying that the purchasing power on the plantations was so limited that it could not sustain industry, is the very same as saying that if purchasing power had been larger there might have been (Fogel's own words) southern industry. The emphasis is on "might have been," which is the reverse of the medal and as such a reasonable assumption, a hypothesis in my terminology. But we deal here with a logically completely different proposition from that of basing a train of thought on a genuinely counterfactual assumption: it is assumed that Napoleon had been the victor at Waterloo or that there had been no railroads, when every school child knows that Napoleon was defeated at Waterloo and that we had railroads as early as the second third of the nineteenth century. In the former case we argue on the basis of a genuine theory (which is non-factual by character); in the latter, on the basis of a figment (the counterfactual).

Certainly Fogel is right when pointing out that one can find hidden counterfactual statements in historical publications. This is the case when a historian expresses a value judgment in extreme terms, such as indispensable, *conditio sine qua non,* and the like. For example, if a historian, waxing enthusiastic about Lincoln, would say, "Thus Lincoln saved the Union," this statement would actually for the non-determinist imply, "Had Lincoln not been president, the Union would have been dissolved," an implied counterfactual statement.[6] If we go further with this discussion, we should arrive at Max Weber's contention that value judgments are not permissible to scholars, but in fact there are a good many cautious historical value judgments that do not have counterfactual implications, such as "played a role," "was important," and the like.

A widely held opinion seems to be that any question that is put to the past is a historical question. I have my doubts about this contention. What is a genuine historical question depends, in my opinion, on what is considered as history. Actually, as is generally known, there are two competing concepts, one wider and one narrower, the former defining history as change over time, the latter as change caused by human action in the past. (I myself prefer the narrower concept, but this matter is not under discussion here and is irrelevant in our context.[7]) In order to be considered historical, a question must, in my opinion, be subsumable under one of these two definitions. If it is not, it may be interesting for the historian, but it is not primarily and genuinely a historical question. Let us give a few examples: When a doctor investigates to learn from what sickness a certain historical personality died, his question is a medical but not a historical one. The same holds true of research on whether or not the Tudors were infected by syphilis. Similarly the matter of whether or not slavery was profitable in the American ante-bellum South is an economic question, and so is that asking for the social savings resulting from the introduction of the railroad or any other modern method of transportation. Questions which are not genuinely and primarily historical questions as here defined, but the answers to which are relevant and perhaps even very relevant for historical research, may be called ante-historical questions. They go before (*ante*) genuine historical research.[8]

Ante-historical research, as here characterized, can result in answers of two kinds. The answer given to the particular question can be factual or it may be contained in a model. King Y died from cancer belongs to the former; the works of Fogel and Fishlow, to the latter category.

Let us now investigate the work of the counterfactualists from still another angle. These scholars take great pride in the fact that they are articulate about their premises and put them on the table. That is correct as far as their technical (economic) assumptions are concerned. But those of methodological and epistemological character, underlying their research, remain hidden, and if they are brought to light, they turn out to be somewhat dubious. First of all, back of the thinking of the counterfactualists is the principle of mono-causation. Every causal factor, save the railroad, and specifically every non-economic causal factor, is thought a way to answer the specific question: What were the social savings due to the introduction of the railroad? We have here, of course, the customary and legitimate thinking of model builders, but it hits societal and historical reality right in the face. In societal and historical reality there is no event or institution that can be explained by one and only one cause. What rules these fields is multi-causation. For this reason alone such research as that of the counterfactualists reveals itself as model-building, even if the historian shamefacedly must concede that up to now very many historians have thought in terms of mono-causation, bad examples being contained in *Bulletin 54* (New York, 1946) of the Social Science Research Council in the article by Howard K. Beale, "What Historians Have Said About the Causes of the Civil War" (pp. 53 ff.).

Yet there is a second equally unrealistic assumption back of the work of the counterfactualists, namely the principle of linear causation, while historical and societal life is ruled by interaction. Again the historian must shamefacedly concede that most of the research of the guild adheres to the former principle; and it appears to me that it is a foremost task of the next generations of historians to rewrite history on the principles of multi-causation (implying an interdisciplinary research basis) and interaction. Thus the justification of the counterfactualists to go on using an antiquated method in an era in which the much admired scientists think in terms of feedback, lies in their building models instead of practicing history, the former being an occupation which can legitimately assume both mono-causation and linear causation.

The recognition that societal and historical life is dominated by multi-causation and interaction leads to the recognition that genuine history writing and research deal with totalities. Historical totality cannot be hacked to pieces if the result is to fall into the realm of historiography.[9] Instinct for the totality of the societal and historical processes is the benchmark of the historian that distinguishes him from the social scientist who is accustomed to break into the process he investigates to analyze it. I cannot express better what I mean than by quoting from the well-known book by Pollock and Maitland: "Such is the unity of all history that anyone who endeavors to tell a piece of it must feel his first sentence tears a seamless web." [10]

This stress on the difference between historical and social-science thinking is important for classifying the work of the counterfactualists. If with the eyes of the genuine historian one sees the historical past as a totality ruled by the principles of multi-causation and interaction, one recognizes that any individual change results in chains of changes. No change can be isolated, if an approximate picture of reality is desired. Consequently, there is no stable *tertium comparationis* with which to compare fictitious figures (in our case, transportation costs if there had been no railroads). The *tertium comparationis* is itself fictitious. Valuable as the resulting model may be, it can be nothing but a model, *i.e.*, a tool for historical research and not an ultimate result. Working on historical material along the principle of linear causation added to that of mono-causation and starting from counterfactual assumptions, leaves the result of the research in question thrice removed from reality.

It should be obvious that an attempt is being made here to establish the borderline between history and the social sciences, which is relevant in view of the recent attempt made in *Bulletin 64* of the Social Science Research Council to absorb history into the social sciences. On the one hand, it is gladly conceded that they overlap, or expressed differently, that we find a border zone rather than a borderline. On the other hand, the extraordinary importance of the social sciences for the understanding and the comprehending of the historical process is not only not denied, but simply taken for granted. But the social sciences serve the historian best when he can use them as an independent master in his own house. Therefore the recognition of a border is required, and for establishing it an earlier thread of our discussion will be taken up again and given another twist. We stated earlier that, except for dyed-in-the-wool Empiricists, there is agreement between traditional and new economic historians that social-science theory plays a legitimate role in the writing of and research in economic and social history. There is disagreement about the kind of role it is to play.

For me the line is to be drawn by asking the question: Who is master and who is maid? If theory is used for causal explanation of established historical facts and for the purpose of arriving at generalization from established historical facts, the researcher remains in the realm of history. (Of course, I am well aware that as far as generalization goes, there is a good deal of disagreement among historians themselves.) But whenever a particular theorem that is applied determines the outcome of the research project, theory has become the master, and for me the project belongs in the field of the social sciences. To understand what I have in mind one should compare the counterfactualists' research on the social savings due to the introduction of the railroad. It will be remembered that Fogel finds a 5 per cent and Fishlow a 15 per cent saving. If this research were history, one or both scholars did a very poor job, because, taken as factual historical information, findings differing in the ratio of 1:3 are irreconcilable. But actually the different results are due to the application of different theories, *i.e.*, in my language: theory was the master of the research. Thus the result belongs in the realm of the social sciences, it is a tool for historians.

The true character of counterfactual research reveals itself right here. We deal with simulation models in that past possibilities are figured, just as present or future possibilities are figured, in current simulation models. If all or most of the possibilities of the past in one area were figured, the historian would be able to use a range of potentialities useful as a guide in answering genuinely historical questions, provided they were possible on the basis of unimpeachable historical sources and answerable by quantitative methods.

When one is familiar with the work of some of the great modern existentialists and agrees with them on the role that the irrational, if not absurd, plays in societal and historical life, one must conclude that, if the goal is explanation rather than description, not every question put to the historical material can be answered rationally, except in a rationally constructed model. In other words, such historically unanswerable questions, including what would have happened if something had happened which did not happen, and others rooting therein as proposed by the counterfactualists, belong for me, if they should be asked at all, in the social sciences.[11]

VI

Let me now summarize my findings from the point of view programmatically stated in the title of this paper. Listening to my presentation, you yourselves may have come to the conclusion that each approach to economic and social history without exception has its potentialities and its limitations, if not pitfalls. Empiricistic, factual, narrative economic history, both of the quantitative and the qualitative variety, has the least potentials to claim, but also few pitfalls to avoid. It will remain useful and applicable, when new material is to be brought to the attention of the scholarly community, and it will by no means die out in the near future. A mere look at what is contained in the historical journals will confirm this expectation. But truly great achievements leading into the future can hardly be anticipated by these approaches.

In my opinion the future belongs to both analytical qualitative and quantitative economic and social history. Each of these two has its specific potentialities and its specific limitations and pitfalls. The former goes after the *understanding* of economic and social phenomena, the meaning and significance of economic and social processes. In principle it aims at the totality of whatever phenomenon it investigates, realizing particularly that economic institutions are part and parcel of social institutions. This, in turn, leads to the recognition of the closeness of what is only artificially separated into economic and social histories. The term "analytical" implies that use is made of modern professional theory, while there is no limitation as to which social science is drawn upon for this purpose. The qualitative method permits one to deal with processes that make for economic development or decay. But the method is unable to provide satisfactory statistical evidence and proofs for its contentions, particularly when statistical material must first be distilled from the raw material and is accessible only through the application of sophisticated mathematical methods. If not cautiously practiced, this approach may involve the danger of the uncertainty in the findings. They are largely dependent on *Weltanschauung,* and on scholarly experience and instinct; and the criterion of their validity and usefulness is the acceptance and application by reputable scholars sharing the *Weltanschauung* with the researcher and author.

What is the strength of the qualitative, is the weakness of the quantitative analytical approach, and vice versa. The latter can provide us with quantitative findings not accessible to the other. The results are testable if one accepts the basic argument. But at least as presently practiced by the self-styled "new" group, it restricts itself, as pointed out earlier, to the purely economic aspects of the phenomena of economic history. This leads into snares that are laid everywhere to trap the extreme specialists. Another pitfall is the belief, which you find expressed at times, that the manipulation of poor quantitative source material with highly sophisticated mathematical methods leads to reliable results. In contrast I contend that the result of mathematical manipulation cannot be better than the source material. Exponents of the quantitative analytical approach usually stop once they have presented figures, they often do not even attempt an understanding of what the figures mean; in other cases their interpretation is very poor, if not misleading. They are unable to get at the historical process in the socio-economic area, because figures represent fundamentally only the result of processes, and putting them together in the form of time series makes them indicative, but not directly expressive and descriptive, of the process concerned.

The problem for practitioners of modern economic and social history lies in the fact that with the exception of a few extraordinary geniuses, such as Joseph Schumpeter, the historical and the mathematical bents of mind are usually not present in one person. Thus, for this reason alone, the two modern approaches to economic history have to become complementary and should be recognized as such. Neither can cover the whole field, and neither can dispense with the other, notwithstanding some very imprudent if not nasty statements that one could easily quote. I do not need to repeat that I reject in principle quasi-economic history, as practiced by some quantitative analysts. Which approach an individual chooses depends on his ability and inclination and also on his pretraining. Today economic historians coming from history will incline toward the qualitative approach; economic historians coming from economics, toward quantitative analytical economic history. As to the former, a good many history departments will go on training exponents of empiricistic narrative economic history. Last but not least, and in making this statement I return to my opening remarks, *Weltanschauung* will largely determine the approach of the individual researcher. The non-Positivist will prefer the humanistic, qualitative approach; the Positivist, the "scientific" quantitative one.

Let me close this paper by emphasizing that it is only a hasty survey of a very broad topic, the epistemology and methodology of economic and social history. It remains to be seen whether or not the present two main approaches are only thesis and antithesis in the Hegelian sense, to be followed in the future by synthesis.

Harvard University (retired)

NOTES

1. "The Schism in American Scholarship," *American Historical Review*, LXXII (1966/67), 3.
2. *Philosophy of Mathematics and the Natural Sciences* (Princeton, 1949), 283. I owe the knowledge of this important passage to an article by Prof. von Haberler.
3. "The New Economic History: Its Findings and Methods," *Economic History Review*, Second Series, XIX (1966), 647–649.
4. See my paper " 'New' and Traditional Approaches to Economic History and Their Interdependence," *Journal of Economic History*, XXV (1965), 484.
The criticism leveled against me by J. A. Dowie in his paper, "As if or not as if; The Economic Historian a Hamlet," *Australian Economic History Review*, VII, No. 1 (1967), 80, 81, is herewith rejected, because the author is also unable to see the difference between nonfactual and counterfactual (hypothesis and figment).
5. Fogel, Robert William, "The Specification Problem in Economic History," *Journal of Economic History*, XXVII (1967), 285–287.
6. It has been pointed out before (p. 99) that determinists and non-determinists in history will look differently at statements of this character.
7. "The very term 'history' means, in fact, human history . . ." If "there is any one subject with which history is concerned, that subject is change—how things ceased to be as they had been before, how they became what they had not been." See Potter, David M., *People of Plenty: Economic Abundance and the American Character* (Chicago, 1954), paperback edition, Introduction, x, xvii.

8. An investigation of *changes* in the profitability of American plantations, say between 1815 and 1860, would be subsumable under history.

9. A good example of what I am criticizing is the recent publication of Douglass North going under the title *Growth and Welfare in the Past: A New Economic History* (Englewood Cliffs, N.J., 1966). The book deals with economic problems of the past that are well handled from the point of view of the economist. They are held together by a historical frame which, unfortunately, is not free from historical errors.

10. Pollock, F. and F. W. Mainland, *A History of English Law before the Time of Edward I,* 2nd. ed. (Cambridge, England, 1898), I, 1.

11. The preceding section V of this paper was not read at the Stanford meeting, but inserted later for publication.

COMMENT

George Green

It strikes me that this session is economic history's counterpart to the Broadway shows *Hello Dolly!* or *Kiss Me Kate.* This is at least the twentieth annual road-show (convention) performance on the topic of methodology. Discussion of these issues of the role of economic theory and statistics in economic history goes back at least to the 1947 meeting of the Economic History Association.

But like *Kiss Me Kate,* our drama has its even more ancient antecedent. Our parallel to Shakespeare's *Taming of the Shrew* is the perennial debate over whether history is one of the humanities or the social sciences. (I suppose the still untamed shrew is theory!) Dr. Redlich's references to the Humanist and Positivist approaches fit perfectly into that familiar plot. But fortunately the positions of today's two papers nearly enable us to avoid another round of that tired old battle.

I hope my own comments will suggest that even the modern version of the old play has got too melodramatic. In its present form the debate between "old" and "new" economic historians is a "sterile argument," as Professor Davis has said. There are some real issues to be fought over, or rather some real methodological problems to be solved by what LBJ calls "reasoning together," but much of the debate has obscured these real issues.

Let me employ a little very amateur social psychology to place the debate in context. Economic history, like many other subjects, has undergone what Richard Hofstadter calls a "status revolution." The prestige of science and the "scientific method" in modern society and thought has threatened the status of the more traditional practitioners, and has favored the rise of the "new" economic historians. Equally important, this

Source. EEH/Second Series, Vol. 6, No. 1. © Graduate Program in Economic History, University of Wisconsin, 1968.

conflict of values has taken a particular institutionalized form. Basically it has become a contest between two well established, formalized social groups—economists and historians. Any individual economic historian has "need of affiliation" and thus "learns the values" of his social group. Economists learn the importance of "scientifically" developing and rigorously testing theories, and of seeking potential policy applications in the contemporary world. Historians learn of the sanctity of primary sources and the facts they contain, of the subtleties of multi-factor and conflicting interpretations, and of literary style. These conflicting ideologies and the social groups that embody them "peacefully coexist" despite occasional battles over university funds and appointments, or over editorships and contents of scholarly journals. To some extent the social conflict becomes a psychological conflict, as economic history has been institutionalized in a single separate department or more often in a joint program or joint appointment in economics and history. Anyone who has lived with one of these recognizes the potential for "intellectual schizophrenia." The political scientists, with their behaviorists and institutionalists, can affirm that "sibling rivalry" within a single department can be just as strong as the conflict between two separate institutions or two departments. As the beneficiary of a joint appointment, I find it in my own psychological and social interest to resolve, or perhaps repress, the methodological conflict.

To that end let me begin by recalling the very important points on which Professors Redlich and Davis, as presumed representatives of the "old" and the "new," the historian and the economist, are in agreement.

First, there are at least three different and legitimate approaches to the study of economic history: the purely empiricist or descriptive approach, the traditional mainly qualitative analytical (theoretical) approach, and the "new" quantitative and even more theoretical approach. Purely empirical history is possible—as in locating new literary or statistical evidence, or arranging such evidence in a simple descriptive and strictly chronological sequence—but Professors Redlich and Davis agree that this approach is uncommon and relatively unexciting.

Second, for most economic historians, "the choice is not between theory and no theory, but between professional or primitive laymen's theories." Professor Davis would say that it is between explicit, well specified theories and implicit, often illogical or incomplete theories. But in any case we are all users of theory.

Third, more explicit or more mathematical theory does not alone distinguish the "new" economic history. It is the combination of such theory with quantitative evidence and statistical inference. This often goes beyond just gathering existing data. In Redlich's words, the new methods can provide quantitative findings "when statistical material must first be distilled from the raw material . . . through application of sophisticated mathematical methods." I might add that this "distilling" of the primary data not only involves calculation of ratios, percentages, etc., but also the synthesis of new numbers through the combination of source numbers and economic theory. The numbers that result from such statistical inference are thus dependent upon the assumptions used in deriving them. I must in fairness add that although Dr. Redlich in his comments here appears to accept and approve such techniques, he has earlier sharply criticized them.[1]

Fourth, if the "new" economic history wins points for being more explicit in its theorizing and more quantitative in its evidence, Redlich and Davis agree that it loses points for other reasons. It is narrowly economic in subject matter and theories. It sometimes uses oversimplified theory, or theory whose assumptions do not fit the historical circumstances.

Having emphasized the broad areas of agreement in today's papers, let me now focus on their sharpest disagreement—the use of the counterfactual conditional, the hypothetical alternative, or what Dr. Redlich calls the "figment." Dr. Redlich flatly asserts that any historical research based on such "figments" is "as-if history, quasi-history, fictional history, not really history at all." It may be historical model building, and may be useful to future historians, but it is *not* history. He says, "It has been generally accepted by historians in the past that the question of what would have happened 'if' is non-permissible." I suspect that many historians would indeed nod in agreement, especially after hearing Dr. Redlich's examples of such counterfactual conditionals as if Napoleon had won at Waterloo, etc. But Dr. Redlich has drawn too sharp a line. Historians *do* reject some particular counterfactual conjectures, but they certainly have not rejected the technique itself. Let me mention a few examples from good old traditional political history: Charles Ramsdell on "the limits of slavery expansion" (what *would* have happened to slavery *if* the Civil War had not been fought?), or indeed the larger discussion about the "repressibility" of that Civil War. Or consider Richard Hofstadter's article, whose very title is a counterfactual conditional: "Could a Protestant Have Beaten Hoover in 1928?" As Professor Davis has said, such conscious, explicit uses of the counterfactual conditional are only the tip of the iceberg; historical writing is filled with unconscious, implicit (and often illogical or irrelevant) arguments of the same type.

Putting the idea in a historian's language may help you to recognize it in disguised form. We commonly say that factor X was an important cause, or the primary cause, or a contributing factor toward the occur-

rence of event Z. In other words, factor X "made a difference" to the
course of history at that point. In other words again, without factor X,
the pattern of events *would have been different.* That statement *implies*
a counterfactual conditional. The "new" economic historian merely follows through to ask: How different? How much different? Answering
these questions necessarily involves a "model" of the hypothetical world
(the real world without factor X, but with all other things unchanged).
And usually the description of this hypothetical world involves the use of
statistical inference.

If we admit that historians *do* use the counterfactual conditional,
then the question becomes: What are the rules of the game? As Professor
Davis has argued, one of the great benefits of the "new" economic history
is that it gets the theory and the assumptions out into the open where
they can be examined and criticized, both as to their logical consistency
and as to their historical realism. There remains a great deal of "art," of
ingenuity, of creativity in the design and estimation of such counterfactual models. It is not at all cut and dried or mechanical, but let us define
some minimum ground rules.

Ground Rule #1—Don't make hypothetical alternatives for which
you have no well specified model. This rules out the familiar cocktail
party questions such as "What if Hitler had taken Britain or if Napoleon
had won at Waterloo?" We simply have no model with which to describe
the hypothetical world without such a factor X. Unfortunately this
ground rule also disqualifies other questions in which historians have
been seriously interested, such as, "What were the most important causes
of the Civil War?" Until we have a general social science model of the
causes of war, this question cannot be answered rigorously. Of course this
will not stop historians from answering it, or from publishing paperback
editions of "Conflicting Interpretations of the Causes of the Civil War,"
in which each article probably favors one particular factor X, one frag-
mentary hypothetical alternative. By contrast the "new" economic historians focus on questions for which they do, it is hoped, have relevant, well
specified models.

Ground Rule #2—Make your crucial assumptions "realistic." Professor Redlich and many other historians have misunderstood one key
point. There is one assumption that is deliberately "unrealistic" in any
causal analysis, the absence of factor X. This is the very essence of the
counterfactual: What would the actual (historical) world have been like
without factor X, all other things unchanged? Thus it is only the assumptions about "all other things" that should be "realistic." By making their
assumptions explicit, the "new" economic historians enable us to judge
the validity of their conclusions. However, they are subject to one criti-

cism in this respect, which Professor Redlich has suggested. They are very explicit about their *economic* assumptions, but entirely implicit about their political, social, and other assumptions. A narrowly economic model with absolutely realistic assumptions might still explain very poorly the economic impact of the Civil War, if it made unrealistic implicit assumptions about the political or social variables.

Ground Rule #3—Select or define your concepts or variables in an "operational" way, so that they are testable—comparable to the largest possible body of historical evidence, whether qualitative or quantitative. Many of our favorite and most fruitless historical controversies have been built around concepts not operationally defined—the "frontier," the "Progressive movement," "Puritanism," or from economic history, "speculation," the "working class," the "Industrial Revolution." In a previous paper Professor Davis has led the way in exposing such inadequacies.[2]

Ground Rule #4—Once the concepts are defined operationally we can worry more about the ground rules for using available evidence, such as: What constitutes an adequate sample of evidence? (Traditional historians, fond of single "well chosen" illustrative proofs, should worry more about this question.) How accurate are the synthetic statistical estimates?—plus or minus how much? "New" economic historians would greatly enhance the acceptability of their estimates if they would provide statistical confidence intervals to show the degree of imprecision or uncertainty arising from their assumptions; only a few have done so. On the other hand, many of the "new" economic historians have actually been beating the historians at their own game: digging up and using new evidence, particularly quantitative evidence. Their fresh theoretical questions have raised the need for new data. Their use of theory has also made them bolder in transforming old data into new synthetic forms.

Let me briefly discuss one case in which the traditional historian makes his hypothetical alternative explicit—he explains one event by historical analogy to another. Today this is more fashionably called comparative history. Note that it is a type of hypothetical alternative. By deriving his theoretical model from similar events in another time or place the historian is assured that his assumptions are "realistic." But comparative history is methodologically much trickier than it looks, and I suspect much harder to use well than the more pure theoretical models of the "new" economic history. First of all, assumptions (or conditions) realistic for one country are not all relevant to another country. Secondly, since the model is less likely to explain theoretically the economic or other processes operating in either country, it is difficult to tell which points of similarity or dissimilarity "made the difference." Although comparative history may seem simpler in theory and more realistic in assumptions, it is usually just the opposite. But at least it can be more explicit than other uses of the hypothetical alternative by historians.

Let me summarize the implications of my remarks about this argument over the counterfactual conditional:

(1) We are all users of theory, and this means builders of historical models that contain their hypothetical alternatives, whether explicit or implicit.

(2) We need to develop better "ground rules" for our common practices. The "new" economic historians, with their better specified models, their explicit assumptions, and their operational definitions of concepts have generally led the way in this direction. More traditional historians, with their intuitively ordered complex interpretations or with their studies in comparative history, have frequently bitten off more theory than they could chew. That is, they have tried to explain events which lie beyond our present theoretical understanding, usually because they are a blend of economic, social, political, and other forces.

(3) There exists a fairly natural division of labor between the new and old approaches to economic history. The "new" economic historians will explain with some precision and finality the narrowly economic impact of historical events. The old economic historians will go on explaining the theoretically unexplainable! After the old historians have told us why Jackson and Biddle fought their "bank war," the new historians will tell us, in millions of dollars, what effects it had on the economy. The old historians will increasingly specialize in the not-strictly-economic factors: the role of ideas, values, politics, etc.—and in the origins of decisions or policies. They will have to leave to the new economic historians the assessment of the *effects* of those decisions or policies. To tell the full story we will obviously need them both.

In conclusion let me just suggest that the traditional historians, instead of being less theoretical, should see themselves as the true pioneers of theory. They are pressing at the frontiers of our present theoretical knowledge, intuitively combining and exploring models from all the social sciences. Their primitive models will necessarily lay the groundwork for Professor Davis' general social science theory, if we ever get to it. By contrast, the new economic historians are *behind* the theoretical frontier, using the narrower theories now available. In this one observation I have neatly reversed the "status revolution" mentioned earlier. I have turned the Humanists into basic research scientists, theoretical explorers, and the Positivists into mere engineers! That should make everybody unhappy!

University of Minnesota

NOTES

1. Fritz Redlich, " 'New' and Traditional Approaches to Economic History and Their Interdependence," *Journal of Economic History,* XXV (1965), 480–495.

2. Lance Davis, "Monopolies, Speculators, Causal Models, Quantitative Evidence and American Economic Growth," paper read to the Organization of American Historians, Chicago, April 28, 1967.

ECONOMETRICS AND SOUTHERN HISTORY*

Alfred H. Conrad

I

I should like to preface my talk this morning by demonstrating that northerners do sometimes have a sense of tradition. I will prove it by making the orthodox gesture of telling a story which may or may not have anything to do with the problem we came here to talk about. This is a Yankee story, about a Harvard law professor in a small Maine seacoast town. The lawyer—who was Judge Thomas Reed Powell—found himself on the edge of an uncomfortably overheated argument about the efficacy of baptism. He tried to remain inconspicuous, hoping thereby to avoid turning at least one-half of the sages of the town into his enemies, but finally someone cornered him and fired point-blank the question, "Judge Powell, do you or do you not believe in baptism?" The lawyer, and he is reputed to have been a great one, hesitated very briefly, and then replied, "Do I believe in it, sir? Why, I assure you, I've seen it done."

Now since you are probably expecting a sermon, that being the usual form of discourse in discussions of methodology, I may as well start by examining closely the title assigned to me in the order of worship. You have been told that I will speak about Econometrics and Southern Economic History. That is a good start. The title offers *Econometrics,* simply, and doesn't beg any questions by naming Econometric *History.* If anybody is to be convinced that econometric history exists, as opposed to

Source. EEH/Second Series, Vol. 6, No. 1. © Graduate Program in Economic History, University of Wisconsin, 1968.

*This paper and the three panel discussion papers following were delivered at the Southern Historical Association meeting in Atlanta, Georgia, on November 9, 1967.

econometric exercises performed upon numbers that are certified to be sufficiently antique, then he must first be shown that it has been done.

The second part of the title presents less difficulty. Nobody can complain about limiting some historical narratives to an area or culture as large and varied and rich in experience as the southern United States. There may be a few backsliders who remember with nostalgia the debates about whether *any* history with an adjective—economic history or constitutional history or religious history—was really possible. But, for many of us, the world is sufficiently complicated, if not confusing, so that we are prepared to concentrate upon one aspect or another of human existence. Those of us who concentrate on economic history do not mean to imply thereby that we think man is simply or always economic man, but only that enough of human life moves in channels that are defined by economic institutions and relationships so that we ought to study how the economic processes and developments have impinged upon, or at least *partly* determined, the history of some group of people, at some time or place.

One last introductory announcement: I would like my sermon to be useful, and not simply exhortatory. I will therefore take liberties under the title and address myself to the following question: How can a historian—who is probably a mathematical layman, to say the least—How can an "ordinary" historian criticize a work of economic history?

II

Econometrics is not simply statistics. Nor is it a newly minted tag for mathematical economics. And, by extension, econometric history is not simply history that is focussed upon economic quantities.

Statistics is a central part of econometrics, obviously. But the econometrician is concerned with quantifying economic theory, in the sense of turning the parameters—the alphas and betas and gammas that characterize functional relationships—from Greek letters into trustworthy numbers. He may do this because somebody has asked him to predict what will happen if a new policy is tried or because he wants to test some piece of received wisdom about the purchase of television sets as incomes go up or the purchase of books as television becomes ubiquitous. Whatever the motive may be, what distinguishes the econometrician is his concern with a model of economic behavior or structure.

Statisticians, as such, do not worry about specification or identification. These are econometric problems that arise when we attempt to construct models. Specification refers to the way in which we translate the algebra—the theoretical picture—into a statistical statement about observable events in an uncertain world. The term points up for us the problems of fitting our measurements, which may be a far cry from the pure variables named in the theory, to the functional model. Specification, then, refers to the match between a formal, causal theory and the corresponding empirical statement drawn from a world full of erratic, possibly random, behavior.

The identification problem is an admission that the parameters we are able to fit may not lead us back (by inference) to one and only one structure, or economic relationship. For example, we may have been given a set of price and quantity figures from a single, well-defined market and still not be able to say whether we are fitting the demand relationship or the supply relationship in that market. In short, we may be unable to identify which of two, or more, structures we are observing, however many observations nature or history may have granted us.

Neither of these problems arises in statistics, per se. There are other specifically econometric crosses to be borne, but I will not mention them now. I have brought in these two simply to make the distinction clear and because they will suggest troubles that I expect must be familiar to anyone who thinks about historical inference.

A listener would have to be very young, or poorly read indeed in economic history, to need a lecture to tell him that distinguished historians were searching for quantities and lining up numbers and arguing from statistics long before the Econometric Society was founded or young men advertised themselves as econometric historians. I have only to name Lewis Gray here or Earl Hamilton or G. Heberton Evans to make my point. But the next step, to invoke them as precursors (much more to list them as econometricians) would apparently be illegitimate, perhaps even tendentious. It would be tempting to invoke tradition again and to claim lineage from these distinguished economic historians, but Fritz Redlich described what Robert Fogel and John Meyer and I have been doing as *quasi*-history, pointedly.[1] That Mr. Redlich knows the literature does not need repeating, and so we had better consider now where the difference lies.

The feature that distinguishes econometric history from the more familiar, even venerable, quantitative work in economic history is the same feature that I discussed when I made the econometrics-statistics distinction—namely, the role of theory or economic models. A model is a formal and, we hope, operational expression of the notions we hold about some economic phenomenon. The model may be held as a hypothesis to be tested, or we may want to use it in order to predict values of the dependent variable. More often—and here the analogy to the physical sciences is obvious—we may use the model to investigate some of the laws or regularities that hold among the variables that enter our phenomenon.

We use the model, essentially, by pushing one of the variables to see what will happen to one of the others. And, since we cannot experiment in an economic laboratory, we are learning how to substitute accumulated observations for the direct methods of experimental physics or biology.

I don't want to give the impression that econometric historians look upon history as a source of evidence or observations with which to test econometric models. We have been directing much more attention to the question of what econometrics, as a way of thinking about economic phenomena, can bring to the study of economic history. The econometricians who have invaded history—invaded, not strayed into—have been concerned with the testing of historical explanations, not with the verification of economic hypotheses, per se. Furthermore, they have been concerned with using econometric techniques to fill in gaps in historical narratives, rather than with mining the narratives as a source of ready-made time series. These claims of usefulness that I have been making suggest a basis for the criticism of econometric history. First, does an econometric paper or monograph tell us something about a stretch of history that we have not been able to find out by other procedures? Second, has the econometrician suggested a way of looking at the available evidence that will be useful in reading another body of historical material?

I would like to proceed now by considering some southern history to see whether econometrics has made a difference. I will conclude by examining critically some of the new methods that econometricians have carried into the reading of history.

III

I want first to look at some work on southern income that has generated unsettling results—unsettling to orthodox views, that is—with the least provocative methodology of the new history. Since the 1850's, historians have been using the statistics of De Bow and Helper and Seaman to shore up their arguments about economic stagnation in the South. Over the last ten years, Richard Easterlin and Robert Gallman have published a series of findings on income and output in the U.S., back to 1834.[2] The pertinent numbers for this discussion are those that show that the South was *not* lagging behind the rest of the nation. The sharp reversal in the southern participation in American income growth, measured in relative or in absolute terms, began with the Civil War, not before.

Where do the new findings come from? Gallman, who has been responsible for most of the recent work on the early nineteenth-century income series, did not turn up new data on incomes, specifically. He has, rather, gone about the task of creating a set of value-added estimates for the major sectors in much the same way that the national income statisticians at the Department of Commerce go about their job: starting from the value of gross output, he subtracted the inputs of fuels and materials consumed in the production process. The result is a measure of goods available for consumption and capital growth—Final Demands, in national income jargon. In this way, duplication was minimized, sectoral detail was maintained, and most important, the income and investment series were extended back to a period for which few, if any, adequate series had been recorded.

The earliest listings in Easterlin's work on regional shares, those for 1840, are essentially reconstructions of Ezra Seaman's estimates using Seaman's procedures.[3] Gallman's results, which are neither income-originating measures nor estimates of the value of final product, were available to check Seaman's series; and in one important case, Gallman's procedure was used to prepare an alternative estimate. The 1860 estimates are derived from Gallman's findings, and for the later years by Easterlin from a number of sources.

The study shows a relative loss in the southern income position, in comparison with the Northeast, but a gain relative to the comparably agricultural West North Central region. The per capita income in the South, as a percentage of the national average, fell from 76 to 72. But the data show a significant absolute rise in per capita income for the South over the two decades before the Civil War. It is in the postwar period that the story changes: the southern position falls from 72 to 51 per cent of the national average, between 1860 and 1880.

If we press the logic of slavery all the way, and count slaves as intermediate goods or capital instruments, but not as consumers, then the ante-bellum South,—the free, white South, that is—appears to have waxed even fatter. Southern income grew by 42 per cent from 1840 to 1860; the national average (again, of course, for free persons) increased by 32 per cent.[4]

The regional data can be used to point some light into another secure corner of orthodoxy. At least from the time of the slavery debates in the Virginia Assembly in 1832, some men have argued that slavery might have been prosperous in the West, but in the Old South the institution was moribund as a commercial proposition, though not as a way of life. Craven, Ramsdell, and Randall all seem to me to be arguing from such a position.[5] When we look at Easterlin's proportions and Gallman's income figures, a rather different story appears. If slaves are counted as people, then for the Old South, the South Atlantic region, the income increase is only slightly below that for the whole nation; if the seaboard region's slaves are counted as inputs in the production process, then that region's per capita income appears to have grown more rapidly than the nation's.

This is not to deny Cassius Clay or Hinton Helper any significance in the southern story, either before the war or since, simply because the income series contradict their assertions. They may have aroused southern doubts before the war, and since the war they have lent weight to the argument that the institution, supposed to have been dying economically, was defended out of a sense of responsibility or in the face of Northern self-righteous provocations. But these new findings should lead historians to ask new questions—about the institutions that enabled the exhausted South Atlantic states to share in the ante-bellum prosperity, and about the commercial foundations of the common cause of the old southeast and the new southwest.

Answers to both of these questions are suggested in a series of econometric contributions starting with a paper by John Meyer and myself that is now ten years old.[6] What we did was to imagine twelve typical southern plantations all growing cotton, but with four different land qualities, represented by the average yield per hand, each facing a range of three different farm-gate prices. Then, using this statistical model, implemented or quantified as best we could with data from contemporary reports and secondary sources, we derived an answer to the following question: Should a Southerner, purchasing land and slaves in the mid-'forties, have expected to make a return on his investment that was at least comparable to what was then being earned on other long-term investments? The answer was *yes*. That answer, or at least the implication it contained—that slavery was profitable in the 1840's in the South—was hardly new. Kenneth Stampp had argued, at the same time that we presented our results in the graduate history seminar at Harvard, that the production of cotton with slave labor was a money-making proposition for slaveholders in the old lands and in the new southwest. He cited in support of his contention, as we did and anyone must, Lewis Gray and Robert Russel, as well as Thomas Govan and Robert W. Smith.[7]

However, the question as we framed it was evidently a strange one for historians to raise. We could not ask whether investments made in 1845, say, were *in fact* profitable, since Emancipation intervened and wiped out the slave-holders' property-rights, long before the economic life of the prime field hand or wench purchased in the mid-'forties had been realized. Nor did we look for plantation records to evaluate as other historians have done, either believing them to be representative, or with a view to combining their earnings experience to get some kind of average for the South. It was our question, then, and the capital model implied in it, that prompted Fritz Redlich to deny us the proud title of professional historian and to label us, instead, as quasi-historians. Part II of our paper, the part I have just described, he refers to as a work of fiction, starting from a hypothesis but based upon figments.[8]

What this piece of econometrics contributed was, evidently, not a new observation about the course of southern history, but rather a new way of approaching the problem. What we did was to apply capital theory to the problem as it was raised by Phillips: that the price of slaves, driven upward by speculative demand and the dictates of conspicuous consumption, would soon have raced so far beyond the price of cotton that the whole system must collapse.[9] Capital theory led us to observe that plantation slavery was based upon a form of capital that not only maintained itself, but was capable of increasing the size of its stock from year to year. The process has been likened to the widow's cruse of oil in the second book of Kings. Starting from this point of view, therefore, we estimated the return on male slaves—prime field hands—and female slaves, separately. The return on male slaves was a relatively straight-forward estimation problem. But the return on females required that we estimate first the number of offspring, the costs of rearing them, their productivity up to the time when they were sold, and their sale prices.

One important test still remained, however; it was not sufficient to demonstrate that slave-women in Virginia and the Carolinas produced salable children. We had to show that an efficient market existed for their sale. Otherwise, in the face of declining agricultural prospects in the East and boom-conditions in the West, stocks should have grown alarmingly in the seaboard region, driving prices down, while Western slave prices would sky-rocket under the pressure of unsatisfied demand. And indeed, the literature about the southerner's contempt for slave-mongering, and the liberal assertions, from J. E. Cairnes at least to U. B. Phillips, that slave capital was immobile, seemed to argue in this direction. In fact, we turned up considerable evidence, not only of regional specialization in the slave trade, but also that the spread between eastern and western slave and land prices did not increase—in short, that the market was efficient.

Before turning to another historical problem and then to the criteria with which we might judge econometric history, let me list a few of the new findings and interpretations that have come forward with regard to the slavery issue. Robert Evans, using an ingenious pricing model based upon the annual hire rate of slaves, approached the Phillips argument from a different direction, with results similar to ours.[10] In addition, his findings suggest that Meyer and I probably *under*estimated the productivity of prime field hands. Attacking the suggestion that our findings on profitability could imply that the system was viable, Yasukichi Yasuba demonstrated that capitalized economic rents were rising in the ante-bellum South, and that far from fading away or threatening to come down with a crash, the peculiar economic institution was becoming more solid, more "blue-chip," as the Civil War approached.[11] In a volume of *reinterpretation* soon to be published, another quasi-historian on the program this morning, Robert Fogel, and his co-author, Stanley Engerman, have taken on Charles Ramsdell and turned the initial premise of his "natural limits" argument into its own refutation.[12] This feat required observations on the relative movements of the demand and supply of American cotton between the Civil War and World War I, and upon the increase in the acreage under cotton after 1860. The data series can hardly raise eyebrows—they are from the Census and James Watkins' *Production and Price of Cotton*. But the test consists of counterfactual predictions of the price and hire rates of slaves between 1860 and 1890. Is Fogel to be put down once again for breaking the rules and indulging himself with *figments?;* or should we both, perhaps, move over to make room for the venerable shade of Charles Ramsdell?

I would like to look into one more concrete example drawn from southern history. That is the still unsettled question of the importance of interregional trade between the West and the South in the ante-bellum period. The antagonists are Robert Fogel and Albert Fishlow.[13] (I am not sure that we can trust Prof. Fogel to refrain from adding fuel, or figures, to the fire this morning.) I introduce this controversy to illustrate how econometricians argue about the numbers they have constructed, not because there is any particular elegance in this exchange. But, since their argument over interregional trade patterns has come up in the context of two of the most sophisticated pieces of econometric history we have had, I first want to talk about the broader issue.

Fishlow and Fogel, independently, undertook to quantify and to question the contribution of the railroads to American economic growth. On the face of it, you might consider this questioning to be a singularly insensitive attempt to resurrect a very dead horse. I, for one, accepted Schumpeter's judgment when I first read it, and later when I balked at Rostow's take-off thesis, it wasn't *because* of the role he assigned to the railroad—indeed, I suspected him of arguing *ad vericundiam,* of hooking a questionable hypothesis to an unimpeachable historical truth.[14] But then Fogel and Fishlow reminded us that economic theorists have defined unambiguous measures of the social benefits that may be derived from investments or innovations, and that some of the assertions on which we'd been raised were rather casual in this regard, to say the least.

Fishlow identified three elements in calculating the contribution of a major addition to the social overhead capital. First, the railroad reduced costs directly and therefore released inputs for use elsewhere in the economy. After the cost reduction, however, it was necessary to estimate what the induced effects might have added to the growth of the American economy. By making greater production possible, more cheaply, the railroad caused markets to expand and, therefore, to specialize. The location of production with respect to the markets, as well as decisions about technological innovation and capital accumulation—all were affected by the cost changes brought about by the railroad. Finally, the transportation network generated demands upon layers or levels of suppliers, suppliers to suppliers, and so on back through the capital goods sectors, almost throughout the economy.

Fishlow computed the returns to railroad investment before 1860, from net earnings and transport costs, simply as a stream of private profits, and then went on to estimate the effects upon supply, especially in agriculture, but also in fuels and minerals. He then quantified the induced, backward-linkages, the chain of demands derived from the railroad investment. Now, some of you may know that the economic jargon I have been tossing at you in the last two paragraphs is part of the tool-kit that every graduate student in economics carries away with his degree. But all of you probably suspect, correctly, that these measures, however well defined, can only be quantified in the presence of continuous series on sectoral outputs, capital formation and equipment, employment, and trade patterns. Those series did not exist, and Professor Fishlow had repeatedly to interpolate and extrapolate from the snatches of information he had in hand. His innovation (not his alone) was to use regression techniques to establish the relationships among the variables, from observations he did have, in order to establish statistical series for the variables (or time periods) that he did not have. For example, he calculated almost half of the annual construction figures for the decade of the thirties from a cubic equation fitted to the limited company data available on total expenditures and the proportions spent over the construction period.

Robert Fogel, in his estimate of the direct benefits, that is, the cost-savings due to the railroads, employed an even more striking set of statistical methods. Since a patently contrary-to-fact hypothesis is at the heart of his procedure—he "constructed" an almost complete system of canals, extending as far west as the Dakotas, in order to estimate the cost savings and to map the commercial limits of cultivation in the imaginary absence of railroads—let me quote an almost exactly parallel use of the counterfactual conditional by David A. Wells, who was many things, but not an econometric historian:

The railroad freight service of the United States for 1887 was therefore equivalent to carrying a thousand tons one mile for every person, or every ton a thousand miles. The average cost of this service was about $10 per annum per person. But if it had been entirely performed by horsepower, even under the most favorable of old-time conditions, its cost would have been about $200 to each inhabitant, which in turn would represent an expenditure greater than the entire value of the then annual product of the country.[15]

If you will agree that neither David Wells nor any of the rest of us can estimate the savings in freight charges in any way except by counting what the charges *would have been* on the displaced mode of transportation, then you must agree to the legitimacy, and not simply the ingenuity, of what Fogel did next.

A market structure, and by this term I mean to include the geographical patterns of production and trade, will move toward an optimal position appropriate to the prices and other conditions at a given moment of time. When there is a major change in costs, and therefore, prices, the structure will change to adapt itself to the new situation. Now, the railroad was obviously a major change, and the pattern of freight movements that was recorded in 1890 was different from what it would have been if there were canals and turnpikes, but not railways. Distances will change, economically, when the cost of moving freight changes from $200 per thousand ton miles to $10. Fogel, therefore, asked what the commercial patterns would have been without the railroad—how far could cultivation have extended, away from the major cities?; what cities would have languished, which others might have grown and flourished? Then, he computed the social saving as the difference between the actual costs of what they would have been in the alternative, contrary-to-fact, *optimal* situation.[16] Is it not obvious that the social savings—or looked at explicitly from the counterfactual side, the loss of income in the absence of rail transportation—are smaller, and historically more valid, when computed from the imagined optimum? (Fritz Redlich dismissed these as figments; we call them counterfactual conditionals. How would David Wells have characterized them?)

Let us turn back now to the specifically southern question, namely, the extent to which the South depended upon western foodstuffs in the ante-bellum period. The question is important, because historians have looked to the regional trade patterns for help in explaining why the small-holding, family farmers of the West should have turned to the industrial East in 1860, rather than to the agricultural people of the South. In 1861 C. J. Vallandigham was still speaking of a natural alliance between the planting South and the West, but by then the *mariage de convenance* had been consummated. Was it made possible by the revulsion felt by democratic freehold farmers in the face of slavery and planter aristocracy? Or did the alignment follow the trade patterns, as Western trade with the South became unimportant and Eastern markets drew the farmers into alliance with the business interests? [17]

Albert Fishlow, while establishing the trade patterns for his estimate of the railroad benefits, faced up to the problem that is hidden behind that last assertion.[18] The problem comes up because the data on trade patterns are very thin, indeed. Much of the evidence, therefore, rests upon a series of inferences from prices and interregional terms of trade, and from indirect indications of the food deficit positions of the different parts of the country. Building upon Kohlmeier's data, Fishlow put together a model of internal trade in which the southern market for western foodstuffs was replaced by the eastern market.[19] But then, in the end, he rejected Kohlmeier's conclusion and declared, "The South was virtually self-sufficient in foodstuffs on the eve of the Civil War. . . . Political overtures to the West were without economic content." What is methodologically novel is Fishlow's use of the limited, scattered data to consider the questions of dependence and self-sufficiency. Starting from annual receipts at New Orleans, drawn from such familiar sources as *Hunt's Merchants' Magazine* and Thomas Berry's *Western Prices . . .* , he went on to southern consumption and output, *intra*-regional transfers, the hog population, river conditions and freight costs, and (peripherally) the southern social structure, to establish six matrices of interregional trade flows covering the period 1839 to 1860.

Striking out from a position of methodological disquiet, Fogel has flatly contradicted Fishlow's findings and conclusions.[20] His first argument is that the model of interregional trade pivoting upon New Orleans is incorrectly specified. Western trade with the South increasingly moved through New York to the South Atlantic cities, Fogel argues. In support of this contention, he cites price differentials and transportation costs. His second argument raises another issue of specification—that is, he charges Fishlow with having combined the state data into regional aggregates in an unacceptably gross structuring. By separating Texas and Arkansas from the rest of the South, he derives a set of cattle inventory figures which he interprets as showing "a steady decline in self-sufficiency in the South Atlantic and Eastern Gulf States" over the period 1840 to 1860.

I have introduced the trade-pattern controversy in the belief that a falling-out among econometricians may yield a bonus in critical insight. As a great Russian historian has taught us, every unhappy family is unhappy after its own fashion. Let me now list some of the origins of our unhappiness, neither to ask indulgence or quarter, nor in a spirit of *mea culpa;* I will go on in my conclusion to face them with some confidence, perhaps even boldly.

The most obvious problem, which required little sophistication to spot, arises with the statistical reconstructions, the patches over the gaps in the primary data sources. Linked to this is the discomfort that must be engendered by what Thomas Berry called "synthetic" statistics—for example, the value-added series that are several operations removed from anything that can be identified as a primary source.[21]

The second difficulty comes in with the use of counterfactuals: Is it really possible to test a proposition that is based upon a contrary-to-fact assertion? Is there any sense in which we can decide to trust an assertion about what might have happened if the country had been tied together by inland waterways, instead of railroads?

The third question brings us back to Tolstoi. We cannot begin to write down all the relationships that tie together the variables that we can name. Therefore, however many observations may come to hand, we cannot say with certainty that the structure or cause we have inferred, is the proper one—the responsible one, if you like—from among all those that linked the variables, in nature. This problem, the identification problem, becomes crucial, even overwhelming, when we deal with innovations and charismatic persons, the outlying events of statistics, and the heroes and turning-points of history.

IV

Let me turn first to the job of defining appropriate criteria by which to judge synthetic statistics. I think we must ask more than, are the numbers true? or, are they reliable? It may be that at the end of a painstaking demonstration that our reconstructed data are indeed firm, we will find ourselves faced with a chilling expression of "So what?" Reliability is necessary, but not sufficient. The econometric historian ought to be asked to show that his numbers are valid—or simply useful—*historically.*

I will take up these two issues in order, now. In classical statistical procedure the manufactured numbers—estimates and fitted coefficients and summary figures, such as averages or measures of variance—are usually accompanied by their "confidence intervals." I would be hard-put to say whether statistical consumers read confidence intervals as authentications or as *caveats.* But the relevant question here is whether as historians we have anything comparable to the formal tests of reliability in statistics. When the numbers are summaries—the average of a sample drawn from a long list of prices-current, say—or where the regression coefficient itself is the interesting result, then the familiar tests of reliability will be applicable. But these are rare cases; more often we are concerned with filling in lacunae, and there the classical tests do not apply directly.

One alternative that has been applied frequently is the device of consistency testing. I have already mentioned the confrontations between Gallman's commodity flows and other income measures, and the use of Seaman's estimates by Richard Easterlin as a consistency check. Similarly, the criticism of Fishlow's construction of the interregional trade series, by Robert Fogel, rests at several points upon the question of consistency— for example, between shipments and regional deficits, and between the deficits and the national populations of cattle and swine.

A second alternative would be to test directly the assumptions upon which the reconstructions depend. There are obvious questions in this regard—whether the postulate of constant consumption ratios is justified or not, say—but it is often the case that we are more interested in the *sensitivity* of the conclusions to a particular assumption (or set of assumptions) than in the reliability of the postulated value, itself, as a point estimate. John Meyer and I tried to anticipate this kind of criticism by computing the returns over a range of cotton prices for each growing-area. But we did not avoid rough handling by some critics with regard to the slave-longevity figures. Nobody, however, as far as I know, has varied the assumptions of length-of-life, to see how the estimated returns might vary.[22] That would be a test of sensitivity. (It is interesting to notice here that sensitivity tests are double-barreled: if an estimate is extremely *in*sensitive to variations in the numerical inputs, then the econometrician begins to worry about the possibility that his results are simply artifacts of the model that he is using.)

In addition to tests of sensitivity and consistency, there are revealing questions that can be put to the procedures themselves. Fishlow has reminded us that the estimating methods are not always neutral.[23] Most econometrics texts start by listing the statistical assumptions under which the maximum-likelihood techniques are legitimate; these are assumptions about the error term, the random element. (The texts usually go on to instruct us as to the dire results that we can expect when the assumptions are violated, and in a few happy situations, what to do next.) In quantitative history, however, there are assumptions about economic processes—substantive assumptions, Fishlow calls them. These are not likely to be neutral. One of the most common violations in this respect is to choose a weighting system for price or output indexes without recognizing, or at least without informing the reader, that choosing weights from the beginning or from the end of the time period will bias the growth rate significantly, by giving undue weight to commodities, say, that may have been disappearing or may have become important only at the end of the period.

That example brings us to the second question I raised at the start of this section, the question about the validity of the numbers, which is dependent upon the historical relevance of the models. In its simplest form, this refers to the specification of the theory used to generate a set of estimates—the single-route model of southern trade with the West, perhaps, or the device of projecting on the basis of relationships drawn from outside the time or the place for which the data are being synthesized. An example already cited is our use of northern longevity relationships to get an expected life for male slaves. A more serious context for this question relates to the use of economic constructs (for example, national income in comparisons of the welfare of the two groups of people or two moments in time) as summary measures for more-than-economic states. The third form in which I have been conscious of this problem becomes glaringly evident when we use, not simply numbers from a different, often later, period, but models of economic processes which may be specific to a different period. Two examples are found in the cases I cited earlier. First, the capital model in the Conrad-Meyer slavery study is not particularly twentieth century in its origins, but it has been seriously questioned whether any capitalist model is appropriate when considering the commercial experience of the plantation culture of the ante-bellum South. Indeed, William Nicholls implies its inappropriateness when he speaks of the peculiarly rigid, agrarian outlook of the South, even in the present century.[24] The other case in hand is Robert Fogel's model of railroad growth as an optimizing process in agricultural space; he has been accused of omitting the speculative elements in the development of the network. I happen to believe that the choice of model was valid in both of these cases. However, I think it is important for historians to remain skeptical until satisfied that the choice of theory has not biased the results away from all relevance for the period. (A brilliant example to be emulated in this regard is Pieter Geyl's history of French political thought in terms of the histories of Napoleon I written down to 1935.) [25]

Let us turn now to the use of counterfactual conditionals.[26] There have been some gross mistakes in the literature in this regard. Fritz Redlich, for example, writes as though every assumption is a counterfactual.[27] That is not correct. The maintained hypothesis in the slavery study, that if the Civil War had not intervened, southern slavery would have quickly fallen of its own weight, is a counterfactual conditional proposition. Similarly, Fogel's measures depend upon the contrary-to-fact statement that if the railroads had not existed, there would have been a network of waterways and a set of bounds to feasible commercial agriculture along the lines that he had postulated. The counterfactual proposition is not an elegant logical device so much as a common habit of speech:—*if* Abraham Lincoln had lived, . . . ; *if* the bombing had not been resumed, . . . ; the value of the farm is the price it would have fetched, *if* a willing buyer had been sought and found. In history, we often use counterfactuals to emphasize, if not indeed to establish, that some person or event was crucial. They are, in any event, more often forced upon us than chosen.

Now, how do we test, or warrant, a counterfactual proposition? Recall that we can never subject the antecedent, the if-clause, to an empirical test: Lincoln *was* shot in Ford's Theatre, the railroads *did* develop and did prove to be too much for the waterways. What the econometrician can do, and must do, if he is going to convince the skeptical historian, is to enumerate the premises upon which the argument rests. These are likely to include a set of relevant or requisite conditions to which estimates of confidence can be attached. Secondly, he must be prepared to state explicitly the law or connecting principle which carries us from the antecedent to the consequent. The problem, then, is to establish the likelihood that the relevant conditions were maintained—in the slavery case, the existence of an efficient slave-market system was the crucial question—and secondly, to demonstrate that the law linking the two parts of the conditional is *not* an empty law. In the counterfactual statements of the viability of slavery, again, it is not uniformly accepted that the economic rules of capitalist economies were relevant to the plantation culture. If capitalist "rules" are not relevant, then the demonstration of profitability may have virtually nothing to do with the counterfactual viability of the institution, economically.

I have argued elsewhere that a counterfactual can be tested by verifying some proposition higher in the deductive chain than the counterfactual itself, and then seeing whether a negative finding at the higher or earlier stage would be co-tenable with the conditional prediction itself.[28] That test is not conclusive in both directions, but it does provide the possibility of dismissing the conditional statement.

Finally, I will turn to one of the most difficult problems imposed upon us when we try to interpret historical change. (I am using the word *interpret* on purpose, to avoid the question of whether historians explain or simply describe what happened in the past. I think that is an empty question.) Econometric historians, like other historians, can only observe what is immediately accessible. But we obviously express ourselves in empirical statements, that go beyond the immediate experience or data. We interpret and evaluate, we ascribe motives and evaluations, and we infer structures and underlying causes, all from the data at hand. The reality or actuality of the hypothetical objects derive from phenomena, which we may not experience directly, but which we believe we can infer from the immediately accessible data. This paper began with a Harvard lawyer among some Yankee pragmatists; we seem now to have got to Heidegger and Sartre, and phenomenology. But we haven't strayed terribly far, really: I think you will agree with me that Karl Marx was an economic historian of some accomplishment. He was also responsible for one of the earliest and most remarkable phenomenological constructs: that the spirit of a society is expressed in its method of production; that the exchange of commodities, of *objectified* labor, is a definition of the particular way in which men co-exist.[29] Now, having satisfied myself that there is some precedent for economists to ask phenomenological questions, let me extend the approach to econometrics and history.

We do not always perceive objects directly, but very often through the screen of some idealized evidence or interpretation. We may find values drawn from a market report or a price-list, or we may turn up letters or newspapers or company reports. The evidence, then, is an *interpretation* of some behavior or of an event, and may often reflect an idealized state. Obviously, the evidence may be in error with regard to the state of the object—the market, say—but still it will be valuable as an expression of what reporters or participants *thought* was going on.

In economics, we often define relationships among the objects, or among the pieces of evidence, simply, and use them to identify deeper causes or motives, which are not themselves observable. If the relationships are sufficiently simple—if we believe there to be only one relationship linking the objects—then with sufficient evidence, which may be as little as two observations, we can claim to have identified the underlying structure or the cause of some action. But what happens when there is more than one link joining the objects or the experienced (perhaps idealized) formulations?; in econometric jargon, what happens when there are other, simultaneously holding relationships between the variables? To repeat the earlier example: when we observe prices and quantities in a market, they are not only linked by a demand relationship; there is also a supply relationship defined between them. In that case, we cannot claim to have identified either relationship with the available evidence. The only way we can deal with this failure of identification is by adding information—not more observations, simply, but external, *a priori* information. It may be sufficient to impose a theoretical restriction —in the single-equation case that is what the theory behind the equation does for us. It is more difficult in the simultaneous equation case, especially if we have not specified all the variables in the other relationships;

in that case, we cannot identify the structure of the observed behavior. In the slavery example, there was more than one relationship between masters and slaves; for that reason, we could not, finally, identify our model as an estimate of the true capital demand relationship. Hence, the continuing discussion about conspicuous consumption, capitalized rent, and planter sanguinity.[30] In the railroad example, Fishlow, especially, was trying to specify the speculative relationships in that investment market, when he examined the hypothesis that the railroads were driven West ahead of any reasonable demand for their services.

In econometrics, then, the usual cure is to add, not more observations, but rather some *a priori* restrictions—an assumption, perhaps, or some information extraneous to the model in hand. In certain historical approaches—business history is an obvious example, as opposed to Marxist history—the assumption is made that one of the relationships shifts more often than the others, or that there is a variable which appears in one of the equations and not in the others, and that that variable varies over a wide range. Entrepreneurial ability would be just such a variable, and enables the business historian to assert with confidence that he has explained what happened in some slice of history when he has located the important entrepreneurs. The additional, implicit assumption, of course, is that the other relationships were essentially stable. I think it is this set of assumptions which informs the abnormalist approaches to explanation and narration, approaches that depend upon the "difference-maker." [31]

Now, why go to the trouble, and what is the resulting information worth? If we were concerned about regularity, simply, and were prepared to accept as a postulate that the basic (unobserved) associations are stable, then we could fill in the gaps in the historical data, or even predict, without worrying about the underlying structure. But, when there are changes—when the rules of the game vary, or quantitative developments become large enough to bring qualitative changes—then the regularities will no longer support either historical interpretation or economic prediction. At that point, which is to me, at least, the point of interest in a narrative, knowledge of the structure is absolutely necessary.

For the coda, let me turn from homiletics to polemics. It is argued, too often, I think, that econometricians, having seduced economics into an excessive imitation of physics, are now trying to reduce history similarly. Because we are charged with the belief that men can be treated, historically, as objects in nature, I tried the shoe, to see if it would really fit. I asked, how could we identify the economic relationships among human objects, and between human objects and physical objects, from the sense-data and idealized constructs that we find in history? Hence, the phenomenological remarks and the return to the problem of identification. I am satisfied that we are not trying to reduce man—not even that poor creature, Economic Man—or history. What I hope to have done in the course of making this point is to have shown you how econometricians behave when they barge into historical inquiry, and to suggest what questions you ought to insist upon, when faced with a piece of econometric history. If the questions have more general relevance, so much the better.

The City College, City University of New York

NOTES

1. Fritz Redlich, " 'New' and Traditional Approaches to Economic History and Their Interdependence," *Journal of Economic History,* December, 1965, pp. 480–495, see p. 488 ff, especially.

2. Richard A. Easterlin, "Regional Income Trends, 1830–1950," in *American Economic History* (S. E. Harris, ed.), p. 525.

———, "Interregional Differences in Per Capita Income, Population, and Total Income, 1840–1950," in *Trends in the American Economy in the 19th Century,* Studies in Income and Wealth, Volume 24, NBER, pp. 73–141.

Robert E. Gallman, "Commodity Output, 1839–1899," *ibid.,* pp. 13–73.

———, "Gross National Product in the U.S., 1834–1909," in *Output, Employment and Productivity in the U.S. After 1800,* Studies in Income and Wealth, Volume 30, NBER, pp. 3–73.

3. Ezra S. Seaman, *Essays on the Progress of Nations . . . ,* 2nd edition, New York, 1852.

4. These estimates, based upon Easterlin's regional shares and Gallman's income estimates, were prepared by Robert Fogel and Stanley Engerman. In addition to offering alternative treatments of slave "income," they added Texas to the South in 1840 (requiring an income estimate for that year) and in 1860. See R. W. Fogel and Stanley Engerman, eds., *The Reinterpretation of American Economic History,* Harper and Row: forthcoming, Introduction to Part VII.

5. Avery Craven, *The Coming of the Civil War,* 2nd edition, University of Chicago, 1966; Charles W. Ramsdell, "The Natural Limits of Slavery Expansion," *Mississippi Valley Historical Review,* September, 1929; James C. Randall, *Lincoln the President, I,* New York, 1945.

6. Alfred H. Conrad and John R. Meyer, *The Economics of Slavery and Other Studies in Econometric History,* Aldine, 1964, Chapter 3.

7. Kenneth M. Stampp, *The Peculiar Institution,* Knopf, 1956.

8. Redlich, *loc. cit.,* p. 489.

9. U. B. Phillips, "The Economic Cost of Slaveholding in the Cotton Belt," *Political Science Quarterly,* June, 1905, and *American Negro Slavery,* New York, 1918.

10. Robert Evans, Jr., "The Economics of American Negro Slavery, 1830–60," in National Bureau of Economic Research, *Aspects of Labor Economics,* Princeton, 1962.

11. Yasukichi Yasuba, "The Profitability and Viability of Plantation Slavery in the United States," *Economic Studies Quarterly* (Japan), XII, 1.

12. Fogel and Engerman, *op. cit.*

13. Albert Fishlow, "Ante-bellum Interregional Trade Reconsidered," and Robert W. Fogel, "Discussion," *American Economic Review, Papers and Proceedings,* May 1964, pp. 352 and 377, respectively.

14. J. A. Schumpeter, *Business Cycles,* New York, 1939, I, p. 341; W. W. Rostow, *The Stages of Economic Growth,* Cambridge, 1960, p. 55.

15. David A. Wells, *Recent Economic Changes,* New York, 1890, pp. 41–42, as quoted in Albert Fishlow, *American Railroads and the Transformation of the Antebellum Economy,* Cambridge, 1965, pp. 56–57.

16. *Sub*-optimal, actually, since the pattern of cultivation is not optimized counterfactually, but is taken as given for the estimation of social saving.

17. Barrington Moore, Jr., *Social Origins of Dictatorship and Democracy,* Boston, 1967, especially, pp. 127–132.

18. Fishlow, *loc. cit.,* and *American Railroads . . . ,* Chapter VII.

19. Fishlow, *loc. cit.;* A. L. Kohlmeier, *The Old Northwest as the Keystone . . . ,* Bloomington, Indiana, 1938.

20. Fogel, "Discussion," *loc. cit.*

21. Thomas S. Berry, "Comment," in National Bureau of Economic Research, *Trends in the American Economy,* p. 334.

22. Robert Evans suggests than an error of 100 per cent in the death rates would change the calculated rates of return by .0175; less extreme errors would change the returns by even less, of course. See Evans, *loc cit.,* p. 219.

23. Albert Fishlow, "Review Article: Trends in the American Economy . . . ," *JEH,* March, 1962, p. 76.

24. William H. Nicholls, *Southern Tradition and Regional Progress,* Chapel Hill, 1960.

25. Pieter Geyl, *Napoleon—For and Against,* New Haven, 1963.

26. See Nelson Goodman, *Fact, Fiction, and Forecast,* Cambridge, 1955, Chapters I and II; Frank P. Ramsey, *Foundations of Mathematics,* London, 1931, p. 237 ff; Conrad and Meyer, *op. cit.,* pp. 23–24.

27. Mr. Redlich has corrected my apparent misinterpretation in private correspondence since this paper was presented. I cannot do better than to quote him: ". . . I make a clear distinction between 'assumption' (assuming what is sensible) and figment (assuming the counter factual). But when I come to deal with your paper I am taking the stand that not only research based on counter-factual assumptions but also such the result of which is based on a heaping of assumptions on assumptions belong [to] the realm of figment."

28. Conrad and Meyer, *loc. cit.*

29. See Maurice Merleau-Ponty, *Sense and Non-Sense,* translated by H. L. Dreyfus and P. A. Dreyfus, Evanston, Illinois, 1964, p. 130 ff.

30. Douglass C. North, "The State of Economic History," *American Economic Review, Papers and Proceedings,* May, 1965, p. 91; Yasuba, *loc. cit.;* Richard Sutch, "The Profitability of Ante-bellum Slavery Revisited," *Southern Economic Journal,* April, 1965; R. Fogel, *Reinterpretations . . . , loc. cit.*

31. See Morton G. White, *Foundations of Historical Knowledge,* New York, 1965, especially Chapter IV.

COMMENT

Robert W. Fogel

Discussants are supposed to approach the paper to which they are assigned with a jaundiced eye. I'm afraid that I can't fulfill that role today for two reasons. First, Professor Conrad has said many nice things about my work and his paper still isn't published; I'm afraid that if I'm critical of him, he'll change it. A second and more serious reason is that I agree with the main points of his paper. Of course, there are some issues on which we differ; but these are little more than quibbles. I would, therefore, rather attempt to expand on three of the points alluded to in the essay. Of course Professor Conrad should not be held responsible for my effort to perform some variations on his theme.

The first point I want to make is that counterfactual conditional statements cannot be banished from history. There has been much criticism of the work that the new economic historians have done with such statements, criticism which implies that they have injected into historiography a type of reasoning that is fundamentally alien to our discipline. The trouble with this viewpoint is that it exaggerates both the novelty of the new economic history and the range of realistic options of choice open to historians. My contention is that we do not really have the freedom to avoid counterfactual conditional statements.

Are we prepared to give up our right as historians to make judgments about mistakes? Are we prepared to say, "We will never hold that any figure in history ever made a mistake." I think it is quite clear that historians are not prepared to rule out such judgments. But what exactly do we mean when we write that President X, or King Y, made a mistake? We mean that the course of action that he followed was inferior to some other course that he might have followed. Once we admit the possibility

Source. EEH/Second Series, Vol. 6, No. 1. © Graduate Program in Economic History, University of Wisconsin, 1968.

that people pursue paths of action that are inferior to alternative ones, we are assuming the existence of counterfactual conditional patterns of behavior.

If we are not prepared to expurgate judgments about "what might have been" from narrative history, it must be clear that the real issue regarding counterfactual conditional statements is not whether we should make them, but the establishment of criteria that enable one to determine the soundness of such statements. That is precisely what the new economic historians have been trying to do. They have not, in general, launched new counterfactual propositions but have devoted themselves to the evaluation of the empirical validity of those propositions that were already explicit or implicit in the existing literature.

My second point concerns the relationship between the testing of counterfactual conditional statements and the comparative method. One prominent economic historian recently suggested that the high road for scholarship in economic history was not the method of counterfactual conditional analysis, but the method of comparative analysis. I fail to see the conflict between these two approaches. Quite the contrary. I would hazard the opinion the econometric historians have employed the comparative method more frequently and extensively than any other group of historians. Their practices in this respect have been obscured by the fact that they usually present their results in mathematical rather than in literary language.

Consider the common econometric procedure of fitting regression equations to cross-sectional data, that is to data describing the activities of various political or business units during a given period of time. That procedure is an application of the comparative method. For the comparative method instructs a scholar to observe different units, such as countries, in order to determine whether such comparison reveals a common pattern. That common pattern is, in mathematical language, an equation. Econometric historians also invoke the comparative method when they compare the parameters of equations fitted to time-series data of two or more regions, industries, or epochs. Indeed, econometrics provides rigorous tests for determining whether or not the differences between the parameters of such equations are statistically significant.

The testing of counterfactual statements leads one naturally into the comparative method. The point is that in order to compare what actually happened with what would have happened in the absence of some specified circumstance, one needs to know the equations that describe the relationships between relevant variables. To determine the stability of these equations it is frequently desirable to estimate their parameters for various time periods, regions, and industries. The comparative method is therefore a crucial feature in evaluating the robustness of the theoretical relationships on which counterfactual conditional arguments are erected.

My third point concerns the debate over whether it is legitimate to use equations to describe historical processes. I believe that this debate is also misdirected. The real issue here is not whether equations can be used but whether in fact the equations that underlie a particular argument are the right equations. Placing the question in this way may be surprising. For I am implying that all historians—not just econometric historians but also purely literary historians—rely on equations in developing their narratives. If the ubiquity of mathematics in history is not more widely recognized, it is because the equations of literary historians are usually camouflaged by words. The camouflage frequently hides the fact that what is often posed as debate regarding the legitimacy of mathematics in history is really a disagreement about the values of the parameters of equations that have, at least implicitly, been employed by all of the disputants.

I'd like to illustrate the last point by turning to Charles Ramsdell's famous essay on the "Natural Limits of Slavery Expansion." In this essay Ramsdell argued that it was the rapid expansion of the cotton culture after 1858, and the subsequent decline of the price of cotton, that heralded the doom of slavery. To support his point he contrasted the last few years of the decade with conditions that prevailed at its start. Ramsdell noted that the 1850's began with a high price for cotton and with a large supply of virgin land suitable for the production of cotton, the latter being located largely in Texas. Moreover, he continued, the production of cotton increased slowly between 1850 and 1857, and its price remained relatively stable, varying from about 10 cents per pound to over thirteen cents. But 1858 began a period of rapid increase in cotton production and a simultaneous decline in price. Ramsdell stressed that the size of the cotton crop doubled between 1850 and 1860. About 70 per cent of the increase took place between 1857 and 1860.

What caused the sudden rise in output? It was due, said Ramsdell, "in part to the rapid building of railroads throughout the South toward the end of the decade, which brought new regions within the reach of markets and increased cotton acreage; but in part it was due to the new fields in Texas." To Ramsdell, prevailing circumstances clearly indicated that the future course of output was up, while that of prices was down. "Had not the war intervened," he continued, "there is every reason to believe that there would have been a continuous overproduction and very low prices throughout the sixties and seventies."

But what, precisely, was the "every reason" for Ramsdell's belief? It was merely his conviction that the virgin lands of Texas would have been

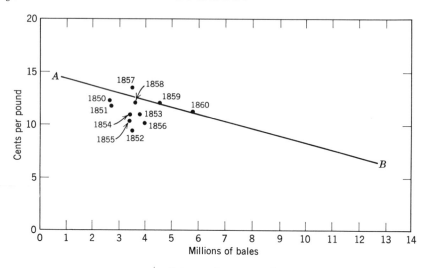

FIGURE 1. Price and output of cotton.

brought into cotton production, and that the increased output of cotton would have led to a decline in its price. Yet, even if one grants Ramsdell's proposition regarding the probably post-1860 expansion of the cotton crop, it does not necessarily follow that prices had to decline. The data on which Ramsdell based his prediction is summarized by Figure 1. What Ramsdell did, in effect, was to fit an equation to the four of these observations. He then used this equation, which is represented in Figure

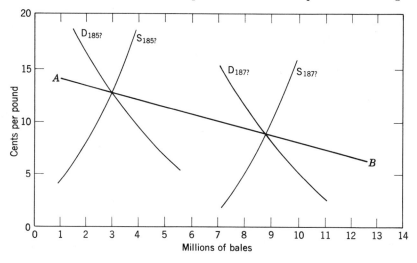

FIGURE 2. Ramsdell's implicit predictions of the shifts in the demand and supply curves of cotton.

1 by the line AB, to justify the proposition that increased production of cotton necessarily would lead to reduced prices.

Now, where do some of us disagree with Ramsdell? Ramsdell, like U. B. Phillips, recognized that it was the forces of supply and demand which determined prices and output. These forces can be represented by curves. Ramsdell's implicit regression thus amounted to a prediction that the supply curve was going to shift outward more rapidly than the demand curve, as is illustrated by Figure 2. I do not believe that the evidence cited by Ramsdell warrants such a conclusion. My disagreement does not turn on whether the forces of demand and supply can be described by equations. It turns on the rates at which certain of the parameters of these equations changed. This disagreement will be resolved not by shunning mathematics, but by employing it intelligently.

University of Chicago

COMMENT

Stuart Bruchey

Ten years ago, as I felt sure Professor Fogel would also remind us, Alfred Conrad and John Meyer launched the era of the *New* economic history with the publication of two articles. The first of these, "Economic Theory, Statistical Inference and Economic History," is less well known than the now famous paper on the profitability of slavery, yet in my opinion it should be required reading for historians generally. That article demonstrated that it is not possible to write history and ignore the causes of change. Causal imputation is implicit in every historical narrative, and all of us need to exhume our hypotheses and scrutinize their adequacy by relating them, under appropriate, structural assumptions, to the conjunctions or regularities that they are believed to typify. The slavery article gave rise to a continuing dialogue concerning slave life expectancy, capital costs, the income returned from slaves, and other variables affecting the computations. Questions concerning the viability of the institution and even of the relevancy of profitability also arose, but I, for one, agree with Stanley Elkins that Conrad and Meyer made a major, conceptual breakthrough. So long as profits were defined in the accounting sense, it was possible to have conducted an endless debate over their typicality. By defining them in the economic sense, and using capital theory as the tool of analysis, the authors raised the problem to a plane where a solution was possible. If these are contributions by quasi-historians, it is time to re-examine the qualifications of so-called professionals.

As with the question of slavery, so too with many others. From the problem of the economic burden of the Navigation Acts to the question of whether any single factor, be it cotton or railroads, played an indispensable role in American economic growth, the *New* economic history

Source. EEH/Second Series, Vol. 6, No. 1. © Graduate Program in Economic History, University of Wisconsin, 1968.

has re-defined the issues and sharpened the analysis. Not every resolution has possessed an equal power of persuasion. Professor Conrad has called attention to controversy among the *New* economic historians themselves, and it is possible to supplement the documentation. I have other reservations as well. Nevertheless, it seems to me the essential contribution that has been made is this; In many cases there has been a specification of the upper and lower limits and a consequent narrowing of the range of probability along which the truth lies. In the social sciences, it is often difficult, if not impossible, to give answers that are right or wrong—or true or false—in the way that a question of fact, for example, can often be disposed of by a crisp citation of accepted authority. Instead, what can be supplied are improved judgments concerning probability. Once again, it is here that the *New* economic history has made its contribution. I'm not myself an econometrician, but a historian, trained in the conventional mode. Yet it seems to me that unless we are willing to turn our backs on exciting and highly important work, and I, for one, am unwilling to do so, we have no alternative but to study statistics and intermediate economic theory, and ask our students to do the same. George R. Taylor has recently observed that the progress made in the last ten or twelve years in this field has been greater than in any comparable period of the past, and that a considerable part of the credit for this must go to the *New* economic history.[1] A considerable part of that credit, in turn, must go to the intellectual leadership provided by the two econometric historians who are with us at this session today. The approach and techniques described by Professor Conrad are no "flash in the pan"; they are here to stay. Without some familiarity with them it will be impossible to assess a large part of future, as well as present, scholarship.

The new techniques, however, are not the only ones that are desirable. Their great strength, it seems to me, is their ability to make possible a rigorous, quantitative analysis of the short-run behavior of economic variables. Their great weakness is their inability to cope with the long-run behavior of non-economic variables. Some of the leaders of the new school are frank to acknowledge the limitations of their technology. The *New* economic history, Lance Davis has remarked, "may not say much, but at least the reader is aware of what has been said." The latter is all to the good, but what do we do about highly important problems that require the saying of much more than a given set of techniques permits?

The business cycle is not the growth cycle. In analyzing the former, one may safely hold as constant the tastes, technology, values, political and legal systems, and social structure of a people. In analyzing the latter, one cannot. The longer the time period involved, the greater the probability of change in the data which, from the point of view of purely economic analysis, it is desirable to hold safely impounded in the category of *ceteris paribus*. It is my belief that the causes of long-run economic change are multiple, that they are not simply economic, but broadly social, that they are interrelated, not always reducible to quantitative modes of expression, and that they require collaborative study by the social sciences generally, and not by economics alone if they are to be understood.

As a tool for causal analysis, the counterfactual proposition seems to me far more efficient for problems of the short run than for those of the long. Suppose, for example, that the question at hand is the degree of responsibility to be credited President Franklin Delano Roosevelt for the liberal, social legislation of the 1930's. (Historians will recognize the example as an instance of the familiar problem of determining the relative importance of individuals and forces in the production of historical events.) Since the period during which this legislation was enacted spanned only a few years, we are concerned here with a short-run problem. In the effort to answer it, a historian creates a counterfactual situation by performing a mental exercise. He imagines the absence of the President from the historical scene and proceeds to ask whether labor laws, tightened control of the banking system, social security, and other legislation would then have been passed. By removing the President from the scene he is able to focus upon the paths of development which might have been taken by other trends and forces. In the absence of the President, which elements would have developed differently from the way in which they did, in fact, develop?—In what direction?—How far?

In his search for answers, he may well consider a number of historical forces of Western European, as well as American origin, that were "bending the times," so to speak, in the direction of the legislation in question. He may take into account the heightened role of government in the United States before and during World War I, as well as the fact of the Great Depression. But his answer, it will be clear, will represent a judgment, a judgment from which some other student who may weigh and balance the pertinent factors somewhat differently, might dissent. In a word, it is not "scientific knowledge" that results from the use of the counterfactual, but rather a sharpened sense of the numerous variables pertinent to the inquiry, and, one would hope, an abridgement and sharper definition of areas of agreement and disagreement. It is not possible to know for certain the causes of social change. While repeated comparisons of similar cases may strengthen one's explanatory hypotheses, the latter must remain far less secure than the statistical probabilities that may reward the search for causes within the realm of the natural sciences.

In the social sciences it is the interdependence of the variables that is crucial.

The problem of explaining economic growth is a typical problem of social science. Commenting on it, Evsey Domar has written that none of the numerous factors pertinent to growth "could possibly be taken as an independent variable, and the required system of simultaneous relationships, whether expressed in symbols or in words, would be impossibly complex, and probably useless." It is this interdependence that creates a social science version of Heisenberg's Principle of Uncertainty. I assume that the "e" or "random error term" that Professor Conrad includes in his notational hypothesis for a stochastic universe is also a symbol of uncertainty. The question that remains is the values of the variables inserted in the equation. Perhaps that has always been the real question. And perhaps the answer, in part, is that a rational world is a world viewed by a rationalist.

But even the relatively more modest achievements possible to the social sciences are more difficult to attain when the technique of the counterfactual is employed for the analysis of long-run problems. The reason, of course, is that when one performs a mental exercise that removes from the historical scene an element present in it for a long period of time, one can be far less certain of his ability to remove it *in toto*. If the element is of sufficient importance to justify historical inquiry, the probability is great that in a period of twenty or thirty years or more it intertwined itself with numerous institutions and trends in ways of thinking, valuing, and acting. President Roosevelt had been in office fewer than a half dozen years before most New Deal legislation was passed, and to create imaginatively a version of the historical scene that would have obtained in his absence is a relatively manageable task.

But what if we consider, as Professor Fogel did, the relationship of railroads to the nation's economic growth, and, beginning with the known size of the GNP as of 1890, proceed to ask: What was the contribution to it made by the railroad? The subjunctive world of what might have been can then be populated only with great risk and uncertainty, and wide areas of disagreement will survive the exercise. For in the many decades that the railroad belonged to the historical scene, it intertwined its presence with so much that belonged to that scene that almost anyone's effort to imagine the consequences of its absence must be inadequate.

In all fairness to Professor Fogel, it must be said that he himself acknowledges that "No evaluation of the impact of railroads in American development can be complete without a consideration of the cultural, political, military, and social consequences of such an innovation." One impugns neither Professor Fogel's ingenuity nor assiduity in suggesting that such an evaluation is probably beyond human capacity. Understandably, then, he has made no effort to compute the economic consequences of the railroad's impact on social and cultural change. Yet, is it not reasonable to believe that the greater ease with which people could move, and information flow, affected the degree of social mobility, the values and incentives of men, and the efficiency with which economic and business life were conducted? Julius Rubin has pointed out that the failure to mention the subject of industrial organization means that Fogel has implicitly equated the size of railroad organizations with those of canal, turnpike, and wagon companies, and thereby has ignored the effects of that experience with large-scale organization and finance that for a long time were provided only by the railroad. Unquestionably, it would be difficult, if not impossible, to measure these effects. Nevertheless, we are bound to ask what the relationship is between that which can be measured and that which can't be; we are bound to wonder if there isn't some way to supplement the admirable techniques of econometrics by taking these other things into account.

I think there is. What it calls for, I believe, is a collaborative effort on the part of the social sciences to work out theories of growth that will include all the variables pertinent to its explanation. What I have in mind is not a single theory that would be so highly generalized as to lose its meaning in specific applications, but rather sub-theories, so to speak, more limited, explanatory frameworks that will reflect the numerous, yet potentially definable, sub-sets of conditions in which different rates of per capita output growth have been discerned. The justification for emphasizing sub-sets is provided by the fact of differential rates of growth within the geographical regions, sub-regions, economic sectors, industries, and firms that compose any economy above the subsistence level of output. These differences are always concealed in figures that represent averages. The Gallman-Easterlin figures cited by Professor Conrad provide a case in point. Average per capita income for the South as a whole in 1860 was $103, but behind this average are the differing fortunes of that area's sub-regions: The figure for the South Atlantic sub-region is $84, for the East-South-Central $89, and for the West-South-Central a whopping $184, highest in the nation. A similar breakdown of the Northern average of $141 shows a large disparity between the $84 of the North-Central states and the $181 of the Northeastern ones. Comparisons require standards, of course, but since the national average of $128 represents such a mix of causal elements, it may be that the more revealing comparison would be between agricultural sub-regions with free and slave labor—a comparison which Professor Conrad does make—and between both types of agricultural sub-regions and the commercial and industrializing Northeast.

These comparisons, I think, should involve not only economic factors, but also interrelated social and cultural factors. Where a large difference between per capita incomes obtains and persists, it may be that differences in other factors are also to be found. An investigation of numerous cases of area income differences, non-American as well as American, may reveal that the correlatives of those differences were entirely economic in nature, for example, the movement of population onto more fertile western land, or the commercial prosperity of Louisiana. Yet the nature of the differences ought not be assumed in advance, especially because they may prove to be social and psychological, as well as economic. In the case of the Northeast, for example, industrial beginnings may prove to have been associated with significant differences in educational inputs and entrepreneurial values. In general, I think we need to investigate sub-regional differences in the distribution of value emphases, psychological drives, social, political, and market structures, degrees of urbanization, and other factors affecting ease of transmission of innovations in technology and administration, to name some of the considerations that may prove pertinent.

In their valuable study of British economic growth, Phyllis Deane and W. A. Cole make an observation that serves to point up my suggestion here:

> While we have reasonable confidence that we have discerned the main features of the growth process and that our measurements, though rough, are generally of the right order of magnitude, the details of the picture are extremely doubtful, and it is the details that may be crucial in suggesting the causal connections of the process.

The closer to the relevant details we can approach in the American case, the more we shall close in on the root causes of regional and sub-regional differences in growth rates.

It may be that drawing cultural regions, or some other organizational framework whose relevance may be suggested by both intra- and international comparisons, would bring us closer to the objective we seek. Fundamentally, it is individual men whose decisions made for growth, and in my view, we need to be able to trace the complex interactions not only between economic factors, but also between men, various groups and institutions, and various ideas and values alive in the regions, sectors, and subcultures of the society. In this quest, we should welcome heartily the theoretical and quantitative rigor provided by the *New* economic history. But I know of no way in which a body of knowledge about the past can be made fast to a rock of ages and secured against the changing needs and insights of changing times. I shall continue to believe that history is fact selected and explained by judging men. And to any advocate of methodological exclusivism I should be tempted to reply as Hamlet to Horatio: "There are more things in heaven and earth than are dreamt of in your philosophy."

Columbia University

NOTES

1. Professor Taylor is not without reservations concerning the *New* economic history, however.

COMMENT

Alfred D. Chandler, Jr.

I should begin by saying that I jotted down these rough notes for my comments on Professor Conrad's paper before I had a chance to read it. I had no choice; I had to complete this task by last weekend. Therefore, I've based these notes on the assumption that Professor Conrad would present a judicious, clear, and persuasive paper on the value of econometric history. And secondly, I, and no doubt many of us here, have been exposed during the past season at many places to the arguments, pro and con, of the value of econometric history. The last three professional meetings have each had a session on this subject: one in Chicago in April at the Organization of American Historians; and another in August at the Pacific Coast Economic Association. Then there was a rather heated one at the Economic History Association meetings in Philadelphia in September. I listened to two and read the papers of another. Frankly, I was a little disappointed at the amount of heat and the relatively little light generated at the sessions. Therefore, before I had the chance to read Professor Conrad's paper, I decided that my comments would be essentially a report of one historian's response to this continuing debate.

Professor Conrad's paper, which I read yesterday, did prove to be judicious and persuasive. Moreover it concentrated on much the same concerns and problems on which I focused my rough notes—that is on the problem of conceptualization, and the nature of concepts, and the apparatus required to use them. I think Conrad puts the basic issue well: The problem is one of identification of a set of relationships and the specific variables to be defined in understanding and working out these relationships.

My basic response, after listening to the debate over the new eco-

Source. EEH/Second Series, Vol. 6, No. 1. © Graduate Program in Economic History, University of Wisconsin, 1968.

nomic history, after reviewing some of the works of some of its practitioners, and now on reading Professor Conrad's paper, is roughly as follows. Historians, particularly in my generation, have keenly felt the need for more precision in identifying the relationships and the variables involved in describing, interpreting, and understanding a specific human situation. So they have given attention to concepts required to synthesize and analyze complex historical data. In seeking help to meet this need they have turned to the social sciences more than to the humanities.

In so doing, I think some historians have learned more from the other social sciences, particularly sociology and psychology, than they have from economics. Nevertheless, the recent work of the economists interested in the past, particularly the new economic historians, has been a great help and has provided invaluable data that historians would find it very difficult, if not impossible, to obtain for themselves. My colleagues in political, social, and intellectual history are now troubling themselves about the methods and meaning of quantification in their areas. I can somewhat smugly point out that historians like myself concerned with things economic have fewer problems. We already have professionally trained, historically-minded statisticians and econometricians to do our numbers work for us. We can, therefore, spend our time working on areas in which *our* kind of data and approach is of particular relevance. In other words, I'm pleased, very pleased, with the partnership which makes up the field of economic history. I see no need to strengthen the union between the two branches and to form a new or special discipline. It seems to me we should encourage an explicit division of labor. Let us each practice our own trade, each stick to our own last, with an awareness of the possibilities and limitations of our own particular fields.

Let me begin this argument by reminding you of something you all know, but something which I think is worth saying because I haven't heard it said at the recent sessions on the new economic history. This is that there are real differences between economists and historians—differences in the data they collect, in the methods they use to make sense of the data, and differences in their aims and purposes in compiling and analyzing data. Consider data—the economists prefer to work with data that are quantifiable and measurable, that may be turned into numbers such as income, output, input, prices, costs, capital, assets, interest rates, and so on. Historians also use these forms of data, but they give far more attention (than economists do) to the written record (in very recent years they have used some of the oral records) such as correspondence, memoranda, journals, diaries, speeches, debates, newspapers, periodicals, etc.

Not much of this information can be expressed in precise numbers.

Consider the differences in methods. The economist concentrates on the manipulation of variables so as to provide useful theories about changes or trends in prices, income, wages, capital formation, and such—theories which help to make understandable the economic processes of production, distribution or investment, and the relationships between them. As Professor Conrad has stressed, economists have moved beyond statistical technique to the use of models based on algebra and calculus. The historian, on the other hand, attempts to re-create a complex human situation that existed in the past. It might be a career of a significant man, the development of institutions—political, social, intellectual—or the development of social systems. He is particularly fascinated, as Professor Bruchey just pointed out, by the enormously complex inter-relationship between personalities, social systems, and cultural attitudes.

The objectives of the two disciplines are also quite different, I think. The economists tend to aim at developing theory, theory that is con-ceptually consistent, rigorous, and, indeed, elegant. They often concen-trate on theory for theory's sake. At least in economics departments I know, the theorists have the highest prestige. These theories are more than explanations. Any theory worth its salt should be able to predict.

Finally, the theories and the models used to develop them should be useful for policy makers in business and government, whether they are used in revising the tax laws, developing an underdeveloped nation, or selling televisions. Let me repeat a couple of sentences from Professor Conrad's paper that make the point:

> The econometrician is concerned with quantifying economic theory, in the sense of turning the parameters—the alphas and betas and gammas that characterize functional relationships—from Greek letters into trustworthy numbers. He may do this because somebody has asked him to predict what will happen if a new policy is tried or because he wants to test some piece of received wisdom about the purchase of television sets as income goes up or the purchase of books as television becomes ubiquitous.

The historian feels he has a different and more modest task. He merely hopes to re-create, or partially re-create, some small part of man's activities in the past. He is skeptical of predictions, particularly those based on past experience; he has seen so many of these go wrong. He is more concerned, I believe, with the real alternatives facing men, and why men took the alternatives that they did. He does not expect the policy makers to make much use, if any, of his findings.

I have reviewed these basic differences, which you all know, in order to emphasize why historians and economists often talk at cross purposes; why the marriage of the disciplines seems to me futile; why an explicit division of labor is really practical in developing economic history; and, finally, to suggest why some historians may have learned more from the social sciences other than economics.

Let me begin on this last point by emphasizing that where the economist has been strong—that is, with his concern for theory and models to identify relationships and the variables involved—is precisely where the historian has been weak. Historians have, in fact, too often failed to specify precisely what they are talking about. They have confused cause and effect, personal with institutional situations, and impact of the overall culture, with that of institutionally defined roles. Worse, still, some have had (no longer, I think, but they did when I was growing up) the intellectually naive idea that the record would speak for itself. So the questions they asked of the data and, therefore, the selection of their information and the synthesis of their findings were affected by their own attitude and values and by those of their times. For example, in my own field of business history, the big question was for many years: Were the creators of the modern corporations robber barons or industrial statesmen? Were they good guys or bad guys? Such a set of concepts is hardly useful in understanding the beginnings and growth of the large organization in our modern, industrial economy.

But surely historians in the past thirty years have tried to be more precise, more rigorous and more sophisticated in compiling and analyzing the in data. It has been this concern for improving methods of historical analysis that turned historians to the social sciences. In this search, many of us have found—even those of us in economic history—that sociology and psychology have as much, if not more, to offer than economics.

I will just speak for myself. My research has carried me into the field of micro-economics, and my teaching into the field of macro-economics. My central research interest has been trying to understand why, when, and how large corporations came to have, and continue to have, such a significant, if not dominating role, in the operation of the modern American economy. This interest, in turn, comes from a feeling that what differentiates the twentieth century from any other century, is the predominance of large-scale organization in the economy, in the power structure and in the society as a whole.

Therefore one place to get a grip on the twentieth century and to understand its activity and its dynamic is to examine how and why these large organizations grew. The data I used for this examination were the records of large corporations themselves—the memoranda and directives of the corporation, of the businessmen, and the managers who ran them.

I also looked at the writings and investigations of those who disliked and were concerned about the growth of large corporations. In my search for approaches and methods to handle this data, I received little help from economics. In dealing with the firm, large or small, the economists had concentrated primarily on price theory, and pricing was only a small part of the activities of the large firm and its managers. The assumptions of the theory almost completely ignored the realities of pricing by a large firm competing with a few other large firms, the standard situation in many American industries. Price theory, as I read it, was more of a model in Conrad's sense than a mere statistical conceptualization. But the competitive model assumed that buyers and sellers had no control over supply and demand, and it assumed profit maximization as the basic motivating force. Clearly, the manufacturers I looked at did control output from the 1870's on; from 1900 on, the written record indicated that the managers of a large firm were more concerned with long-term company growth, volume of sales, and share of the market, than with short-term profit maximization. During the 1930's the economists began to develop a new model—one of oligopoly, or imperfect competition. But they agreed that it was imperfect, that it led to inefficiencies in the allocation of resources, and they still based their suggestions for public policy on profit maximization. Only in recent years have economists begun to tie pricing in an oligopolistic situation to managerial goals. The works of William Baumol, Robin Marris, Jack Downey, Edith Penrose, and of younger economists like Alfred Eichner at Columbia and Robert Averitt at Smith are very useful to historians. But, alas, such writings were too late for my work in investigating the rise of the large corporation.

Compare this experience to my initial readings in sociology: Max Weber's single chapter on bureaucracy written before World War I had more useful information and a more significant approach to the problem of the growth of the large corporation than almost anything written in price theory. Weber raised questions about the structure and function of a large corporation by suggesting the regularities of human action in any large-scale organization. Such regularities included recruitment, training and career patterns of its personnel, the development of its files, the uses of its power and its strength and weaknesses in adjusting to social and cultural change. As important, Weber suggested a way to identify relationships and to isolate variables.

I found Weber's ideal type an extremely useful, analytical construct for analyzing non-quantitative data. It seemed to me to do pretty much the same kind of thing that Conrad asks of a mathematical model, and I would like to know whether he sees any validity in this comparison. By the same token, I found the writings in organizational theory and small-group theory, also more meaningful than price theory. The writings and conceptual constructs of Elton Mayo, Chester Barnard, Robert Gordon, Herbert Simon, James March, Robert Homans, and Robert Bales provide me with more information and more in the way of method than even Joan Robinson or Edward Chamberlain.

Let us turn to macro-economics. Here the economist has certainly been of more use to the historian, thanks, I believe, to the Keynesian revolution and the postwar concern with economic development. My interest has been not so much in development but in the transformation of the American economy from a rural, agrarian one to an industrial, urban one. The large corporation played a central role in this transformation. Of more importance, the great transformation provides a very useful theme around which to teach a course in American economic history. In developing the data and approach for teaching the course, the work of the statistical historians has been invaluable. The works of Easterlin and Gallman, which Professor Conrad mentioned, are absolutely basic; as are certainly the pioneering studies of Simon Kuznets, Moses Abramovitz, and Raymond Goldsmith. These findings helped me to pin down, with some precision, part of the economic environment in which the American farmers, workers, government officials and businessmen had to work. I'm still a little uncertain about the value of econometric history in analyzing this transformation, but still, I will continue to make use of this brand of history wherever I can.

I do have a couple of complaints: So far, the econometricians have tended to concentrate on the period before 1860. North's first book stops at that date; two-thirds of his volume on *Growth and Welfare* is devoted to the period before the Civil War, so too, Robert Fogel's set of readings are heavily weighted on the ante-bellum side. The section on industrialism has very little or nothing on the twentieth century and rather little on the late nineteenth. All I'm urging is that new economic historians put their talents and attention to the more recent period where the data are richer and the basic problems more complex and where more variables need to be sorted out and their relationships analyzed.

Secondly, the methods and approaches of the econometricians often seem to be more valuable at the moment than their findings. Indeed, Conrad has suggested this, and Lance Davis made the same point at the Pacific Coast meetings. Davis pointed out that three of the new economic historians who had looked at the question of the indispensability of railroads, had come up with three different answers: Bob Fogel said the railroads were *not* indispensable in 1890; Albert Fishlow said that they were *not* in 1859 but *were* by 1890: and Stanley Lebergott said that they *were* before 1859. The difference, Davis points out, lies in the nature of the model selected, and in each author's view of relative alternatives. The importance of argument is the explicit unveiling of hypotheses. I would certainly agree with the value of such precision. Historians (as Bob Fogel was suggesting about Ramsdell), have not been so explicit, and surely this new approach is very essential. In so doing, the economists have said a good deal about the impact of the railroads. However, we still don't know whether the railroads were indispensable or not; but by this time, I'm not sure that it is that important a question anyhow.

Further, the reading of these three exercises has convinced me that historians should leave the matter of predicting what might have happened in the past to the economists. They're trained in this business and historians are not. I'm even willing to leave counterfactual questions such as what might have happened if Lincoln had lived, to the econometricians. I'm sure that Conrad and Fogel will do a much better job on this type of question, than Ramsdell or Phillips. The only viable predictions that a historian should get involved in, are those made on a comparative short-term basis, as Stuart Bruchey mentioned, such as those based on comparing the southern economy with the northern economy at about the same period of time. So, too, it would seem to me, we should leave the making of mathematical models to the economist. Again, they are trained, and we are not. They are not only better equipped to do these things for us, but if they do them for us, we can then devote our time to defining concepts and constructs that are more relevant to the kinds of data and the kinds of questions we have traditionally used and asked.

For example, in analyzing and describing the great transformation from the agrarian to an industrial economy, I've learned more from Talcott Parsons' attempt to do something with a general theory of social action than I have from the works of any economist. Whatever one thinks of the results, Parsons' efforts to define and interrelate personalities, social systems, institutions, and cultural values—as well as to explain the dynamics of change—is a very impressive intellectual effort. Parsons does try to identify the complex relationships and variables involved, and he does this without relying on quantified material. He is concerned with the basic historical questions of why and how patterns of action changed over time.

This gets me back to my original point about the advantage the historians dealing in things economic have over those who are primarily concerned with political, social, and intellectual matters. We have trained experts to pin down the statistically definable environment. More

than this the economists can supply us with intriguing predictions of
what might have happened so as to sharpen our own thoughts about
what did happen. Thanks to them, we have more time to analyze the
historical problems which provide our own special interests. Historians
can learn from the social sciences. However, we shouldn't become economists, sociologists, political scientists, psychologists or anthropologists;
and in my own experience, I have found that the return on the limited
time I can invest in exploiting other disciplines is a little higher from
sociology than from any other social science.

Let me conclude by a quotation; not a philosophical one from Tol-
stoy, but what one eminent economist said about another. This is Joseph
Schumpeter talking about Lord Keynes:

> Every comprehensive theory of an economic state of society consists of
> two complementary, but essentially distinct, elements. There are first the
> theorist's view about the basic features of that state of society about what
> is, and what is not, important in order to understand its life at a given
> time. Let us call this his vision. And there's a second, the theorist's tech-
> nique, an apparatus by which he conceptualizes his vision and which turns
> the latter into concrete propositions or theories.

> In the pages of the *Economic Consequences of the Peace* [Keynes' famous
> book on the Versailles Treaty], we find nothing of a theoretical apparatus
> of a general theory, but we find the whole vision of things, social and eco-
> nomic, of which that apparatus is a technical complement. The *General
> Theory* is the final result of a long struggle to make that vision of our age
> analytically operative.

Vision—we have little choice where it comes from, childhood experience
on up; but we do have some choice in the selection of our apparatus. Unfortunately that provided by our own discipline of history gives us very
little help. So we historians have turned to the social sciences. For the
moment, my own experience is that the most significant lessons are to be
learned from sociology—from the works of men such as Weber and Talcott Parsons.

Johns Hopkins University

THE NEW ECONOMIC HISTORY:
AN ECONOMETRIC APPRAISAL *

G. N. von Tunzelmann

For the purposes of this article, the "new economic history" is defined as that branch of economic history involving the use of theoretically ordered quantitative data to reject or provisionally accept its given hypothesis (or set of hypotheses). Within the field of the new economic history, overriding interest for the present is with "econometric history." Some authors use the latter term interchangeably with "new economic history." In this case, however, I limit econometric history to examples in which the theoretical ordering of the data follows the precepts of current econometric theory, as defined say by Goldberger [1]—specifically, regression and correlation analysis. In doing so I am understating the diversity of quantitative approach already attempted by the new economic historians, extending to techniques such as linear programming and spectral analysis.

Even so, econometric history has, until quite recently, made little use of many relationships on which applied econometricians have centered their attention. This is particularly true of the "behavioral" relations, among which the demand curve is a most familiar example.[2] Nevertheless I do not intend to investigate the breadth of scope for econometric work in historical research. My interest is depth rather than breadth. The thesis to be propounded in this article is that whatever topic the historian chooses to study by means of regression techniques, in doing so he should satisfy the prevailing standards set in applied econometrics. If any-

Source. EEH/Second Series, Vol. 5, No. 2. © Graduate Program in Economic History, University of Wisconsin, 1968.

* This article revises a portion of my dissertation for M.A. at the University of Canterbury, 1966. I am especially grateful to Professor A. D. Brownlie, who supervised the dissertation. Any remaining failings are my own responsibility.

thing, the historian's attention to detail may have to be even greater. The reason is that the historian tends to be much more concerned with the path of the variables he is investigating through time and at each moment of time.[3] For example, the historian may wish to emphasize not so much the relationship between two variables (established by regression) as notable exceptions to that relationship. He might be examining trade between Rome and Egypt in the first century B.C. to discover the effect of the length of Cleopatra's nose.

The rigor being advocated here is not to be interpreted as "rigor mortis." In the first instance, it is true that further study may reveal that some of the results obtained cannot satisfy closer analysis. It would be unusual for this situation to compel rejection of the results *in toto*, however. In many cases where the assumptions of the statistical procedure are shown to be invalid, there may be a range of techniques supplied by econometric theory to bypass the difficulty, e.g. by transforming the variables. I intend to stress these alternative or consequent methods that are at one's disposal in the quest for greater accuracy. Even where it is not so easy to remove the difficulty, it may sometimes be possible to use the results as they are, but with full awareness of the biases that may be introduced. For example, one might find multicollinearity among the independent variables of an estimated relationship, yet still be able to extract usable results, while appreciating the tendency to indeterminancy of the estimates.

Secondly, there is a positive aspect to increasing the level of rigor, in that by doing so one may be led to further fruitful results within a specified relationship, or even to new relationships. In examining data for evidence of autocorrelated residuals later in this article, I have been able to show a regular cyclical influence on the dependent variable, ignored in the original study. Only by greater attention to such detailed analysis can econometrics fully contribute to historical research.

As hinted above, the use of stochastic relationships ties the econometrician to his historical context. One very important explanation he puts forward for the existence of a disturbance term consists of just this: he is dealing generally with the actions (or results of actions) of human beings, and these are going to be influenced by an extremely wide range of determining factors, many non-economic, many not readily quantifiable. Even if, in the extreme case, some direct or indirect method were found to quantify all these conditioning factors, there would be no statistical means of solving for them all in the typical econometric situation of small observational samples. Interpretation of the observed residuals must rest heavily on the historian's insight into the background conditions of his period of study. Insofar as he has neglected to examine the residual, the econometric historian has failed to recruit all the econometric armory available for attacking historical problems. Use of residuals in this manner has indeed been rather sparing. Exceptions, which provide excellent examples of appropriate procedures, occur in the work of Davis, Kelley, and Fogel.

Davis' regression model [4] tests for long-term aspects of the relative importance of equities, loans, and retained earnings in a representative firm's financial structure. By contrast, the residuals are charted to evaluate short-term aspects, viz. the cyclical influences of changes in financial conditions and of the general state of business activity on these variables. Kelley's hypothesis [5] concerns the Australian labor market, and its influence on immigration. Where his regression equation generates large negative residuals, immigration into Australia is lower than "on the average" employment conditions would have led one to expect. These periods of low immigration, with certain explicable exceptions, coincide with high immigration rates into the U.S.A. Fogel,[6] on the other hand, is not dealing in residuals from any particular regression equation, but in discrepancies between estimates of rail consumption generated by himself and available figures on rail production. These differences can be interpreted as inventory accumulations (or decumulations) in each year. Fogel is thus able to unearth a previously unsuspected cycle in inventories within his observation period.

The point is clear. There is much more to be gained from the use of regression methods than simply a measure of goodness of fit, or even a practical set of coefficients. Emphasis will center on examining the properties of the disturbance term and their infringement. In this light I shall query the performance of some of the econometric historians, and illustrate from their work. In fairness I must point out that the examples were originally chosen not because I thought them outstandingly bad, but because their authors were among those who at least had the honesty to publish their data. It is the opposite of my intention to imply that any of the illustrations are unique.

To hold good, least-squares regression techniques require certain well-recognized assumptions about the disturbances. If, for example, the disturbances are correlated with the independent variables, the coefficients estimated for these independent variables will be biased and inconsistent. It can be shown that when the independent variables are erroneously measured, this will be the case.

Many series which the econometric historian will be called upon to study—possibly even the majority—will be imperfect. Methods of collecting data in the nineteenth century and earlier were far from systematic. Patchy coverage, double-counting, and similar blunders have been struck

time and time again by the present-day analyst.[7] Use of avowed samples
runs the risk of their being unrepresentative, since the records of the
larger, more prosperous firms are more likely to have survived, while the
smaller-scale firms might more accurately reflect prevailing business conditions and practices.[8] Most disquieting of all, the relevant material may
be completely missing. Extrapolation backwards ("postcasting," as it has
been called), or total reconstruction of the missing series, may involve assumptions of heroic stature.

One method commonly resorted to by econometric historians is
using "variable-surrogates." Frequently surrogate variables take the form
of a component of the required series, a part for the whole, e.g. building
to represent gross capital formation. In regression work the bias would
arise not from differences in absolute magnitudes between the two series
but from the alteration of their proportional year-to-year movements.
Conceivably, inventories (for example) may move so strongly in the opposite direction to building, between one observation period and the
next, as to reverse the movement in gross capital formation as a whole.
Often more satisfactory than to regress on a variety of variable-surrogates
(perhaps done in the hope of individual discrepancies being cancelled
out by sheer weight of number), is to employ one or more of these surrogates as instrumental variables.

The best established series on pig iron output in the U.S.A. in the
1840's can be used to illustrate the biases introduced by use of ordinary
least-squares regression when the independent variables are subject to
measurement errors. The series of Carey and Grosvenor were selected [9]
and contrasted with a series reconstructed by Fogel,[10] which for the time
being is taken as a "true" series. Like Fogel, I am interested in evaluating
the importance of railroad consumption (R) in the total output (P).
Unlike Fogel, I adopt regression methods to do so. R was regressed on P
for each available series of P: Carey's (subscript c), Grosvenor's (g), and
Fogel's (f). Then, for the years 1840–50: [11]

$$(1) \ldots \ldots \quad R = -2.5 + .049 \, P_c \qquad R^2 = .580$$
$$(2) \ldots \ldots \quad R = -39.5 + .124 \, P_g \qquad R^2 = .709$$
$$(3) \ldots \ldots \quad R = -5.5 + .057 \, P_f \qquad R^2 = .527$$

The coefficient estimated in the simple regression on Grosvenor's series is almost three times as large as in regressing on Carey's figures. It is
clear that at least one of these estimates must be biased, and to some considerable degree.

If there were no series at all available on total production or total
consumption of pig iron, it might be suggested that railroad consump-

tion stand as a surrogate for aggregate production. The example is by no means untypical of the kind of substitute that is commonly employed. Yet equation (3) indicates that here this substitution would be unsatisfactory. Indeed it would more closely resemble the apparently misleading series by Grosvenor.

Alternatively, if it were not possible to reconstruct pig iron production, so that Fogel's series would not exist, it might be thought reasonable to select from Carey's and Grosvenor's series, depending on which gave the higher correlation with R. The researcher might appeal to the common sense of a heuristic relationship between pig iron production and its consumption by railroads. Then he must accept the Grosvenor series, since $R^2(R, P_g)$ is greater than $R^2(R, P_c)$. In fact, if Fogel's series is to be taken as the datum, Carey's series is much the better. The R^2 of P_c on P_f is .980, compared to an R^2 of .819 for P_g on P_f.

Of the several approaches suggested in econometric theory to combat the inconsistency introduced by errors in the variables,[12] the use of instrumental variables seems most suitable for the economic historian. With this technique one attempts to overcome the interdependence between independent variable and disturbance by selecting a third variable, uncorrelated with observational errors in the original independent variable.

One series that on a priori grounds appealed as an instrument in the present circumstances was pig iron imports into the U.S.A.,[13] interpolating fiscal-year figures to provide estimates of calendar-year data. The essence of the instrumental-variable method is a two-stage procedure regressing the independent variable containing errors of measurement on the instrument, then substituting estimates of the independent variables from this regression—appropriately cleansed and purified—back into the original regression equation. In this case, the procedure can be simplified into one operation by a short-cut formula [14] but to convey the flavor of the approach the two-stage method is adopted here.

First, P_c and P_g were regressed on M, the calendar-year imports of pig iron:

$$(4) \quad \ldots\ldots \quad P_c = 406.6 + 5.159 \text{ M} \qquad R^2 = .397$$
$$(5) \quad \ldots\ldots \quad P_g = 430.2 + 2.733 \text{ M} \qquad R^2 = .575$$

By substituting the given values for M in each period into these equations, one obtains "average" estimates for P_c and P_g. The latter are used in the final step as independent variables in the regression of R, as originally required:

$$(6) \quad \ldots \ldots \quad R = -7.7 + .057 \ \overline{P_c}$$
$$(7) \quad \ldots \ldots \quad R = -30.9 + .108 \ \overline{P_g}$$

(Where the bars on P_c and P_g represent estimated values taken from equations (4) and (5) respectively). The same procedure gives an estimated coefficient of 0.073 for P_f, in contrast to the direct least-squares estimate of 0.057.

The major difficulty of the instrumental-variable method is selecting an appropriate instrument. The choice of instrument unfortunately has much to do with the results that emerge, since the approach is designed to produce consistent estimates, i.e. estimates that are unbiased only in large samples. In small samples, bias may still remain. The fundamental requirement, that the instrumental variable should be uncorrelated with the disturbances of the original regression, is untestable in such situations, since the residual is but an estimate of the disturbance term. There are clear advantages in having a perfectly-measured instrument, since zero correlation of measurement errors between independent variable and instrumental variable at least is guaranteed. In most practical historical work only instruments such as "time" are likely to satisfy this condition. The second requirement for an instrumental variable is that it should be strongly correlated with the independent variable it is being used to doctor. If not, the estimating technique breaks down. This requirement tends to conflict with the first. For this reason, Fisher [15] advocates that only variables that causally influence the independent should be used as instrumental variables, although even this can give no more than a measure of compromise.

In the above example, the instrumental variable, M, is significantly correlated with P_c at the .05 level and with P_g at the .01 level in the zero-order matrix. At the same time, M is not significant at these levels in a simple regression on the dependent variable, R. This is partial justification for proceeding as above, and not including M as a second explanatory variable. However, these correlations of imports on pig iron production are positive. This means that some third factor reflecting American demand for pig iron must be brought in to explain why the two variables should have moved in the same direction in each year. In the event of no data on the causal variable, Fisher does allow that one of the jointly influenced variables may have to be used instead.

Yet even though tests on the observed results seem not unsatisfactory, the example serves to demonstrate that econometric history cannot expect halcyon days solely on account of instrumental variables. The latitude for bias in the estimates has been narrowed to a factor of approximately twice instead of three times the magnitude of the lowest coefficient, but this is still overly large. Various methods might conceivably be adopted to improve the chances for success. One of the most popular among the econometric historians is placing an upper or lower bound on the set of observations—whichever extreme happens to be least favorable to the acceptance of one's hypothesis.[16] One can go further and evaluate the effect of feasibly extreme values in the context of the particular problem at hand.[17] This may be so small that the degree of error is perfectly tolerable in the given calculation.

Whatever the approach, there seems little reason why the vulnerability of the data to errors of observation should have induced econometric hypochondria. As Goran Ohlin says: [18] ". . . Any understanding of statistical information is founded on distrust, and the classical problem of statistics is that of making valid inferences from observations that are known to be poor."

In many cases it seems that the problem of biased estimates is smaller than the problem of fear of such a bias.

The "time series problem" of serially correlated residuals will be encountered as normal fare by the econometric historian. Common explanations for the presence of autocorrelated residuals arise from misspecified forms of the regression equation, from significant variables being omitted from the equation, and from errors of measurement. When the residuals are autocorrelated, the significance level estimated for each independent variable is likely to be biased. In many examples autocorrelated residuals increase the probability of usual tests of significance accepting a hypothesis where it should be rejected. M. Lovell, in noting that his original estimates generate residuals that are serially correlated, says "there is a tendency for this [t] test to overestimate the significance of the relationship." [19] But this is true only under certain rather exigent assumptions. When Lovell removes the autocorrelation, the R^2 rises quite sharply.

Tests for autocorrelation of residuals were applied to the simple regressions tabled by J. G. Williamson of deflated U.S. imports on various surrogates used for domestic activity during the nineteenth century.[20] Both dependent and independent variables have their trends removed by quadratic time functions and then are smoothed by five-year moving averages. Williamson experiments by lagging the independent variable a varying number of years to represent lags in the reaction of imports to American capital formation, then selects the equation with the highest correlation coefficient as denoting the best lag. This is a justifiable beginning, but the statistical analysis ought to be taken further, as Williamson explicitly admits.

The first set of regressions he provides is of imports on the Riggleman building index, 1830–70. Results of applying the Durbin-Watson statistic, d, to each of these regressions are given in the table:

Lag (years)	Coefficient of Independent Variable	R^2	d
0	.4787	.760	.24
1	.5205	.904	.52
2	.5133	.878	.54

With the very low values calculated for d, one is compelled to reject the null hypothesis of no serial correlation being present in the residuals at every significance level for which Durbin and Watson provide critical values.[21]

To overcome bias and inefficiency introduced by autocorrelated residuals, obviously the first step is to ensure that all significant variables are included in the estimating equation. An attempt was made to include short-term capital inflow into the first of Williamson's equations above (i.e. unlagged U.S. building).[22] It was hypothesized that American capital imports between 1830 and 1870 were determined by American business conditions, and that in the short run capital imports substituted for commodity imports. The result of this test was disappointing:

$$M = 55.63 + .547 \ B - .037 \ C \qquad\qquad R^2 = .776$$
$$ (.050) \qquad (.043) \qquad\qquad d = .28$$

M = Commodity imports into the U.S.;
B = Riggleman index of U.S. building, unlagged;
C = Net capital inflow into the U.S.[23]

C was of the specified sign but its standard error was estimated as greater than the coefficient. The Durbin-Watson statistic rose only marginally. (A number of very strong reasons can be advanced to explain why capital inflow has contributed very little, statistically, to the explanation of commodity imports.[24]) However the low value of d indicates that other variables, as yet undetected, may very well be significant in a multiple regression.

Assuming for the meantime that no further improvement can be made by increasing the number of independent variables, nor for that matter by altering the form of the equation or improving measurements, there may still remain evidence of autocorrelated residuals. A straightforward technique designed to remove this is to transform the variables to their first differences.[25] This transformation is theoretically entirely valid only when it can be taken that the disturbances have an autocorrelation coefficient of unity. A more general transformation procedure has been developed by Durbin,[26] using the autocorrelation coefficient of the residuals as an approximation to the equivalent coefficient for the disturbances.

For Williamson's first equation, the results of these two transformations are compared with Williamson's original estimates in the next table:

Method	Coefficient of Independent Variable	R^2	d
Original Regression	.4787	.760	0.24
First Differences	.4791	.546	1.68
Durbin's Transformation	.4847	.579	1.54

For both transformation methods one can accept the null hypothesis of no serial correlation at the .01 level. It would therefore be safer to rely upon the significance levels estimated from the transformed variables rather than from the original variables. Since in a simple regression significance levels are provided directly by the correlation coefficient, one can assert a large reduction in the level of significance as a consequence of removing the autocorrelation. (N.B.: Unless by sheer chance the autocorrelation coefficient is actually unity, the R^2 from the regression in first differences is also a biased indicator of variance.)

A few of the econometric historians have tested for autocorrelated residuals, using various adaptations of the von Neumann ratio (such as the Durbin-Watson statistic). Notable examples include L. Davis, in his study of industrial finance; M. Lovell in examining the discount policy of the Bank of England; and A. Kelley for Australian immigration patterns.[27] All three have found evidence of positive serial correlation. This sample, although very small, is highly suggestive. It is not difficult to find other examples where tests had not been carried out, as in Williamson's case.

A further restriction on the disturbance term is that its variance shall be uniform. When this condition is satisfied, the disturbances are said to be homoscedastic; when it is infringed, they are heteroscedastic.

Heteroscedasticity is believed to be quite common in econometric work. For example, at higher levels of income one might expect the propensities of individuals to save to vary much more than at low income levels, since in the latter case a relatively large proportion of the income will be detailed for expenditure on necessities and thus be beyond the scope for a pool of savings. At high income levels, the consumption ex-

penditures on essentials are comparatively slight and much of the re-
mainder is available to spend lavishly or to save.

The problem with heteroscedasticity is that it is impossible to detect
with more than a modicum of probability in practical economic work.
Even allowing that residuals are merely an estimate of disturbances does
not get one very far. The basic difficulty is that one does not and cannot
know the variance of each residual: there is only the single observation,
and from single observations, statistical inference is not possible.

One must therefore be prepared to act on "hunches" that heteroscedasticity may be present. Perhaps one may be able to divide the sample
set into subsets of greater homogeneity and calculate the variances of
each subset.

H. J. Cranmer [28] incorporates "engineering" data into a cost function to estimate the total cost of constructing American canals in the first
half of the nineteenth century, by performing a multiple regression on
the length of the canal, its area of prism (i.e. cross-section) and amount
of lockage included. He notes that the shorter canals did not do very well
in the multiple regression. It may therefore be suggested that short and
long canals have distinguishable statistical properties. Of course, this is
entirely conjectural—it assumes away just what one wants to know; but
this is exactly what happens in any applied investigation of heteroscedasticity.

Cranmer's observations were tabulated in the first instance according
to length of canal. The forty-four observations were then divided in two
at the mid-point, to approximate Cranmer's distinction between short
and long canals. Standard deviations were then calculated for the residuals in each category. For small canals, the standard deviation of the residual was \$67,060; for long canals, \$188,250. Thus if one could regard
each of these two subsets as being homogeneous within itself, one might
conclude that the residuals were heteroscedastic in the direction of increasing variance with respect to length.

Quite the most straightforward means for dealing with heteroscedasticity is by transforming the variables to their reciprocals. For the hypothesis of increasing variance with respect to length, one can divide
through each of the other variables by length of canal.

Regressing the results gave:

$$\frac{TC}{L} = \frac{-10.5}{L} + 1.7714 + .4413\frac{P}{L} - .0252\frac{LK}{L} \qquad\qquad R^2 = .675$$

Compared to Cranmer's original equation:

$$TC = -35.1 + 1.7454L + .5176P + .0818LK \qquad\qquad R^2 = .656$$

where TC = total cost of canal ($000);

    L = length, miles;
    P = area of prism, sq. feet;
    LK = lockage, feet.

Use of average cost per mile as the dependent variable has caused a slight rise in the R^2. If heteroscedasticity has induced inefficiency in Cranmer's equation, while the revised equation goes some way to overcoming it, this result might be expected. On the other hand, the marginal improvement may be merely the result of converting the variables on each side of the equation to ratios. Perhaps of more concern is that the estimate for lockage per mile is of the wrong sign, although it happens to be not significantly different from zero at the 1 per cent level.[29] Note that the inclusion of economic variables in addition to the engineering data might further improve the correlation. A simple regression on average cost per mile of wages of common laborers on the Erie Canal, published by Smith for the years after 1828,[30] gave an R^2 of .459.

Of more immediate interest is the effect on the variances. Resuming the twofold division of the observations, the standard deviation of the residual for short canals was now, at $2,000 per mile, greater than that of long canals, at $1,488. If the initial supposition of heteroscedasticity was correct, the technique adopted to eliminate it has bent over backwards to do so.

Other procedures are also available to overcome heteroscedasticity, depending on the assumptions one makes about how the variances alter. The method used here is equivalent to assuming that the standard deviation of the disturbance is proportional to the value of the independent variable, i.e. to length of canal. This and other possibilities can be generalized in the form of a transformation matrix. Any transformation, however, requires that one has prior knowledge on the disease one is trying to cure, and this is equally impossible in all cases.

The econometric historian would therefore seem to have had good reason in avoiding any consideration to date of whether his results are affected by heteroscedasticity. Even so, it may be of considerable value to check the residuals, and see if any relationship emerges between their absolute magnitudes and any of the independent variables, or time. This really amounts to an elaboration of the general procedure recommended to historians of interpreting their residuals very carefully in the hope of extracting further information (perhaps from the reclassification of samples, as attempted in the Cranmer example), or of formulating new relationships (as in introducing the reciprocal form).

The existence of multiple relations among the variables being analyzed may present larger problems to the historian in being more difficult to remedy than, say, autocorrelated residuals or heteroscedasticity. Multicollinearity among the independent variables has been one of the more persistent problems faced by econometric historians. The traditional time-series dimension itself encourages multicollinearity although not all examples in economic history occur in time-series studies.[31] The relative scarcity of their data may perhaps be partly to blame for the vulnerability of the econometric historians. There may also be multicollinearity latent where a variable-surrogate happens to reflect the influence of variables other than its progenitor.

Multicollinearity may arise either from one of the explanatory variables[32] regulating (in some direct manner) the movements of another, or from two or more variables being jointly influenced by some factor not explicitly included. The former kind does not bias the estimates: they are still "best linear unbiased." Thus A. Fishlow admits to multicollinearity in an equation he derives, then uses the results for mean and variance in his subsequent discussion.[33] It does, however, make the estimates hypersensitive. When two independent variables are perfectly collinear, usual estimating techniques by ordinary least-squares break down. In the general situation of high but less than perfect collinearity the estimates tend to indeterminancy—variances tend to be large and coefficients change markedly as the collinear variable is alternately included and excluded. If the included variable is acting partly as a proxy for some other variable not made explicit in the relationship, i.e. if the equation is misspecified, then the coefficient may well be biased and its significance level overstated. This, of course, is the fault of the hypothesis and not of the method of estimation, but data deficiencies may preclude any allowances being made in much historical work.

The indeterminancy thus induced in the estimates is well illustrated by Williamson's discussion[34] of capital movements into the United States, 1871–1914. Williamson's hypothesis is a composite one, but for present purposes two of the major strands are sufficient: that American net capital inflow in this period was significantly affected by the requirements of investment outlays on the railroads; secondly, that this capital flow responded inversely to the willingness of British investors to invest at home. The first equation tests the "pull" hypothesis, the second yokes "push" and "pull" together:

$$(1) \quad \dot{K}^t = 6.7487 + 1.0189 \ I_{us}{}^{t-1} \qquad\qquad \overline{R}^2 = .624$$
$$(.1271)$$

$$(2) \quad \dot{K}^t = 953.5 - 0.073 \ I_{us}{}^{t-1} - 9.206 \ I_{gb}{}^t \qquad \overline{R}^2 = .739$$
$$(.242) \qquad\qquad (.628)$$

$\dot{K}^t =$ Net capital inflow into the U.S.A. in year t;
$I_{us}{}^{t-1} =$ Ulmer's series of net capital expenditure on
    American steam railroads, lagged one year;
$I_{gb}{}^t =$ Cairncross' series of British home investment inv.[35]

In the first equation, the coefficient of U.S. investment is of the specified sign and is significantly different from zero at the .01 level $(t = 8.017)$. By itself, American railroad investment seems to explain about five-eighths of the variance in net capital movements. Equation (2), which is my own recomputation to allow direct comparison with (1), shows that these conclusions are premature. The power of explanation attributed to $I_{us}{}^{t-1}$ pales into insignificance $(t = 0.302)$ beside that for British investment. Its sign contravenes specification. The reason is that in the first equation lagged railroad investment is serving in part as a proxy for current British home investment. The correlation coefficient for the regression of $I_{us}{}^{t-1}$ on $I_{gb}{}^t$ is —.888.

Nor can there be any strong *a priori* supposition that the matter rests as in (2). If a third independent variable, plausibly influential in determining net capital inflow into the U.S.A., is added to the regression equation, $I_{gb}{}^t$ could conceivably become insignificant in turn, if it has hitherto been acting as a proxy variable for this third factor or alternately $I_{us}{}^{t-1}$ may revert to significance at an appropriate level.

Williamson's solution to this dilemma is to scrap the idea and start afresh. Other investigators may not have the same opportunity to try elsewhere. It is wise to be methodical in dealing with variables that are inclined to move together over time. Of the several systematic approaches that are possible, one would be to use a step-wise procedure. In the early stages one incorporates those variables having relatively high simple correlation with the dependent variable into the regression equation. In later steps this end is compromised by selecting further independent variables which are also least intercorrelated with one another. Laying out the R^2's obtained from simple regressions of each variable on the other in triangular matrix form gives: [36]

One would begin the process by taking the simple regression of $\dot{K}^t$ on $I_{gb}{}^{x-1}$, since this leads to a coefficient of determination of .796, or

	$I_{us}{}^{t-1}$	$I_{gb}{}^{t-1}$	$M_{us}{}^{t-1}$	$M_{gb}{}^{t-1}$	$\dot{K}^t$
$I_{us}{}^{t-1}$	1.000	0.618*	0.247	0.013	0.586
$I_{gb}{}^{t-1}$		1.000	0.142*	0.169	0.796*
$M_{us}{}^{t-1}$			1.000	0.339	0.436
$M_{gb}{}^{t-1}$				1.000	0.049*
$\dot{K}^t$					1.000

*Where M = commodity imports into the relevant countries, and all independent variables are lagged one year.

.785 corrected for the additional degree of freedom used up. The next best fit to $\dot{K}^t$ is the one tried initially by Williamson, $I_{us}{}^{t-1}$. However this variable is highly inversely correlated with $I_{gb}{}^{t-1}$, already included, so that bringing it in as well immediately exposes one to the risk of multicollinearity. To see the effect, the regression was carried out:

$$(3) \quad \ldots \ldots \quad \dot{K}^t = 794.5 + .222 \ I_{us}{}^{t-1} - 7.640 \ I_{gb}{}^{t-1} \qquad \overline{R}^2 = .796$$
$$\phantom{(3) \quad \ldots \ldots \quad \dot{K}^t = 794.5 + } (.158) \qquad (.387)$$

As expected, U.S. investment proves to be not significant at the .05 level. However the equation is an improvement over (2) above. By lagging British investment, the coefficient estimated for $I_{us}{}^{t-1}$ has the right sign and is at least larger than its standard error. More importantly, the $\overline{R}^2$ is appreciably higher.

At the next stage I have gone beyond Williamson's model to study the effects on estimated coefficients and standard errors of the variables included when further independent variables are introduced. Lagged U.S. commodity imports is next highest on the list of simple correlations with the dependent variable. It is significantly correlated with both $I_{us}{}^{t-1}$ and $I_{gb}{}^{t-1}$ at the .05 level, but the R^2 in each case is lower than in a simple regression on $\dot{K}^t$. Therefore:

$$(4) \quad \ldots \ldots \quad \dot{K}^t = 544.5 - .055 \ I_{us}{}^{t-1} - 7.745 \ I_{gb}{}^{t-1} + 2.573 \ M_{us}{}^{t-1}$$
$$\phantom{(4) \quad \ldots \ldots \quad \dot{K}^t = 544.5 } (.111) \qquad (.799) \qquad (.363)$$
$$\overline{R}^2 = .908$$

Thus, lagged U.S. imports are significant at the .01 level in explaining capital imports, subject to the hypothesis being refuted by the possible discovery of additional significant variables. In comparison with the previous equation, the coefficient estimated for U.S. railroad investment has reversed in sign and now contradicts its positive specification. Its standard error is twice as large as the coefficient itself. For British domestic investment, the coefficient has changed little but its standard error has risen because of the inverse association with M_{us}^{t-1}. Finally, the overall fit has risen quite markedly, even after allowing for the extra degree of freedom used up.

Symmetry demanded that one investigate whether these conclusions were altered by going further and including lagged British imports. This could be rationalized on the grounds that the American capital inflow was significantly directed into the export sector. But M_{gb}^{t-1} is not significant at the .05 level in a simple regression on K^t, while it is significantly intercorrelated with both I_{gb}^{t-1} and M_{us}^{t-1} at the same level. Nevertheless, the regression was run through to trace the effect of including this variable:

$$(5) \quad \dot{K}^t = -290.79 - .061\ I_{us}^{t-1} - 8.628\ I_{gb}^{t-1} + 1.977\ M_{us}^{t-1}$$
$$\phantom{(5) \quad \dot{K}^t =}(.110)\qquad\quad (1.187)\qquad\quad (.700)$$
$$\phantom{(5) \quad \dot{K}^t =}+\ 1.177\ M_{gb}^{t-1}\qquad\qquad\qquad \bar{R}^2 = .912$$
$$\phantom{(5) \quad \dot{K}^t =}(1.261)$$

For the additional variable, the standard error is estimated to be higher than the coefficient. As the low intercorrelation of this variable with I_{us}^{t-1} would suggest, there has been very little effect on either the coefficient of the standard error for the latter variable. However, since M_{gb}^{t-1} is significantly correlated with the other two variables, these show larger changes in their coefficients and higher standard errors.

Obviously, then, Williamson's analysis was incomplete as it stood. By experimenting with other lags and combinations of lags, and by casting around for other significant variables, the R^2 might be improved quite considerably even yet. However the above analysis only modifies Williamson's conclusions, especially in the substitution of lagged for unlagged British investment. It does not undermine his result that the "push" caused by a reduction in British domestic investment significantly influenced American net capital inflow in this period, whereas the "pull" generated by American outlays on railroad investment did not. I leave this to the next section.

The problem to which the applied econometrician addresses most of his attention is that of multiple relationships, but of a different sort. Simultaneity occurs wherever the dependent variable in some direct or indirect way influences the values taken by the "independent" variable.

That is, causation is no longer unidirectional. When variables appear in two-way relationships to each other, one can show that in the probability limit this constitutes an infringement of the assumption that independent variables and disturbances should be uncorrelated. Least-squares estimates are biased and inconsistent; more refined estimation techniques must be devised.

A few econometric historians have shown themselves well aware of simultaneity and its effects. Generally they have been led to attempt to avoid the difficulty. By reformulating the structure of their relationships they can hope to by-pass the source of bias. In at least one way this is a very suitable policy for the historian to pursue, since as stressed in the following discussion even the more advanced estimating techniques are not completely satisfactory.

The success of such an outflanking maneuver rests largely on the historical plausibility of the reformation. On the surface it seems reasonable to argue that lags of response were more characteristic of the world a century ago—with the slower transportation and communications systems, and still more two centuries ago, with very much slower methods of production—than of the world today. The historical dimension itself builds longer supply and response lags into the structure. Thus econometric historians would defend their use of ordinary least-squares estimation methods on grounds that the economies they are studying are not sufficiently complex to warrant the investigation of two-way relationships. However, dangers lurk in weeding out simultaneity. In studying the composition of iron and steel products in the late nineteenth century, Temin [37] attempted to isolate changes due to shifts in the demand schedule by asserting that technical progress shifted supply curves for each product line in similar proportions. As Smolensky points out in a brilliant commentary,[38] Temin's justification for his assertion, that relative prices of the products remained nearly constant, is inadequate. Proportional effects of technological progress on the marginal costs of the iron and steel industry do not imply proportional effects on the supply curves of each firm, because of the imperfectly competitive conditions.

A more general consideration is that the economies that many a statistician is likely to be investigating *are* complex and will involve him in simultaneous determination. While dozens of exceptions can undoubtedly be found, the great majority of historical series good enough for econometric treatment relate to the last hundred years or so. After the middle of the nineteenth century the leading economies are advanced, industrializing rapidly, and becoming heavily capital-intensive. The macro variables interact along Keynesian lines (witness the transition from the economics of underdevelopment to the economics of growth to describe Britain before and after 1850).[39] The historian engaged in these fields, at least, may have little opportunity to escape the ravages of simultaneity. As historians edge towards the construction of full-blown simultaneous equation models,[40] the need for satisfactory techniques of estimation becomes increasingly acute.

For an example, refer back to Williamson's model of capital flows between the U.K. and the U.S.A. in the late nineteenth and early twentieth centuries.[41] In Williamson's formulation, British home investment is unlagged and regarded as an exogenous variable determining net capital flows from Britain to the U.S. It seems valid to argue that the reverse causation could also have been true: that British domestic investment is partly determined by the outflow of capital from Britain. Cairncross, in his classic study of British home and foreign investment, 1870–1914, might well have agreed: "[The boom of 1900] was the nearest approach to a purely domestic boom. All other booms from 1870 onwards seem to have been communicated through the export trades from America and other centers of investment." [42]

Tinbergen, in his econometric study of the British economy from 1870 to 1914,[43] considered *only* the one-way relationship with foreign investment as the independent variable causing home investment. Clearly the counter-example stands in good company.

Accordingly I have formulated a Cairncross-type long-run relationship expressing British investment in terms of net capital flows to the U.S.A. and a number of exogenous variables. By Cairncross' argument, an increase in British investment results from an improvement in Britain's terms of trade, from a reduction in previous-year unemployment, and from a smaller level of emigration from Britain.[44] Using the modification introduced in the last section including lagged U.S. commodity imports to explain the inflow into the U.S.A., I began by estimating each equation independently by ordinary least-squares:

$$(1.1) \quad \dot{K}^t = 707.7 - .232\ I_{us}^{t-1} - 9.079\ I_{gb}^t + 2.239\ M_{us}^{t-1}$$
$$\phantom{(1.1) \quad \dot{K}^t = 707.7}(.151)(1.533)(.307)$$
$$\overline{R}^2 = .900$$

$$(1.2) \quad I_{gb}^t = 104.3 + .185\ t_{gb} - .962\ U_{gb}^{t-1} - .116\ E^t - .050\ \dot{K}^t$$
$$\phantom{(1.2) \quad I_{gb}^t = 104.3}(.174)(.743)(.048)(.013)$$
$$\overline{R}^2 = .790$$

t_{gb} = British terms of trade;
U_{gb}^{t-1} = lagged percentage unemployed in Britain;
E^t = emigration from U.K. to U.S.A.[45]

The result of (1.1) is much as before, with British investment now not lagged. In (1.2) the Cairncross thesis of a positive association between the terms of trade and British domestic investment is found to be statistically insignificant at the usual levels. One would surmise that lagged unemployment was not significant at the 5 per cent level in explaining British investment, the reason being multicollinearity with the emigration and capital flow variables. Net capital movement into the U.S. provisionally justifies its inclusion by being significant at the .01 level.

The ordinary least-squares estimates are, however, inconsistent. British investment is used to explain capital flows in (1.1) while the reverse is true of (1.2). To obtain consistent estimates of the coefficients, more refined estimating techniques must be adopted. The equations (1) were re-estimated by Two-Stage Least-Squares: [46]

$$(2.1) \quad \dots \quad \dot{K}^t = -351.7 + .967\ I_{us}^{t-1} + 1.203\ I_{gb}^{t-1} + 2.281\ M_{us}^{t-1}$$
$$\qquad\qquad\qquad (.185) \qquad\quad (1.120) \qquad\quad\ (.557)$$

$$(2.2) \quad \dots \quad I_{gb}^t = 123.3 + .063 t_{gb} - 2.118 U_{gb}^{t-1} - 128\ E^t - .045\ \dot{K}^t$$
$$\qquad\qquad\qquad\ (.133) \quad\ (.569) \qquad\quad\ (.036) \qquad\quad (.010)$$

In (2.2) the terms of trade variable has an even poorer fit than in estimating by single-stage least-squares (1.2); its standard error is twice as large as the estimated coefficient. Lagged unemployment, however, has become significant at the .01 level, while emigration has improved to significance at this level also. In spite of these changes, presumably due to reduced intercorrelation with $\dot{K}^t$ and in spite of $\dot{K}^t$ being one of the jointly-determined variables, its coefficient has scarcely changed in value or significance.

The dramatic change occurs in going from (1.1) to (2.1). Williamson's argument—that the push effect of British domestic investment is significant in explaining net capital flows whereas the pull of American investment is not—is turned on its head. The sign of the coefficient estimated for I_{gb}^t now contradicts specification; that for I_{us}^t changes sign to become significant. In absence of further results, Williamson's econometric conclusions have to be reversed.

To show the effect of these changes in terms of their proportional influence on $\dot{K}^t$, I have adapted Goldberger's method.[47] The causative influence of variables on the right-hand side of the equation is then given as the summed cross-product of estimated coefficient and modulus of first differences of each variable. Estimated coefficients found to be significant were assumed to be best linear unbiased; insignificant estimates were taken to be zero.[48] Finally, proportional shares in explanation were allocated on a percentage basis. The impact of the re-estimation process can be gauged from the table:

	Ordinary Least-Squares	Two-Stage Least-Squares
Lagged U.S. investment	—	74.36
Lagged U.S. imports	25.31	25.64
British domestic investment	74.69	—

While Goldberger's method does not lead directly to probability levels attached to these weights, it does make the switch between American and British investment stand out markedly.

For the present, methods rather than results are important. In the first instance, note that the outcome would have been very different if I had followed the customary procedure of eliminating insignificant variables after ordinary least-squares regression. Lagged American investment would not then have appeared to be found significant in the Two-Stage calculation, nor would lagged British unemployment. The effect of dropping these two variables at the preliminary stage is evident. The example demonstrates very effectively that econometric techniques cannot always give final answers. By specifying the model in other ways, one might obtain further results contradicting those so far.

In the present case, since the equation for capital movement is over identified, different methods of simultaneous estimation will in general lead to different point estimates. Consistency in large samples does not necessarily imply lack of bias in small-sample situations. To date there is little theoretical information available on the exact small-sample properties of various estimators. In practice the historian is unlikely to go beyond single equation methods. The systems methods (Full Information Maximum-Likelihood and Three-Stage Least-Squares) appear prone to specification errors, and with data shortcomings such errors can be expected in most historical work. In the model used here, more complete specification might involve additional equations explaining unlagged American investment, emigration, and so forth. Moreover, computational difficulty will generally rule out such procedures for the historian.

Of the single-equation methods, Two-Stage Least-Squares has probably performed as well as any other in Monte Carlo studies.[49] In relevance to the above model, Klein and Nakamura [50] have argued that in certain circumstances Two-Stage Least-Squares is preferable to Limited-Information Maximum-Likelihood (for example), in coping with multicollinearity. On the other hand, Fisher [51] has recently theorized that there is no basis on which one can uniformly prefer one or the other insofar as specification error is concerned. In another recent paper, Cragg[52] has made a Monte Carlo study of several estimating methods applied to variables containing measurement errors. He finds little difference in the relative capabilities of the procedures tested. The importance of this result to economic historians should be apparent from the preceding discussion in this article. Similarly Cragg discovers little advantage of any one method in handling heteroscedastic or autocorrelated disturbances. On grounds of neatness and seeming effectiveness, Two-Stage Least-Squares appears perhaps most suitable for the econometric historian's purpose. One further attribute is that of relative computational simplicity: except for Indirect Least-Squares (applicable only in exactly-identified equations), the Two-Stage method is probably the least burdensome in this respect. Certainly, with ready access to modern computing equipment, the additional calculation should be no excuse for the painstaking historian (some of the computations for Two-Stage Least-Squares above were performed on an I.B.M. 1620).

This overview of the econometric tools available to the historian cannot be completed without at least passing reference to the variables themselves. Econometricians have developed several standard techniques of allowing in some respects for certain variables to appear in a relationship; variables which are believed to be of significance but which cannot be quantified directly. One of the most useful of these techniques to the economic historian is that of dummy variables. These may be used in at least two leading ways:

(a) to discriminate between recognizably different phenomena that have a time dimension, e.g. to single out seasonal influences in quarterly data, or to distinguish between prosperity and depression;

(b) to represent qualitative variables, e.g. the form of agrarian tenure, or even quantitative variables where the pattern of correlation may be irregular, e.g. in life-cycle models of savings.

Temin, for example, has used dummy variables with some success in economic history,[53] although he formulates the problem in such a way as to risk multicollinearity. Dummy variables have a range of flexibility that may seem well suited to the historian's needs: they can be extended from their usual employment as constant terms to acting as dependent variables (although not without additional statistical complications).[54] In many cases they may, however, be too blunt an instrument to satisfy the historian's requirements. He will often be concerned with shades of influences, with differential impacts.[55] Short of developing a whole proliferation of dummy variables, the historian will usually have to fall back on analyzing the residuals, as before.

An even more obviously useful econometric device is that of lagged variables. Delayed response of one variable to another is likely to be increasingly common the further back in time the historian goes. It is quite legitimate to try out various conceivable lags to see which provides the highest R^2, as done by e.g. Williamson and Kelley.[56] However one should not disregard other tests for significance.

Current emphasis of econometricians is on formulating more realistic lagged functions, designed to cope with what are felt to be more accurate approximations of the real world, in both behavioral and technical functions. These are the class of distributed lags, corresponding to reactions spread over a (regular) number of past periods of observation.[57] Kelley experiments with fractional and distributed lags in describing the "pull" influence of the Australian labor market in attracting migrants to Australia. Using the Durbin-Watson statistic as one relevant criterion, he settled on the general distributed-lag form in which the endogenous variable appears lagged one period as a predetermined variable, along with the lagged exogenous variable. It can be shown that in such cases the least-squares estimates of the coefficient of the lagged endogenous variable are biased. If the disturbances are normally distributed, the bias will be negative, if the coefficient of the lagged dependent variable is positive. Now, Kelley's d value for his equation (1.67) suggests an acceptably normal distribution on this account; in these circumstances, however, the d value is also biased, towards accepting the null hypothesis of no serial correlation in the residuals.

Taylor and Wilson [58] have developed the method they call "Three-Pass Least-Squares" to derive consistent estimates of coefficients of lagged endogenous variables, making use of the estimated autoregressive structure. An attempt was made to recompute Kelley's general distributed-lag model by Three-Pass Least-Squares, using data for the relatively short period, 1921–35. Unfortunately the estimates "blew up" in the first pass due to multicollinearity. Nevertheless, re-estimation by Three-Pass Least-Squares for the whole of Kelley's period (1865–1935) might still be a worthwhile venture.

The potential for econometrics in the new economic history should be clear. By no means do I intend to convey the impression that the above exhausts its possibilities. Except for the brief glance at dummy and lagged variables I have scarcely touched on the formulation of relationships. P. A. David's study of capital accumulation in Chicago, 1870–93,[59] shows that econometrics can be a powerful tool just in establishing some series. David estimates capital stock in each year by inverting the C.E.S. production function, employing his own form of the usual side conditions. His technique will no doubt be adopted by many econometric historians thirsty for data on capital formation.

At the same time it is quite evident that the role of the historian will continue to dominate any historical enquiry. Many other writers have made this clear.[60] The historian is of primary importance in that he alone is able to elucidate the background conditions. Basmann takes this even further. To begin with, he supposes that the economic statistician is free to choose whatever hypothesis he desires so long as its logic is not refuted by economic theory. Then:

". . . the whole *metier* of the economic historian, his intellectual participation in every stage of the testing of proffered 'economic laws' is required: in the formulation of such 'laws,' in their empirical interpretation, and in the evaluation of their agreement with what actually happened in the past." [61]

I justify my emphasis on the reverse direction by its comparative neglect.

University of Canterbury, New Zealand

NOTES

1. A. S. Goldberger: "Econometric Theory," New York, Wiley, 1964.

2. Recent exceptions include work by P. Temin and J. Williamson.

3. On the other hand, the economic historian is less frequently called upon to undergo the acid test of prediction outside the sample.

4. L. E. Davis: "The Sources of Industrial Finance: The American Textile Industry, a Case Study," *Explorations in Entrepreneurial History*, April, 1957.

5. A. C. Kelley: "International Migration and Economic Growth: Australia, 1865–1935," *Journal of Economic History*, Volume XXV, No. 3, September, 1965.

6. R. W. Fogel: "Railroads and American Economic Growth: Essays in Econometric History," Baltimore, Johns Hopkins, 1964, pp. 185–8.

7. G. Ohlin, e.g.: "No Safety in Numbers: Some Pitfalls of Historical Statistics," in H. Rosovsky (ed.): "Industrialization in Two Systems: Essays in Honour of Alexander Gerschenkron," New York, Wiley, 1966.

8. A good example is provided by S. Pollard's re-examination of fixed capital during the British Industrial Revolution. Pollard shows that the conclusions reached by H. Heaton applied only to a relatively small number of excessively large firms, and that a different picture of capital supply emerges if the average-sized firm is considered. See S. Pollard: "Fixed Capital in the Industrial Revolution in Britain," *Journal of Economic History*, Volume XXIV, No. 3, September, 1964.

9. From the various series given in P. Temin: "Iron and Steel in Nineteenth Century America: An Economic Enquiry," Cambridge (Mass.), M.I.T., 1964, pp. 264–65.

10. Fogel, *op. cit.*, Chapter 5.

11. Gaps in the Carey series were filled out by naive interpolation.

12. See e.g., J. Johnston, "Econometric Methods," McGraw-Hill, New York, 1963, Chapter 6; E. Malinvaud: "Statistical Methods of Econometrics," Amsterdam, North Holland, English translation, 1966, Chapter 10.

13. From Temin, *op. cit.*, p. 281 ('000 gross tons).

14. Given in J. Johnston, *op. cit.*, p. 166.

15. F. M. Fisher: "The Choice of Instrumental Variables in the Estimation of

Economy-Wide Econometric Models," *International Economic Review*, Volume 6, No. 3, September, 1965.

16. E.g., R. P. Thomas: "A Quantitative Approach to the Study of the Effects of British Imperial Policy Upon Colonial Welfare: Some Preliminary Findings," *Journal of Economic History*, Volume XXV, No. 4, December, 1965.

17. E.g., P. A. David: "Economic History Through the Looking-Glass," paper delivered to the Econometric Society, December, 1963.

18. Ohlin, *op. cit.*, p. 69.

19. M. C. Lovell: "The Role of the Bank of England as Lender of Last Resort in the Crises of the Eighteenth Century," *Explorations in Entrepreneurial History*, October, 1957.

20. J. G. Williamson: "American Growth and the Balance of Payments, 1820–1913: A Study of the Long Swing," Chapel Hill (N.C.), University of North Carolina, 1964, p. 81.

21. J. Durbin and G. S. Watson: "Testing for Serial Correlation in Least-Squares Regression," *Biometrika*, Volume 37, 1950, and Volume 38, 1951.

22. C.f., Williamson, *op. cit.*, pp. 89 ff.

23. Source: Williamson, *op. cit.*, Table B-1.

24. E.g., the fact that C is dominated by long-term capital imports, which may have a positive correlation with commodity imports—the admixture of short and long term capital biases the estimate towards zero.

25. As used by Lovell, *op. cit.*

26. J. Durbin: "Estimation of Parameters in Time-Series Regression Models," *Journal of Royal Statistical Society*, Series B, Volume 22, No. 1, 1960. Johnston, *op. cit.*, Chapter 7, gives a less terse exposition, laying stress on practical estimation procedure. For an application with rather interesting econometric and historical results, see my "On a Thesis by Matthews," forthcoming in the *Economic History Review*, Volume XX, Number 3, December, 1967.

27. *Op. cit.*

28. H. J. Cranmer: "Canal Investment, 1815–1860," in "Trends in the American Economy in the Nineteenth Century: Studies in Income and Wealth," Volume 24, Princeton (National Bureau of Economic Research), Princeton University, 1961, Part IV.

29. This result may be partly due to the rather artificial nature of the variable, lockage per mile. However, the lockage variable in Cranmer's original regression, although of the correct sign, is not on recalculation significant at the five per cent level.

30. W. B. Smith: "Wage Rates on the Erie Canal, 1828–1881," *Journal of Economic History*, Volume XXIII, No. 3, September, 1963. This and similar results may improve predictions of canal construction costs. See e.g., Fogel, *op. cit.*, p. 98.

31. E.g., the example provided by A. Fishlow: "The Trustee Savings Banks, 1817–1861," *Journal of Economic History*, Volume XXI, No. 1, March, 1961.

32. Strictly speaking, "One of the regressors. . . ."

33. *Op. cit.*

34. Williamson, *op. cit.*, pp. 147–8.

35. *Op. cit.*, Tables B-1, B-14, B-24.

36. Asterisks denote inverse simple correlations. Import variables are from Williamson, Tables B-3, B-20.

37. P. Temin: "The Composition of Iron and Steel Products, 1869–1909," *Journal of Economic History*, Volume XXIII, No. 4, December, 1963.

38. E. Smolensky, Discussion on the above paper by Temin, *loc. cit.*

39. To illustrate with examples from the New Economic History, compare M. Blaug: "The Myth of the Old Poor Law and the Making of the New," *Journal of Economic History,* Volume XXIII, No. 2, June, 1963, with P. Temin: "The Decline of the British Steel Industry," in H. Rosovsky (ed.): "Industrialization in Two Systems. . . ."

40. E.g., P. Temin: "The Causes of Cotton-Price Fluctuations in the 1830's," paper delivered to the Econometric Society, December, 1966.

41. Williamson, *op. cit.*

42. A. K. Cairncross: "Home and Foreign Investment, 1870–1913: Studies in Capital Accumulation," Cambridge, C.U.P., 1953, p. 196.

43. J. Tinbergen: "Business Cycles in the United Kingdom, 1870–1914," Amsterdam, North Holland, 1951.

44. Cairncross, *op. cit.*, chapter 7. Perhaps it is timely to recall the warning note sounded by Cairncross in the Introduction to his book concerning ". . . the simpleminded who lie in wait for the man with the hardihood to speak in figures; who treat every statistical series, however ill-founded, with a sort of reverence, and who cannot see a statistical nut without itching to crack it under a mathematical steamhammer." Duly humbled, we nod to Sir Alexander.

45. Sources: (i) Terms of trade—Cairncross, *op. cit.*, p. 206; (ii) Unemployment—B. R. Mitchell with P. Deane: "Abstract of British Historical Statistics," Cambridge, 1962, pp. 64–5; (iii) Emigration—*ibid.*, p. 50.

46. Developed by H. Theil. See e.g., "Economic Forecasts and Policy," Amsterdam, North Holland, 2nd revised edition, 1961.

47. A. S. Goldberger: "Impact Multipliers and Dynamic Properties of the Klein-Goldberger Model," Amsterdam, North Holland, 1959, Chapter 4. Notice that, since I am not interested in forecasting, etc., I have compared the structural rather than reduced-form equations.

48. Alternative procedures are conceivable, e.g., eliminating nonsignificant variables and re-estimating. However, in the Two-Stage case this would lead to a rather bizarre recursive model.

49. Surveyed in Johnston, *op. cit.*, Chapter 10.

50. L. R. Klein and M. Nakamura: "Singularity in the Equation Systems of Econometrics: Some Aspects of the Problem of Multicollinearity," *International Economic Review,* Volume 3, No. 3, September, 1962.

51. F. M. Fisher: "The Relative Sensitivity to Specification Error of Different k-Class Estimators," *Journal of American Statistical Association,* Volume 61, No. 314, Part I, June, 1966.

52. J. G. Cragg: "On the Sensitivity of Simultaneous-Equation Estimates to the Stochastic Assumptions of the Models," *Journal of American Statistical Association,* Volume 61, No. 313, March, 1966.

53. P. Temin: "Iron and Steel. . . . ," pp. 270 ff.

54. Goldberger: "Econometric Theory," pp. 218–231, 248–255.

55. See e.g., M. Lovell, *op. cit.*

56. *Op. cit.*

57. There are several well-known references. A summary appears in Malinvaud, *op. cit.*, Chapters 14–15.

58. L. D. Taylor and T. A. Wilson: "Three-Pass Least-Squares: A Method for Estimating Models with a Laggerd Dependent Variable," *Review of Economics and Statistics,* Volume LXVI, No. 4, November, 1964.

59. David, *op. cit.* An extract appears in *Econometrica,* Volume 32, No. 4, October, 1964.

60. E.g., J. R. T. Hughes: "Fact and Theory in Economic History," *Explorations in Entrepreneurial History,* Second Series, Volume 3, No. 2, Winter, 1966. An interesting attempt to apply such criteria to econometric building is M. Nerlove's critique of Tinbergen (et al.) in "Two Models of the British Economy: A Fragment of a Critical Survey," *International Economic Review,* Volume 6, No. 2, May, 1965. Nerlove's discussion of British history, 1870–1914, would benefit from consideration of recent authors such as A. G. Ford and A. I. Bloomfield, but if he himself is to be believed, he would not apologize for such lacunae.

61. R. L. Basmann: "The Role of the Economic Historian in the Testing of Proffered 'Economic Laws,'" *Explorations in Entrepreneurial History,* Second Series, Volume 2, No. 3, Spring/Summer 1965, p. 160.

BIBLIOGRAPHY OF OTHER RECENT PAPERS ON METHODOLOGY IN ECONOMIC HISTORY

Ralph Andreano, "Four Recent Studies in Economic History: Some Conceptual Implications," in Ralph Andreano (ed.), *New Views on American Economic Development* (Cambridge, 1965), pp. 13–26.

Thomas C. Cochran, "Economic History, Old and New," *American Historical Review,* Vol. LXXIV, No. 5 (June, 1969), pp. 1561–1572.

Arthur H. Cole, "Economic History in the United States: Formative Years of a Discipline," *Journal of Economic History,* Vol. XXVIII, No. 4 (December, 1968), pp. 556–589.

Lance Davis, "Professor Fogel and the New Economic History," *Economic History Review, Second Series,* Vol. XIX, No. 3 (December, 1966), pp. 657–663.

Meghnad Desai, "Some Issues in Econometric History," *Economic History Review, Second Series,* Vol. XXI, No. 1 (April, 1968), pp. 1–16.

Robert W. Fogel, "The New Economic History: Its Findings and Methods," *Economic History Review, Second Series,* Vol. XIX, No. 3 (December, 1966), pp. 642–656.

———, "A Provisional View of the 'New' Economic History," *American Economic Review,* Vol. LIV, No. 3 (May, 1964), pp. 377–389.

———, "The Reunification of Economic History With Economic Theory," *American Economic Review,* Vol. LV, No. 2 (May, 1965), pp. 92–98.

———, "The Specification Problem in Economic History," *Journal of Economic History,* Vol. XXVII, No. 3 (September, 1967), pp. 283–308.

Louis Galambos, "Business History and the Theory of the Growth of the Firm," *Explorations in Entrepreneurial History, Second Series,* Vol. IV, No. 1 (1966–1967), pp. 3–16.

Louis M. Hacker, "The New Revolution in Economic History: A Review Article Based on *Railroads and Economic Growth: Essays in Econometric History* by Robert William Fogel," *Explorations in Entrepreneurial History, Second Series,* Vol. III, No. 3 (1966), pp. 159–175.

Douglass C. North, "The State of Economic History," *American Economic Review,* Vol. LV, No. 2 (May, 1965), pp. 86–98.

William N. Parker, "American Economic Growth: Recent Trends in Its Historiography," *Journal of Economic History* (forthcoming).

Fritz Redlich, " 'New' and Traditional Approaches to Economic History and
Their Interdependence," *Journal of Economic History,* Vol. XXV, No. 4
(December, 1965), pp. 480–495.

Harry Scheiber, "On the New Economic History," *Agricultural History,* Vol.
XLI (October, 1967), pp. 383–395.